IN THE
RHODODENDRONS

IN THE
RHODODENDRONS

A Memoir with
Appearances by
Virginia Woolf

HEATHER CHRISTLE

ALGONQUIN BOOKS OF CHAPEL HILL 2025

Algonquin Books of Chapel Hill / Little, Brown and Company
Hachette Book Group
1290 Avenue of the Americas, New York, NY 10104
algonquinbooks.com

First Edition: April 2025.

Algonquin Books of Chapel Hill is an imprint of Little, Brown and Company, a division of Hachette Book Group, Inc. The Algonquin Books name and logo are trademarks of Hachette Book Group, Inc.

The publisher is not responsible for websites (or their content) that are not owned by the publisher.

The Hachette Speakers Bureau provides a wide range of authors for speaking events. To find out more, go to hachettespeakersbureau.com or email hachettespeakers@hbgusa.com.

Little, Brown and Company books may be purchased in bulk for business, educational, or promotional use. For information, please contact your local bookseller or the Hachette Book Group Special Markets Department at special.markets@hbgusa.com.

Design by Steve Godwin.

ISBN 9781643755922 (hardcover) ISBN 9781643755953 (ebook)
LCCN 2024055310 (hardcover) LCCN 2024055311 (ebook)

Printing 1, 2025

LSC-C

Printed in the United States of America

CONTENTS

IN THE
RHODODENDRONS

PROLOGUE

THE FIRST TIME PERSEPHONE was kidnapped, it was by Hades, god of the Underworld, who found her picking flowers in a meadow and carried her into the earth in his golden chariot. Her mother, Demeter—goddess of the harvest—was furious. Eventually she negotiated for her daughter's return, but only for half of each year. Ever since, for the months they are kept apart, Demeter has withheld her warmth and left the land to its fate.

The second time Persephone was kidnapped it was by Thomas Bruce, the British Lord Elgin, who pried her from her home in the Parthenon and dragged her marble form from Athens to the British Museum. This time, at least, her mother came too. They and their marble neighbors sit now in a massive hall near small signs that tell parts of their story, among which one can find no mention of Greece's ongoing demand for their return. That homecoming, the signs imply, is unnecessary: "[T]hese remarkable portrayals of human form have transcended their ancient past to become a representation of humanity itself."

In my childhood, I lived in New Hampshire with my American father and my English mother, who would return with my sister and me to her home country every other year or so, visiting family, historic sites, stately homes and galleries, so that we might absorb a full sense of ourselves as belonging to the place, but somehow she never took us to the British Museum. Perhaps she thought it not British enough, its holdings mostly scraped from an imperial elsewhere and forced into transcendence. In any case, when I walked into the museum one rainy day in March of 2023, it was for the first time.

To all appearances I came alone. This is what the security guards and cameras would say, but these days, as soon as I step foot in England, Virginia Woolf's voice echoes inside me, whispering about what once happened here, or conjuring characters I watch pass about the room. I know she has been dead since she drowned herself in 1941, but over my years of reading her thousands of pages of novels, essays, letters, and diaries, my years of travel—real and imagined—back to the land of my mother's birth, I have grown accustomed to playing the rhythms of her language as mental soundtrack to the scenes of my own life.

The British Museum's Room 18, where the Parthenon Marbles are held, wasn't built until 1939, late in Woolf's life, and so her encounters with what she (and everyone around her) then called the Elgin Marbles occurred in a different space, adorned with different signs. The marbles themselves have also shifted. Entire heads have disappeared. Books too. In Woolf's lifetime the holdings of the British Library were still housed inside the Museum, but in 1997 they were moved a bit farther north to their own building at St. Pancras. I love my visits to that newer building, touching words written in Woolf's own hand, but I can't help longing for an hour or two of working beneath the great dome of the old reading room, which still stands, but has been repurposed for archival storage, closed off for more than a decade.

It's to that old, circular space that Woolf brings her title character in her 1922 novel *Jacob's Room*. She sets the young Jacob to copying passages of poetry, while nearby an elderly Miss Marchmont works through her too-large pile of books—gathered in a wooly-headed attempt to construct a philosophy of color, music, and sound—a pile so precariously stacked that it tumbles over into Jacob's compartment. Woolf seems to pity Miss Marchmont a bit, and I sometimes fear I resemble the woman, with my own embarrassingly overabundant stack of books. How much more comfortable to imagine, then, that I am like the narrator[1] of Woolf's *A Room of One's Own*, who describes "an avalanche of books sliding down on to the desk" where she too sits in the same reading room, trying to figure things out. (For if "truth is not to be found on the shelves of the British Museum," she asks, wide-eyed and deadpan, then where is truth?)

In *Jacob's Room*, when the reading room closes for the day, Miss Marchmont picks up her shabby umbrella and goes for a quick visit to the Parthenon Marbles on her way out. She waves hello, greeting the statues aloud, and the woman's eccentric address to the inanimate draws young Jacob's attention. He turns around, struck by the oddness of her behavior, and though I brace

---

1   That narrator is a slippery figure, one who declares that "'I' is only a convenient term for somebody who has no real being." "Lies," she goes on, "will flow from my lips, but there may perhaps be some truth mixed up with them; it is for you to seek out this truth and to decide whether any part of it is worth keeping." She has little interest in acquiring stable identification: "[C]all me Mary Beton, Mary Seton, Mary Carmichael, or by any name you please," she says. "It is not a matter of any importance."

myself for a descent into shame, Miss Marchmont doesn't seem to mind his gaze. She smiles at him, "amiably," and when I think of this moment, it feels as if somewhere back behind the page Woolf smiles too, as if she notices her readers' distress and subsequent relief, as if she could actually *see* us, as if it were no great matter to reach through the words and touch another's time.

That day in March, as I stood in Room 18, gazing around the crowd of human figures (some marble, most flesh) the thought of Miss Marchmont's eccentricity—and Woolf's smile—gave me a little burst of courage. I walked around to see the marble gods from the back, a generally unpopulated area. Not forbidden, by any means, but just odd enough that I felt the eyes of a guard upon me. I tried to pretend he was not there. It was Demeter and Persephone I wanted to see. Mother and daughter are headless, footless, somewhat ravaged, but Demeter still rests her arm on Persephone's shoulder, loving and relaxed. I could detect no anxious protection, no bodily tension indicating defense. It must be spring, I decided, the season when Persephone returns from the Underworld and her mother lets the rage and grief of winter go.

I WAS NEVER KIDNAPPED, but I have been to the Underworld. In the summer of 1995, when I was fourteen, my grandfather died, and my mother and I flew to England for the funeral. My father (a merchant mariner) was at sea, and my sister was signed up for a week of camp, so I was my mother's sole companion. When we arrived, my mother settled into her parents' flat, while I was sent to stay with my cousin and his girlfriend. They were both in their early twenties and I treated myself to imagining I was one of their glamorous friends. It was exciting. I'd never been in London without my mother before. My cousin and his girlfriend took me out one night in Camden Town, let me drink myself into oblivion. I remember very little, but I know that we walked to the World's End—a semi-legendary pub—and I borrowed someone's ID to enter the Underworld, the basement club below.

It was there, in the Underworld, that I danced with a man whose face time has worn away, but whose hands I remember later in an alleyway reaching beneath my dress to pull down my underwear. I remember the feeling of my back against the wall. I don't remember what happened next, but I can easily recall the immense shame I felt back at my cousin's flat when I looked down at the bright spots of blood. I was supposed to be grown-up. I was afraid that my underwear, white cotton and high-waisted, had given me away as a child. I was afraid I was in trouble. I was still drunk.

The next day, my cousin and his girlfriend went to a family dinner, everyone gathered around the table, around the fact of my grandfather's death. I spent the evening alone in their basement flat, vomiting from the combined effects of alcohol and the morning-after pill. I watched *Pulp Fiction*.

I waited for my mother. Her rage. Not with the man, but maybe my cousin, or with me. How terribly I had misbehaved. I waited for winter. I did not know the myth, but instinctively I wanted her to tear England apart, like Demeter in Ovid's telling, to "forbid the fields to bear a crop / of any kind" so that "[this] island that had boasted its plenty / Throughout the world [would] lay barren." Or just for her to want to find me. She did not come. Summer rolled onward.

There was an emptiness in the years that followed, all through high school. My sister went away to boarding school, and with my father so often at sea, for months at a time our house was home to only my mother and myself. I struggled with feelings I did not know how to name, let alone control. The more I acted out, the further away my mother drew. She made certain I received the education she desired for me, at great cost—as I was often reminded—but beyond that I could expect little in the way of emotional support. I had, I came to understand, gone bad. She found me upsetting.

Over time, and in particular over the years of writing this book, I have learned to gather subjects through which I can perceive my mother indirectly, the way people will watch an eclipse through a pinhole viewer so the sun cannot burn their eyes. The life of Virginia Woolf has proved to be an especially reliable space within which I can make my explorations: she is geographically proximate (both Woolf and my mother spent years living near Kew Gardens), and their biographies overlap at certain points of shared suffering, but between the two women there are enough differences in class, artistic practice, and historical moment that if, as I worked, their overlaid paths began to feel too dangerously bright I could step off onto a shadier route. The other day, among my notebooks full of research and other acts of composition, I found a sentence I had written to myself along the way, something between a joke and prayer: *Virginia Woolf can't hurt me (haha).*

DOWN THE STREET FROM the British Museum, a lingering winter threatened the early March daffodils. It was cold and wet enough that I ought to have caught a taxi back to my hotel, but I had another statue to visit, the bust of Virginia Woolf that stands a few blocks away, at one corner of Tavistock Square. It was not our first meeting. Every time I see this casting of her I wish she had not been left frozen in this haunted expression. It's good, of course, the sculptor Stephen Tomlin's talent undeniable, but I don't want so many people to meet her this way. I don't want her public presence to be so locked into sorrow. It too easily narrows her life down to her death, as if she were forever about to walk into the River Ouse and drown. There are other ways she walked, other places. I have tried to learn those paths, and my mother's too. Restless with what I have been told—even by my own memories—I have wanted to go and see for myself.

This book contains several journeys to the UK: one with my mother and sister in September of 2018, and then three on my own: October 2019, September–October 2021, and March 2023 (the visit I have been describing here). Each return has brought with it new understanding, new ways to view old stories.

When Woolf was twenty-three she traveled to Athens, visiting the Parthenon, the temple from which Elgin snatched the gods. Some figures still remained; in her diary Woolf wrote of "fat Maidens" who hold up the portico, smiling "with tranquil ease, for their burden is just meet for their strength." She let her imagination fill the scene in further, so that "the warm blue sky flows into all the crevices of the marble; yet they detach themselves, & spring in to the air, with crisp edges, unblunted, & still virile & young."

If you look closely or for long enough at anything, time can't help but flood in, carrying the detritus of the past and future with it. One day in the British Library at St. Pancras, I unlatched the brass fastenings of *The Mausoleum Book*, an autobiography handwritten by Woolf's father, Leslie Stephen, who was so in the habit of profuse composition that even as he lay dying he insisted his words be taken down to the page. The final entry is written in Woolf's dutiful hand, her father's voice moving her pen to record an address to her and her siblings: "I have only to say to you, my children, that you have all been as good & tender to me as anyone could be during their last months & indeed years." It was after he ceased dictating that Woolf's pen was able to go fully and freely in search of new lines. I have not yet suffered my mother's death. It may be that when I do I will feel my pen's weight shift. Perhaps, alongside my grief, there will be a release from the fear of hurting her.

She has always been a sensitive person. Once, as a child, she snuck into her parents' bedroom to read letters they wrote to one another during the early years of their marriage, through the trials of the Blitz and my grandfather's time in the army. Years before my mother's birth, my grandfather wrote to his young wife to say how completely content he was with their lives, their two children—my aunt and uncle—and that he could not imagine wanting anything more. Between the lines, my mother interposed a meaning that upset her: she was unwanted, a burden or a mistake. She could not ask her parents to allay her fears without revealing her trespass, and so she cried through this alone.

Through the course of writing this book, I have gradually asked my mother for permission to read letters and diaries she wrote during my childhood and adolescence, hoping to find a more detailed understanding of events whose lines had disintegrated in my memory over time. Over time she agreed. She is sensitive; she is also brave. Because she placed her pages in my hands, and because she has allowed me to tip their sentences into the work you now hold, I have not had to hide what I learned, nor the pain we have both felt.

My mother says she likes having the words to go back and visit, a feeling common to many diarists. I have only ever made sporadic attempts at keeping a diary myself, but I often think of visiting the past, of seeing then through now, and now through then. In 1932, decades after her first trip to the Parthenon, Virginia Woolf returned to Athens with her husband and friends. This time she wrote, "Yes, but what can I say of the Parthenon—that my own ghost met me, the girl of 23; with all her life to come: that; & then, this is more compact & splendid & robust than I remembered . . . Now I'm 50 . . . now I'm greyhaired & well through life I suppose I like the vital, the flourish in the face of death." She found, among the statues, a shifted understanding of her own figure. It's not possible to describe what one perceives when returning to a place, or to the past, without also learning what has changed in oneself.

ON MY LAST DAY of my March trip to London I went to the Underworld alone, no Woolf. I walked beneath my red umbrella northward for two miles, from Trafalgar through Leicester Square, up Hampstead Road past a sign that said WE'RE TIME TRAVELERS, an advertisement whose intended purpose I did not try to determine. I find joy in such encounters, taking the sign's presence as an invitation to imagine, the world in its generosity endlessly offering language that might be read a different way. Even if a sign's words remain the same, their meaning can shift, the letters cracking enough to let us inside and rearrange what was thought to be settled.

It had been twenty-eight years since I last came to the Underworld. I calculated this as I approached the site, crossing back and forth over the street to avoid long stretches of construction work. The earth around me was broken open, letting myth flood in. I thought of the six red pomegranate seeds Persephone ate, evidence used against her after she was rescued to sentence her to perpetual return. In my mind I had returned to the Underworld so many times I'd lost count, but those visits always occurred in the strange atmosphere of incomplete memory, a space from which seasons and weather drift away.

In the present, the rain was coming down harder, my freezing hands holding tight to my red umbrella, which the wind pulled nearly inside out. I circled the Underworld, looking for the alleyway, feeling self-conscious as I went around the back. *What are you doing here?* I feared some authoritative voice demanding. What would I say? How do you explain this kind of returning? I'm not as old as Woolf at the Parthenon—my hair's only flecked with gray—but enough years have passed that I did wonder if I might meet my own ghost, the girl of fourteen with all her life to come. Could I offer that as my reason? *Yes sir, I'm looking for my ghost.* I suspected this explanation would be met with a better reaction than the other I considered: I am a mother now myself and I have a mother's rage. *Sir, I am here to break your windows and let this furious winter in.* I looked around for a rock.

Then I saw the alleyway, across the side street, sudden and unmistakable. I walked over and touched the brick wall. I pressed my hand against it. I looked around again. I could not see her—no ghost, no girl—and my eyes fell instead upon a sign painted onto a wall just around the corner. Years had worn its message away, though not completely. Amid what had faded to white one word remained, continued speaking. I read it to myself silently. Then, with sudden decision, I read it aloud, not caring if passersby gazed at me or thought me strange.

Please I said. That was the word. Nothing happened. I was cold. I put down the red umbrella, pressing it shut on the ground. I stood back up. If anyone approached me, my hands would give nothing away. It was still winter. Rain fell on my head. I read the white sign. Nobody came. I tried again.

PART ONE

"There was a garden where they used to walk,
a walled-in place . . ."

—WOOLF, *Mrs. Dalloway*

Gate

꧂꧂

ONE NIGHT, ALONE IN their room, my child Hattie wrote DOTFRGET on a torn bit of paper. Still in preschool, they had not yet learned the custom of leaving spaces between words, they did not hear the *n* in *don't*. Come morning they carried their sign out to Chris and me, laughing, "But I forgot!"

None of us—not me, not Chris, not Hattie—will ever know what they had so wanted to remember, but the sign marked the moment when they crossed some threshold out of the constant present into a small hope—fear?—for the future.

For months after, they continued making DOTFRGET signs, and the growing collection led me to picture a wall that would some-day be covered with them. In the gallery of my mind it stood next to an imaginary display of the telegrams the artist On Kawara sent over and over again, each telling its recipient I AM STILL ALIVE.

What is it that I love, that these two sentences share? Their optimism and their doom.

I love signs for what they do not quite mean to say. I collect them, which is to say I take photographs so I won't forget.

I seek their instruction as if they were telegrams from an other world.

IN SEPTEMBER OF 2018, my mother, my sister, and I took a trip from our various homes in the United States to visit Richmond and Kew in England, where my mother grew up. My father—who had by then retired from the Merchant Marines—did not come, continuing a pattern we were accustomed to, since during our childhood trips to visit my mother's family he was often away at sea.

It had been more than two decades since the three of us last made this journey together. For ten years after my grandfather's death in 1995 I did not step foot in the country. From 2005–07, I twice flew to see my grandmother, who funded the travel. Another decade passed. Then, in 2018, my mother grew suddenly generous, buying plane tickets neither my sister nor I could have otherwise afforded. Chris and I were living on his single income as a professor of creative writing at a struggling public university, supplemented by whatever I could make from publishing poems and short-term teaching and reading gigs. My sister, Michele (or Chelly), worked for a nonprofit, and her partner was employed by the state wildlife department. We teetered along in our generation's precarious iteration of middle-class life. When we landed in London, she flying in from Maine, me from Ohio, our mother gave us each one hundred pounds, spending money for meals and souvenirs. "Nannie money," she called it, meaning she'd withdrawn it from the account where she kept what she'd inherited when her own mother died.

She had arrived a few days before us, and was already firmly oriented in both time and space, while Chelly and I were moving through unfamiliar streets, our bodies' clocks lagging five hours behind. We followed her onto a bus and then off again when we reached a shopping plaza on the outskirts of Kew. Hunger had us in further disarray. Our mother led us to eat at the windowless cafeteria of a Marks & Spencer—a department store space she finds comfortingly familiar—but Chelly and I pulled out our phones and insisted on a little restaurant near the train station.

More grounded, we walked away from lunch and through our mother's childhood world: her family's flat, her school, the garage over which her grandmother lived. The slowness with which my mother walked, and the uncertainty about when I would have the funds to return, tinged everything with urgency. I feared we would not come here together again. We took pictures, images I thought would be useful as I worked to memorize a map of the place and its stories: the laundry she heaved from home to the cleaners' and back again, the birthday parties she attended in other children's gardens, envious of their beautiful dresses, their large, vibrant lawns.

"And that," she said, pausing us across from an alleyway I didn't notice until she lifted her hand and pointed, "is where a man molested me when I was eight."

The map crumpled.

I looked at my sister, and she looked back, our gazes swiftly knitting together. Without speaking, we agreed we would carry her. When our mother stepped away from the place we arranged ourselves, one daughter on each side, listening. She told us she did not tell anyone, that she bore this alone. She saw the man once after, she said, or thought she did, on a trip with a friend to the ballet at London's Covent Garden. When I think of this now I picture—from above—the route they would have walked, curving around obstacles like a dancer's spine, like a tree bending to keep toward light. She warned her friend to stay away from the man. She did not tell her why.

As we walked away from the alley, a scene returned to me, murky and slow. I checked to see that Chelly was still holding my mother in conversation and let myself fall into solitary recollection. My mother and I were sitting on the steep white staircase of the house in New Hampshire, she above, me below, months after my grandfather's funeral and the night in Camden Town. What precipitated the conversation I could not remember. I only remembered the stairs, and that I told her I had had sex. I didn't know what other words to use. It was the fastest way to say it. She said something about a man "interfering" with her when she was young, but I didn't want to hear it. I was angry that she was talking about herself, angry that I still needed her, angry at the story I could feel assembling itself in her mind, one of connection and comfort. When she hugged me it felt as if she were pulling a vision of herself out through my skin. Where had she been, I thought, when I was alone in my cousin's flat? Anger filled the space where connection could have formed.

NANNIE'S ASHES ARE BURIED in the churchyard of Saint Anne's on Kew Green, the church where my mother attended Sunday school as a child, the church where she and both of her siblings were wed. I had no recollection of coming to Saint Anne's in our childhood, but knew the place well from my mother's enormous collection of photo albums. Out of the corner of memory's eye I spied her standing on a staircase to the church in her wedding dress, gazing flatly down at her sunlit bouquet, while directly ahead of me, in the overcast present, she wore an indigo raincoat and walked toward her mother's ashes. We would find her, she said, not far from the graves of the painters Thomas Gainsborough and Johan Zoffany. She would have liked that, said my mother. Nannie loved to paint, to visit exhibitions at the Royal Academy, to drink cappuccinos in the cafeteria.

"When did you bury her ashes?" I asked, wondering what other stories she might need to say. I knew there had been a gap between her mother's death and interment. For years Nannie had lived semi-independently in a flat near my uncle and his wife, a situation made difficult by her worsening dementia. In 2007 she moved in with my aunt in South Africa and was diagnosed soon after with cancer. She died in March of 2009. Neither my sister nor I could afford to make the journey to England for the burial.

"My birthday," said my mother.

"Your birthday?" I must have known this, but when left without physical connection my sense of events easily drifts off and evaporates.

"Yes," she said, and—seeing the questioning looks on our faces—went on. "I just . . . wanted to feel connected to her? I thought . . ."

She shut and reopened her eyes, collecting herself.

"I thought it would be nice to say goodbye on the same day we met. To sort of close the circle."

Pangs struck me from several directions: love for the figure of a daughter seeking a final closeness with the woman who'd birthed her, worry that her siblings might have wanted such closeness for themselves, recognition of my mother's position as youngest child, much-indulged. I turned and my eyes fell upon my first sign of the trip, a warning to churchyard visitors:

Tombstones can be
DANGEROUS
Please do not let
your children play on them.

Despite our adulthood and my own motherhood, despite my sister's belly swollen with six months of pregnancy casting its round shadow on the graves, I couldn't help feeling that the sign's message was meant for my mother, an instruction to keep us, her children, safe, or to have done so in the past. Then it flipped and I felt it the other way around: my mother as the the threatened child.

"Here she is," said my mother, and knelt down with difficulty to touch the ground. Chelly and I crouched too. The grass was wet and cool and unkempt. I wanted Nannie to rise up and go rescue her daughter, but she did not stir. Even the grass kept still.

When we stood up and tried the door to the church we found it locked, so we went around the side to peer through the windows.

It was dark and I strained to read the signs, until my eyes adjusted and I spotted plaques on the wall, commemorating the lives and work of William and Joseph Hooker, father and son, Victorian-era scientists who oversaw Kew Gardens, the three hundred acre botanical wonderland just across the Green. They were buried in the opposite direction, not far from my grandmother's ashes.

Making a small joke about the Hookers' name, my mother offered my sister and me a way into a different conversation, a tacit request to step away from death and what the alleyway let her disclose. We smiled. We followed. She recited a different story, well-established in familial myth.

Once, when my mother's belly was swollen with the early months of me, she wandered around a rest stop somewhere between Texas and New Hampshire, searching for the cat who had escaped my parents' car as they made their way north, uncertain of where they'd live. The cat had come from a ship my father worked on, and the sailors had named it for its one claw.

"Hooker!" my mother yelled into the rest stop parking lot, her English accent softening her cry, "Hooker, come on!"

We cut across the cricket green between the church and Kew Gardens, Chelly and I laughing with our mother and then glancing at each other, eyes declaring we'd later speak more.

Our parents never found the cat, but they found, in a small New Hampshire town, a derelict house with its name hung up on a sign: MERRY LEE COTTAGE. My father fixed it halfway up and headed off to sea. A columnist for the local paper reported on the house and my mother's arrival with misspelled and mildly incoherent delight:

[T]he little five-room homestead neglected for such a long time is being steadily converted into a reproduction, or rather, a very lovely copy of an English cottage with a great deal of natural charm.

[...]

One of the prominent club women in town, Mrs. Evelyn Mooney, noted: "Mrs. Crystal will be a great asset to the community."

Indeed, wrote the columnist, "The 'bonnie lass' from across the 'herring pond,' is captivating everyone she meets."

Englishness has—in the entirety of my awareness of my mother—stood at the forefront of her identity. It's the first thing I tell people about when I'm describing her, a convenient headline for what is always a more complicated story. I often wonder which parts of her I might have more readily perceived had she raised us in her home country, which parts of her I took for Englishness, but were in fact particular to her own psyche and experience.

Months after the newspaper column appeared, I was born. Just over a year after that, my sister. Our mother taught us to record our voices onto cassette tapes to send to our father, whose frequent absences at sea meant she had to learn to manage our care on her own. All behavioral matters, my parents decided, would be considered her domain. She had high expectations. In one recording, made on a summer evening after we had spent the day at a wedding with her visiting parents, she says, "You tell Papa if you were good or bad at the wedding."

"Good," I whisper.

"You think so?" she asks.

"Let's pretend," I say.

My grandfather's voice chimes in from across the room. "No,

you *were* good, you were good at the wedding. It was only when you came home . . .ˮ

"Well they weren't *so* good at the reception," my mother says. "They were pulling and tugging. Stuff like that."

I was four years old. Chelly was three. We had not yet fully comprehended what a sin it was to display poor manners in public, but we would soon absorb the lesson. At the table, good behavior meant English behavior. Soup spoons moved *away* from oneself across the bowl. Bread was to be buttered one small piece at a time. Forks were not to leave one's left hand. One remained infinitely in one's seat until released by the authority of an adult. My mother loves to tell the story of a lunch at the Melbourne Yacht Club during a visit to Florida. (We were guests of a boat captain, my father's former employer, though I vaguely remember a sense of playacting that we were members.) Still age four, I waited for a pause in the grown-ups' conversation, and, lifting my napkin from my lap to place it on the table, said, "May I please be excused? I need to go throw up."

WE MADE OUR WAY into Kew Gardens through Elizabeth Gate, first opened in 1846 and known until Elizabeth II's Diamond Jubilee as Main Gate. Before *gate* came to mean the structure that keeps a wall opening shut it meant simply and only the opening. You could say the opening comes first, but that would be wrong. First comes the wall.

A garden was among the first examples Foucault gave when he was developing his concept of *heterotopia*—a space that is apart from but nonetheless shaped by the society that made it. (Some others: a library, a ship, a prison.) A heterotopia, he wrote, must be entered ritually, and though there was not much ritual to the passing of a credit card to the woman in the ticket booth, we had only made it to the moment by walking through my mother's childhood, her wedding, her own mother's death. My jet lag was returning and my mind was offering up glitched captions of the scenes. The tour she gave us was a baptism, I thought, trying out the idea, feeling over-pixelated and a little unhinged.

It was wildly expensive to enter.

"When she was a child it cost a penny!" I exclaimed, gesturing to my mother. I wasn't trying to complain, but rather to mark and celebrate my mother's return, the length of her life. In my mind she was a celebrity of this place. I wanted the woman to know. I wanted my mother to feel important and captivating. We were having an occasion.

The woman in the ticket booth thought I was talking about money. She must have this conversation daily. Its well-worn ruts carried us from her explanation of cuts in government support and the neglected state of the gardens during the penny-entrance era until she reached the Great Storm of 1987, which knocked down more than seven hundred of the Gardens' historic trees.

How funny that a tree could be historic, but in such a concentrated space I suppose the label is inevitable. Everything can be noticed and noted. Layers of time accumulate, and—having nowhere to drift—they harden like a diamond, are transferred into the archival vault.

The Great Storm, the woman told us, destroyed her garden shed at home. We performed understanding noises. I felt my mother's pleasure at being told this personal anecdote, imagined her future recounting of the conversation. "Oh we talked and talked," she'd say. "Just like old friends. I don't know why people tell me these things!" she'd marvel, and then try out a theory. "I think she just felt *comfortable*?" And everyone would nod.

ON MY WALL BACK home in Ohio I had left behind a halfway painted mural of a 1933 London Transport poster advertising Kew Gardens as "A Pageant of Flowers." It is possible to buy the same image reproduced in many forms from the Gardens' gift shop: jigsaw puzzle, tea towel, postcard, magnet. I left the mural unfinished because the faculty at the university where Chris taught were about to go on strike. We had no idea what ruinous cuts and demands the board of trustees would make in future years, and so were looking for work elsewhere. I couldn't face the thought of finishing the mural and then having to repaint the wall white, erasing the work and making the house blank enough to appeal to prospective buyers.

I tried to find beauty in its unfinished state. One English gardener wrote that "the aim of all gardeners should be a garden that is always presentable—not a (. . .) garden that has been, or will be, but never is at its best." She believed "a good garden is the garden you enjoy looking at even in the depths of winter. There ought never to be a moment when it is not pleasant and interesting." I tried to think of my wall this way too.

It did not work. I felt closer in spirit to Jamaica Kincaid, the Antiguan-born writer and gardener, who resists the English argument and scoffs "it is so willful, this admiration of the garden in winter, this assertion that the garden is a beautiful place then." I did not want to wait in the quiet. I wanted to know the future. I wanted to paint the wall.

At one point in his tenure as Director of the Gardens, Joseph Hooker faced pressure from the public to open Kew earlier, and to replace his forbidding brick wall with iron fencing through which people could regard the grounds, even if they were not able in that moment to enter.

Hooker was not sympathetic to the public's demands. The

gardens, he thought, were to be used *scientifically*, not for the plea-sure of a dirty mass of drunks who would trample his specimens like a farrow of piglets. Eventually he relented, shifting the public hours to start earlier on bank holidays, but as he opened time he further closed space, instructing workers to raise the brick wall another three feet. For decades after, his suspicion of the public lingered on, so that even in the 1930s, gatekeepers were instructed to keep a close watch for forbidden behaviors including "Eating & drinking, Shouting, Smoking, Singing, playing, running over borders, and loose or rude conduct of all kinds."

By the time my mother was born, just after the end of the Second World War, it seems the rules against play had softened. She and her two siblings, she told Chelly and me, knew the best places for hide and seek, and we watched her hand gesture in the direction of the trees and bushes behind which she once could take cover. I felt an urge to go pull back the leaves and look for her, but we were already walking onward.

It was money and property that pressed against the Hookers' wall to make possible Cumberland Gate, the opening through which my mother as a child would enter the gardens. In the 1860s John Gardner Dillman Engleheart, whose family had long owned the land east of the wall, had workers build a road and line it with houses. Knowing his structures would increase in value if residents were provided easy access to paradise, he paid for a new entrance to be cut through the brick himself. Engleheart's road, where my mother would later live, ended not with a wall, but a way in. Cumberland Gate is still there, but it's no longer open to the pub-lic. We had to walk past the Princess of Wales Conservatory and through the Rock Garden to reach its inner side.

Not far from Cumberland Gate, atop a small, man-made mound, sits the Temple of Aeolus. Standing with my sister and mother at the foot of its little hill, I remembered a photograph from one of my mother's many albums, taken here in 1979, just months before she married my father and moved permanently to the US. In the foreground of the picture, in precisely the space where we were standing, a bright pink clutch of rhododendrons burst into view. There was no sign of those flowers now.

In *Mrs. Dalloway*, Virginia Woolf's 1925 novel of a single day in London, it's from "behind the rhododendrons" that her character, Septimus Warren Smith, suffering terribly from his experiences in the First World War, hears the voices of the dead, singing. I listened and could not hear them, but imagined they must be here somewhere, along with a full chorus of my mother's past selves. I wanted to run off and find them. I wanted them to teach me the words to their song.

Half

A COUPLE OF MILES from Kew Gardens, in Richmond, my sister and I wandered through the cloudy morning with coffee, following the path of the Thames, enjoying our independence. Our mother was staying with our cousin Scott, but we had rented a flat nearby, needing a bit more space to let the density of the experience diffuse. Later we had plans to meet up with our mother, Scott, and his wife Kate.

We sat down on a bench not far from where later we would picnic, and where later still an artist would install a sculpture of Virginia Woolf as a marker of the years she spent living in Richmond. I felt a little thrill to be in this proximity to the physical world she inhabited, to lay the map of my life momentarily over hers. My sense of affinity with Woolf grows not only out of admiration for the words she wrote, but recognition of the moods she rode through her life, high and low, waves that sometimes wet the pages of my biography as well, and—I place this at the sentence's end so it does not crest at pathologizing either one of us—the many ways she approached reading. The sculpture's design has her sitting on a bench, book in lap, but her face is turned up and to the side, pausing as if she has reached the point in reading she describes in her essay, "On Being Ill": "We rifle the poets of their flowers. We break off a line or two and let them open in the depths of the mind, spread their bright wings, swim like colored fish in green waters."

How at ease I felt with my sister by these waters, how restless when later all the needs of the family buzzed in the air and everyone reached up frantically to meet them. *Is anyone still hungry? Look at this picture! Should we move further down the hill? The grass is patchy. We should find my mother a seat. No, she is happy on the ground. Is she lying? Kate isn't eating. Should we—can we—find shade?*

In groups of people, particularly of family, my mind can sometimes feel like a garden wilting in relentless sun. I need solitude, or movement, or ideally both to restore my thoughts to their unshriveled state. My sister's company causes no such problem. There, on the quiet bench, we let conversation rest. My eye wandered down the riverside walk to picture how the statue of Woolf would appear. An ice cream truck was parked nearby, and though I knew time and reality kept the truck and the writer apart, I couldn't help imagining ordering an ice cream and offering Woolf a lick.

Even now, when I look at an image of the sculpture as it was eventually installed, she gazes in that direction, toward the truck, and I want that pleasure for her. Want the story to turn otherwise.

When I read Quentin Bell's biography of Woolf, I stop at 1940 because I don't want to kill her. If I hold back the page, she'll never reach the river.

In that same year where I ask Woolf to stay, in September, Nazis dropped an incendiary bomb on the British Museum and firefighters hosed the blaze. Later, examining the damage to the collection, workers came across an envelope with botanical materials extracted during a diplomatic expedition to China in 1793. After almost 150 years in the quiet and dark of the envelope, the seeds of the *Albizia julibrissin* had replied to the fire and water with germination, sending up leaves like tiny green signal flags.

The three seedlings were planted in the Chelsea Physic Garden—which predates Kew by more than a century and is London's oldest botanical garden—where they thrived until the following May, when two were destroyed by another bomb. I do not know the fate of the third. By then Virginia Woolf was dead.

IT IS RARE FOR a thought to enter my mind without knowing— or soon discovering—that Woolf had something to say on the subject. In her early short story, "The Mark on the Wall," for instance, Woolf demonstrated her own concern with historical plants, turning to them to illustrate the pleasure of setting certain thoughts to the page:

> "What flowers grew in the reign of Charles the First?" I asked—(but, I don't remember the answer). Tall flowers with purple tassels to them perhaps. And so it goes on. All the time I'm dressing up the figure of myself in my own mind, lovingly, stealthily, not openly adoring it, for if I did that, I should catch myself out, and stretch my hand at once for a book in self-protection.

How good, the books behind which one can hide! One from my own childhood I recall barely in terms of plot, save that it featured a group of teenagers putting on a production of *Romeo and Juliet*, and that it made a vicar in the audience weep to see the roles played by actors the same age as their characters. I do remember its material presence, remember checking it out from the library near my grandparents' suburban flat and holding it aboard a ship crossing the English Channel one afternoon in 1989. I remember my short hair and my silence while my sister chattered happily with the captain. In a little lull he looked over at me and remarked, "Your brother doesn't talk much, does he?" I felt a flash of simultaneous indignation and pride, a sudden awareness of a transformative power I'd not known I possessed. I'd not yet read *Orlando*, the iconic mock-biography in which Woolf sails her title character over to the continent, sending him to sleep as a man, waking her as a woman. (Here, on the question of pronouns, I follow Woolf's lead, pausing to admire the single paragraph in which, as she composes Orlando's transition, she refers to her protagonist as *they*, briefly calling forth the expansive pronoun my own child now stretches across the whole of their life.)

In a cassette recording made just after our 1989 trip, addressed this time not to our father but some imaginary figure on the other side of sound, my younger self speaks with almost unbearably precise, mannered enunciation: "I had a haircut before we went to England, and now everybody thinks—well, quite a few people think—that I look like a boy." Chelly chimes in: "I had a haircut too, but it looks normal."

We went on to explain that we were the sole passengers on the boat because we had not been allowed to disembark as planned at Calais. Laws had shifted, unbeknown to my mother, and while she, her parents, and her brother (who held British passports) could lightly step ashore, the United States passports held by my father, sister, and me were insufficient without a visa. I remember feeling perplexed. As a child, I understood *British* to mean *English*, a metonymical slip that placed England as the central and prototypical nation within the UK, Britain, the Commonwealth, or the empire. It was not an accidental slip; that path was heavily trodden, though at the time all I knew was that our mother told us we were "half English," never "half British." I imagined my sister and myself as of both places, even, perhaps, more English than American, a good story for why I had so few friends back home. They weren't my people.

Still, no matter how strong a child's belief, it cannot break through a policed border. We sailed back and spent the day on the Dover shore, in the shadow of the white cliffs.

Had we been born to a British father we would have been eligible for dual citizenship, a gift they would not permit our British mother to bestow. She gave us instead the habits and tastes of her own distant childhood: margarine and cardigans and proper shoes. Out of place at home, here we were out of time. When we went to the playground the children around us wore sneakers—trainers. We would always arrive, it seemed, too late.

IN THE EVENING, CHELLY and I stepped into a little pub for a drink and to talk over a draft of the book she was revising—a memoir of going to sea with our merchant mariner father. The society of my sister was delicious, and the beer and the sitting—after the hours of larger family company—satisfied every kind of thirst. We imagined paths for Chelly's book, sighed over the tales she had to leave out. How deep the waters, I thought, beneath the ship's course. How vast the book that lived in my sister's mind and body.

We raised a toast to the work, then turned our conversation elsewhere, jostling childhood memories loose. The trip was sending things to the surface.

"Do you remember Lilliput Lane?" I asked.

"With the sandalwood girl and the iron boy?" She thought I was talking about a series of children's stories, published by Ladybird Books, whose uniform size continued across decades of publishing and formed the most visually satisfying shelf of our childhood library.

"No," I said. "That was *Puddle Lane*. I mean the little houses Mom had up on the mantel?" A row of miniature cottages stood over the top of the fireplace, a tiny linear village.

"Yes! Green felt on the bottom. Next to the music box."

"The music box?"

I had forgotten. So much drops away from my memory, not just these small objects, but events whose significance makes it seem I ought to be able to hold them with a more certain grip. It helps, then, that there are two of us. What one of us leaves out the other will often catch.

"Dad brought it back from Switzerland? Shaped like a chalet? They had a fight about it," said Chelly. "It cost so much money, and she said they were broke."

"But *she* got to spend money," I said, thinking of her collecting habits, her antiques, her boxes of fabric, her ebony statue of St. George and the dragon. Then I felt bad.

"We should get her some licorice all-sorts while we're here," I said, grasping about for ways to be kind. "Oh! Dolly mixtures!"[1] This was the candy our grandparents gave us whenever we saw them, and their annual appearance in our lives gave them near-mythic status, like the Turkish delight in *The Lion, The Witch, and the Wardrobe.*

"They're a little bit gross," said Chelly.

"Entirely sugar," I agreed. Still.

"It was our password, remember?" she added, leaning in a little closer. *"Dolly mixtures."*

I had forgotten. It was the phrase a grown-up had to utter if we were to trust them, if they asked us to go with them, if they said they were taking us to our mother. I can recall only a single instance in which I put it to use, one day when my mother and I had a mix-up about how I was to get home when my after-school ballet class ended.

"Dolly mixtures," said the driver of the last bus, and so I climbed aboard. There was no way an American would know the words unless she had told them. The language kept us safe.

---

[1]   The name, officially, is "dolly mixture," but we made it plural in childhood and I can't bring myself to correct it now.

A Sketch of the Past

AT TIMES, ON THAT first day of our September trip, as my mother, Chelly, and I walked through Kew Gardens, the stimuli overwhelmed me: the glinting glass houses, the sharp yellow of the yarrow. When the three of us stepped into the Orangery—built in 1761 by William Chambers as a place of light and warmth for citrus against the kingdom's gloom and chill, but since remade into a café—my consciousness gobbled everything at once: the vast, high ceiling; the white walls and towering windows; the way the tiny people seemed to tremble in the chairs beneath them; everyone's hands trembling as they lifted teacups to lips; the tropical botanical print of the upholstery faded and a little shabby; the pigeons people tried to ignore as if for the sake of some vital decorum; the laser-printed bees on top of the iced buns; my mother; my sister; the trays; the empire; the bright green reaching up to the horizon line through the window as if the gardens were a rising flood; and I, myself among it, grown from it, grown away; I found myself turning to my sister to exclaim, "Our imagination *comes* from here," when a pigeon nearly flew into my skull. I ducked. I felt I might be sick, that there could be no space for a single further thought to be added to the room.

It felt akin to the "moments of being" Virginia Woolf describes in her short memoir, "A Sketch of the Past," moments in which she feels she has been struck by "a token of some real thing behind appearances" and makes it "real by putting it into words." She recalls three instances from her childhood, two of which (including her terrified association of an apple tree with news of a neighbor's suicide) brought her to despair. One, however, led her to "a state of satisfaction":

> I was looking at the flower bed by the front door; "That is the whole," I said. I was looking at a plant with a spread of leaves; and it seemed suddenly plain that the flower itself was a part of the earth; that a ring enclosed what was the flower; and that was the real flower; part earth; part flower.

Woolf comes to the subject of these moments only after having passed through a sequence of other early memories. She recollects the flowers printed on her mother's dress, the sound of waves breaking at the family's seaside summer home. She writes through an attempt to understand her horror of mirrors, which she associates in part with having been molested by her half-brother, Gerald, when she was "very small." In a separate memoir, she wrote—in an oddly comic mode, arranging her syntax to play up the sentence's shocking effect—of how later her other half-brother,

George, would go on to assault both her and Vanessa. "Yes," she says, "the old ladies of Kensington and Belgravia never knew that George Duckworth was not only father and mother, brother and sister to those poor Stephen girls, he was their lover also."

I do not want to plant these stories of her half-brothers' acts in the center of Woolf's life, and especially not at the cost of displacing the wholeness she perceived and composed.

I do not want such stories to displace whatever wholeness grows in the soil of my own life, nor my mother's. Let there be room for it all, I tell myself. Let there be seasons.

The first of my own moments of being I can recall happened in a little brown car, a Colt Vista. My mother was driving us somewhere in the November or February light that is gray and purple and gold and seems mainly to exist along the near-bare sides of highways. I remember staring out the window and feeling the texture of the seat material beneath me with my fingertips, a tight-woven bumpy grid of pale gray and dark brown, and when we reached a certain point along the road—an intersection near the small regional airport—something within me aligned with the exterior in such a way that whoever I was dissolved into the perception of the entirety. Myself and my surroundings appeared as if through a stereoscope, the Victorian invention that presents each eye with a slightly different perspective on the same image for the brain to resolve into a scene with dimension and depth. Each object looked flat and strange and distributed across planes of what seemed infinite distance. I was not a flatness but an empty depth between. My breath quickened and slowed, trying to hold the moment. Years later, in the same car, in the same light, we passed the same site again, and though I recognized the convergence and braced myself for the returning sensation, it never arrived.

MY MOTHER, MY SISTER, and I walked a little aimlessly through the gardens, letting ourselves drift toward the Palm House, an enormous construction of glass and iron, inside which trees grow until they reach the roof, when they are felled so as to keep the building intact.[1] It was built from 1844 to 1848, in a moment of new material possibilities: sheets of glass had grown larger, and cast iron could now be used in combination with wrought. This was the age of spectacular glass, culminating in the construction of what became known as the Crystal Palace, built to house Britain's Great Exhibition in 1851. As one of the passages the critic and philosopher Walter Benjamin gathered into his *Arcades Project* explained:

> It seemed then that the world we knew from old fairy tales—of the princesses in the glass coffin, of queens and elves dwelling in crystal houses—had come to life. . . . It has taken four decades, numerous fires, and many depredations to ruin this magic, although even today it is still not completely vanished.

The author of this passage was writing in 1900, as the Crystal Palace was declining into shops and shabbiness. In 1936 it burned to the ground. The blaze could be seen from as far as Brighton.

Hermione Lee, author of the magnificent *Virginia Woolf*, warns against the biographer's pitfall of feeling a need to stage, interpret—or overinterpret—her subject's death, instead of reading it "as perhaps it should be read, as without content, merely contingent, just the next fact in a series of facts." On a similar note, in a book paradoxically entwined with Woolf's death in

---

[1]   Palm trees cannot be kept short through pruning; they grow from a single point at the top, ever upward and unbranching. If that crown is cut, the tree will die.

the River Ouse, Olivia Laing declares that "the future is by its nature contingent and to read every event in terms of what is yet to occur disjoints the moment in which life is lived, divesting it of that uncertain, glancing quality that is the hallmark of the present." Despite my desire to heed these words, my mind lists in the direction they warn against.

When I imagine the Crystal Palace it feels (as with that moment in the Colt Vista) like looking through a stereoscope: one eye sees the palace as it hung on walls across the continent, while the other palace was built to exhibit flames. I feel the two layer themselves over each other and combine. A cluster of glass, iron, and fire holds itself closely together in me, concentrated. Alight.

But then England is so small; perhaps there's no real room for just the glancing present, and time can't help but pile up on itself. Still, I can work to sort through the heap, to lift details and detritus from memory and examine them as if I did not yet know where the story were headed. I can think for instance, of the comforting rituals with which my mother, my sister and I used to travel across the Atlantic together. At the airport in Boston our mother would buy us chewing gum: Big Red for me, Wrigley's Spearmint for Chelly. This was medicinal gum, purchased to help our ears with the plane's changing air pressure, but we received it as a treat. At home, gum was forbidden, a disgusting American habit. In return for this indulgence, it was our job to earn compliments from fellow travelers for our mother. "They are so well-behaved!" British Airways provided even those of us sitting in economy seats with diminutive metal cutlery, and we ate carefully, napkins on our laps, elbows held to our sides. Our mother was most pleased when strangers heard us speak and gasped, "I had no idea they were American."

Then the present insists upon itself. Standing in front of her childhood home on Kew Gardens Road, my mother asked Chelly and me, "Do you remember that photo of me in the baby carriage? It was right here," and touched the railing outside the house.

My mother is, in her family, the guardian of photo albums and letters.

"Why do you think Nannie and Grandad chose you to keep the letters?" I asked, pretending I was a journalist, a role I often find more comfortable than daughter.

"Well, they trusted me," she said. "I think they just knew I would take good care of them?" When she compliments herself, or says something disapproving of others, she lifts the end of her sentences into questions.

Chelly pointed up. "Was that your window?"

"Yes," she said, "And that one there was Nannie and Grandad's."

"Do you think we could read their letters some time?" asked Chelly.

"Yes," she said. "The ones he wrote during the war—and Nannie's replies—will just break your heart. They were so young."

"Are you going to pass the letters onto us?" I asked, edging toward what I knew were unacceptable questions.

"Yes," she said, and gave my hand a little squeeze.

"And your diaries?"

"I don't think so. I don't know." She hesitated, let my hand go. "There's some stuff in there I wouldn't want you to read."

"From your twenties?" I asked, thinking of her drug use, the breakdown she suffered in 1968, which led to her spending months in a psychiatric hospital where she underwent electroconvulsive therapy. I tried to broadcast sympathy from my face.

"No," she said. "From when you were a teenager. You were horrible?"

She wanted me to pretend this was funny and she wanted me to confirm it was true. I looked away. A sign across the road began *Polite Notice*. I thought of the years after Grandad's death in which she came to England alone. As teenagers, Chelly and I ceased to behave, becoming sources of embarrassment rather than pride. We drank, swore, fucked, smoked.

When I was sixteen, as soon as school finished for the summer, I moved out to live with a boyfriend at a punk house in Maine, and just a few weeks later—when he kicked me out for cheating—the streets and parks of Boston. I hadn't exactly meant to run away. It was more that I couldn't face the thought of going home. My mother came and found me in Harvard Square and begged me to go back with her. When I refused, she made me promise I would find an apartment and a job to pay rent, saying that if I didn't she would report my running away to the police. She wanted me to be safe, to be protected. I wanted her to leave me alone.

I made up a job offer and then an apartment. Only Chelly knew the truth. She took a bus to come and see me. I made her memorize the layout of my imaginary home from a map I'd drawn on a scrap of paper, so that our stories would align if our parents asked. I scavenged food from abandoned containers of takeout and joined traveler kids in asking passing strangers for spare change for beer.

I remember a man in a suit offering another girl and me twenty dollars for a blowjob. We declined. All summer I carried a legal notepad with me, writing in a voice that cycled through performances of the selves I thought I should be. I played at being tough and blasé on one page (predicting someone will "end up a little junkie out in SF"), before growing ponderous on the next: "The question has been asked by many writers & travelers far more eloquent than me, but I ask it anyway. What is the point of all this?" I listed the many men I had sex with. The one woman I left out.

I went home in time to begin my junior year at the local private high school. I was a work-study student, but some expenses were not covered, and I thought my mother would not forgive me if I abandoned my studies after two years of sunk costs. More importantly, I was exhausted. I couldn't remember my last night of good sleep or sobriety. A person I'd considered a friend attacked me one night, trying to steal my blanket. "A fucking blanket," I wrote. "It makes me sick." It would be my final paragraph in the notepad.

At one point that summer my mother had asked me what it would take for me to come home. I don't know why, but I said I wanted my own cat. When I came back we went to the animal shelter together. I named the cat Tess, after Thomas Hardy's *Tess of the D'Urbervilles*, a novel that ends with Tess being executed for the murder of her rapist. I thought the name was pretty, and that the reference would make me sound like a sophisticated, literary adult. My mother would later say that my request for a cat was a reminder of "the child still in me." I must have been confused about how old I was supposed to be.

I realized I was still looking at the sign. *Polite Notice*. I turned back around to face my mother on the sidewalk by her childhood home. She had registered my silence.

"I do have something I wrote that you could read," my mother said. "A description of the house from when I was little, and how we'd go play for hours in the Gardens. I was going to make it a gift for Nannie and Grandad's golden wedding anniversary, but I never finished. Would you want to see that?"

"Yes please," I said.

THE DAY AFTER WE walked through Kew, my mother, my sister, and I made our way toward the London Design Biennale at Somerset House, which sits by the Thames just over the bridge from Waterloo Station. I was tired and distracted and could not get the lyrics to the Kinks' "Waterloo Sunset" out of my head, which meant, if I decided to believe my recitation, that I was in paradise.

According to the blue dot on my phone's map this was not true. We were in Covent Garden, taking a detour for lunch on our way to the exhibition. The air was chilly and damp and I was developing a sinus infection, so when we found a little spot where we could get noodle soup with a spicy broth, I insisted this was the place. My mother was not sure, but I was grumpy and hungry and demanded it. We carried our steaming bowls to the long thin table facing the window, arranged ourselves in a row on the tall stools. *This is better*, I thought. *Having eaten I will remember how to behave.*

It worked. Released from my hunger I could think beyond myself. As my consciousness inched outward it was struck. *Covent Garden. My mother. She's just a child.* I straightened my spine, remembering the man she thought she saw. When I went to fetch more napkins to soak up what the soup was making my nostrils release, I felt I was abandoning my post as lookout, watching the passersby in case one was him, or a man who brought that one to mind. My mother's, I mean. *I will kill him*, I thought. He never arrived.

At Somerset House we found our quarry: a stack of newspapers that had been printed to accompany the room's art installation (a giant slab of pink agar under plexiglass, a petri dish on which remnants of visitors' microbiomes were invited to grow). Midway through each copy of the newspaper were poems Chris and I wrote at the request of a friend, whose editorial collective helped conceive of the installation.

The room belonged to Switzerland. Each room in the massive building—which William Chambers designed after finishing his follies at Kew—was given over to a single country, who had been asked to represent themselves, or their history, or art generally, by filling the space with material objects, but the Swiss installation had run into difficulties. It was not possible to view the agar clearly; the inside of the plexiglass box was covered with condensation. The dampness of the day.

The light outside had gone golden, and I took pictures of my sister and mother reading the newspaper with sun haloing their hair. Chelly's belly gleaming beneath her black shirt. My mother was proud. I could see it. Her children in this elite English place for all the world to see. Her pride was the cause of this light.

Paradise

VIRGINIA WOOLF HAD NO children, but she loved her sister Vanessa Bell's deeply. Late in his life, Quentin Bell—her nephew and biographer—said, "Her laugh made a paradise of Richmond."

Virginia and Vanessa (as well as their brothers Thoby and Adrian) were at the core of what would become known as the Bloomsbury Group, which began in 1905, as the orphaned siblings hosted evening gatherings of Thoby's friends from Cambridge. Guests included Clive Bell (the art critic whom Vanessa would go on to marry, who fathered her two sons), and Duncan Grant (the artist with whom she'd later live and have a daughter). (Should mention: Grant's first love affair with the Stephen family was not with Vanessa, but her younger brother, Adrian.) In late 1906, the twenty-six-year-old Thoby died of typhoid, a loss that brought the group closer together in their shared grief.

The group's borders are blurry and long-contested, but one can cry out an incomplete roll call of its members: Leonard Woolf (who was abroad working as a colonial administrator when the evenings began, but who would return and wed Virginia, who excitedly described him as "a penniless Jew"), Lytton Strachey (eminent biographer, briefly Virginia's fiancé, Duncan Grant's cousin and—for a time—his lover), Maynard Keynes (also Grant's sometime lover, more frequently an economist, and eventually husband to Lydia Lopokova, the Russian ballerina), Roger Fry (art critic whose affair with Vanessa would later complicate Virginia's task of writing his biography), Carrington (an artist who illustrated the first edition of *Kew Gardens* and lived with Lytton Strachey), and David Garnett (an uninteresting writer who was Grant's lover in the early years of his living with Vanessa Bell, and who would, decades later, marry their daughter). I could continue on into that second generation, or outward to further associates, but it would be, I think, unwise and overwhelming.

It is famously difficult to keep track of these tangled relationships, though it seems helpful to work from a general assumption that at one point or another any given person was probably in love with the irresistible Duncan Grant. Marriages were open and almost nobody entirely straight. Maynard Keynes actually maintained a spreadsheet of his sexual encounters, which sounds clarifying, but is so populous that it only makes my head spin. Among the group, goes the legend, everything—sex, literature, philosophy, the color of one's living room—could be subject to discussion and therefore (should their talk lead them to new understanding) to subsequent change. The whole world might be transformed! One night in 1918, Woolf returned home from hearing Roger Fry and Vanessa Bell rhapsodize as they unpacked a Cézanne painting Maynard Keynes had just brought back from

France. She picked up her diary to record her thoughts in the moment: "What can 6 apples not be? I began to wonder."[1]

While the Bloomsbury Group was named for the London neighborhood where it began, its members also made their homes elsewhere. Leonard and Virginia Woolf had a series of country houses in East Sussex.[2] Not far from the last of those, Monk's House, stood Charleston Farm, home to Vanessa Bell, her family and its extended, sometimes messy circles. Maynard Keynes and Lydia Lopokova lived nearby as well. In addition to these rural outposts, early on in their marriage, Leonard and Virginia Woolf moved to London's western periphery, seeking quiet in suburban Richmond, where they first lived on the Green. For most of their Richmond years, from 1915 to 1924, they made their home at Hogarth House, at 34 Paradise Road, an easy walk to Kew.

It wasn't until 1917, when she had recovered from one of her major breakdowns, that Virginia and Leonard founded the press they named after the house. Two years later, the Woolfs printed a short story she'd written for the press, "Kew Gardens," which speaks of many dynamic beings in the botanic space—a married couple, a father and son, a snail crossing a leaf—but feels (until its last paragraph) anchored in the body of a single observer, a person sitting in stillness, perhaps on a bench, like the unmoving figure at the center of a snow globe.

Just before the Woolfs moved to Richmond, in 1913, some suffragettes—who evaded capture and have never been identified—broke into Kew's Orchid Houses, smashing the glass walls and destroying the plants inside. Almost two weeks later, in the quiet of

---

1   People like to note that Cézanne's painting actually had seven apples in it. I like to pretend Woolf left one out on purpose, as if the last apple refused to be anything but itself.

2   The second of these they never actually lived in. Virginia bought it on a whim and they sold it soon after finding Monk's House.

the night, Olive Wharry and Lilian Lenton set fire to the Gardens' Refreshment Pavilion. They were caught, imprisoned, and went on hunger strike, as did many suffragettes in this moment. Prison doctors subjected both women to forced feeding, prying their mouths open with screws and inserting rubber tubes down their throats. This was not only a violent practice, but a dangerous one, as food could easily end up forced into a person's airway. In Lenton's case this led to pneumonia and subsequent release.

In Woolf's "Kew Gardens," it's possible to detect subtle evidence of the Pavilion fire. Two of her characters, a young couple on an awkward date, decide—awkwardly—that they ought to go have their tea "like other people," but don't know where to go. "Wherever *does* one have one's tea?" asks the girl, "vaguely looking around." It is difficult to have one's tea in a building that isn't there.

ONE MORNING, LATE IN our September trip, I left behind Richmond, my mother, and my sister, so I could pass the sunny day with friends. Near the London Eye I met up with Kaveh, Paige, and Raewyn, and we climbed aboard a ferry to ride down the Thames. Raewyn was visiting from New Zealand (by way of an artist's residency), while Paige and Kaveh had flown in from the US to give poetry readings. I felt nervous about managing conversation, but their talk soared along with little need of my support. I could let my mind coast back and forth between ferry and shore, present and past, imagination and memory.

When we passed the Tower of London I caught a flash of my nine-year-old self standing in the spot where a swordsman executed Anne Boleyn. I remembered learning she paid him to replace the usual axe wielder in hopes of a swift death. I remembered he was French and I remembered that every time I think of the story of her life, something in me wills it to turn otherwise. Something in me always hopes that she will live. But the ferry was swift and we were already passing Greenwich, which insists that time is always and only ever measured in distance from itself.

My memory pushed me onward, from the summer of our Tower of London visit to the following Christmas, when my English godmother sent me a book about C. S. (Clive Staples) Lewis and Narnia. I had read all of the Chronicles and this new tome was an immersive treasure. I flipped back and forth between map and timeline, trying to hold both in my mind at once. The danger of leaving Narnia is that time moves differently there, so to step out of the wardrobe for even a day means upon your return you'll find months have passed. It is an elsewhere with an elsewhen.

England is not—was not—my Narnia. Rather, returning to visit my grandparents every other year, my own body was the place I found strangely shifted. The letter slot in my grandparents' door remained the same height, but my head shot up to it and then beyond.

Before Lewis invented Narnia, he and his brother Warnie loved to make stories in each other's company: Clive's set in a place called Animal-Land, Warnie's in the India he conjured across imperial distance. Vexed by the problem of how to join their stories, they decided the best solution was to set the borders of Animal-Land and India together. They drew the map to fit, made India an imaginary country.

England is not my Narnia, but on the map my memory makes, all its rivers are connected, from the Thames to the Ouse, and I can send my finger along them to reach anywhere I like, or, for that matter, hate. Wherever and whenever I land, says the map, YOU ARE HERE. It marks *here*, or *you*, with an X.

Sinking further out of conversation with friends, and staring over the edge of the ferry into the depths of the Thames, I felt myself drop into the water and backstroke toward Fleet Street, where Wynkyn de Worde set up his printing press in 1500, a street that borrowed its name from the river it crossed. As industrialization and other forces filled the river with sewage and waste, it was gradually covered over, taken underground.

Mind swimming beneath the city, against the current of the Fleet and toward its origins, I surfaced in Camden Town. Somewhere within its boundaries was the brick wall of the building against which I had passed minutes that night, drunk and fourteen. There was no sign, or if there was I couldn't read what it said. Maybe *here*. Maybe *X*. My cousin Scott had been somewhere nearby. Maybe, I thought, he could tell me more. I had always been too scared to ask. I did not want to upset anyone. I thought of my mother as a child, running out of the alley, thought perhaps she had felt the same way.

"We're here," said Kaveh, and the bricks rippled back to river. We climbed off the boat and pulled up maps on our phones. We were looking for our friend Jack's house. He'd invited us to come pass the afternoon beneath a tree in the back garden, with ice cream, tea, and cake.

I FIND IT HARD to remain as close to myself as it seems these memories might demand, though I try. It's easier to distance my thoughts with Woolf or with some kind of theory, to gaze at events as though through glass. I can stand and nod next to Foucault, for instance, as he gestures to his exhibit of *crisis heterotopias*, "privileged or sacred or forbidden places, reserved for individuals who are, in relation to society and to the human environment in which they live, in a state of crisis." Mulling over honeymoons, he considers whether "the honeymoon trip wasn't both a heterotopia and a heterochronia of sorts: it was necessary that the deflowering did not take place in the very house in which the girl was born; this deflowering had in some way to take place *nowhere*." I keep nodding, but the glass is not strong enough, or my thoughts grow too fast, before I can cut them down. The glass cracks on that word, *deflower*:

Deflower: *verb* : 1 : to deprive of virginity. 2 : to take away the prime beauty of.

When Americans use the word *pants* it makes English people giggle; it's the equivalent of saying *panties*. *Underwear* is the word I have always used. An example: "My white underwear was spotted with blood."

No sooner do I say this than I feel the glass reassembling itself, and behind it the return of my map. I can gaze at it and wonder—as if it had almost nothing to do with me—how long it would take to walk from my X to Woolf's to my mother's. It might be too far; her knees have grown tired and sore.

If I let my eyes drift farther north, they fall upon a town named Harrow, a word one can read in several ways. As a verb it means both *to raid or pillage* and *to prepare soil for planting by breaking it apart*. Holding the two meanings in mind, I can perceive the word's suggestion that what begins in violence makes way for new growth. *Fascinating*, I can think, as if the word were a rare specimen displayed in a glass case. It's pinned down, dead. It cannot hurt me.

MY MOTHER MARKS THE linear progress of time at Kew by the noise of airplanes overhead. (She is Americanized enough that the extra syllable of *aeroplane* has fallen from her speech.) In her youth, she says, the gardens were quiet, a place of peaceful repose. Some imp within me always wants to disturb it; when she complained of contemporary noise to Chelly and me as we stood in the Gardens together, I felt an adolescent compulsion to remind her that even Woolf's Kew was not a peaceful refuge. A whole century ago, wrote Woolf in "Kew Gardens," the sky overhead spoke through "the drone of an aeroplane," and in truth "there was no silence; all the time the motor omnibuses were turning their wheels and changing their gear."

It was easier for me to trust Woolf's perception than my mother's. Though my mother stood before me in the flesh, and Woolf was made of words inside my skull, those words felt alive and vital. They twitched and took wing, while my mother's smooth recollection felt as if she were reading from a museum placard, reciting the flat narrative of a past paradise degraded by an impure, industrial fall.

It could be that my mother's memory of quiet is not wholly her own. It could be that she is flying further back, past Woolf, all the way to the sentences of the Victorian nature writer Richard Jefferies, who in 1887 declared:

A short walk from Kew station brings the visitor to Cumberland Gate [. . .] It is not necessary to go further in; this spot at the very entrance is equally calm and still, for there is no margin of partial disturbance—repose begins at the edge. Perhaps it is best to be at once content and to move no further; to remain, like the lime tree, in one spot, with the sunshine and the sky, to close the eyes and listen to the thrush.

I did not want to be content. I did not want to be still. My mother's pace along the path was slow—her knee again—and I itched to leave Chelly by her side and run onward, gathering all I could perceive, alone with my leaping thoughts. More noise! More planes! Sunlight flashing from the lake!

Once, in 1938, a plane crashed near Kew's Palm House, falling from the sky with its advertising banner trailing behind. (Nobody was hurt.) It makes me think of the plane Woolf sent through the London sky in *Mrs. Dalloway*, skywriting letters made of smoke. She has people below crane their necks, working to read its message, which emerges slowly, one letter at a time:

But what letters? A C was it? an E, then an L? Only for a moment did they lie still; then they moved and melted and were rubbed out up in the sky, and the aeroplane shot further away and again, in a fresh space of sky, began writing a K, an E, a Y perhaps?

"Glaxo," reads one person below. "Kreemo," reads another. "It's toffee," says a third. To Septimus Warren Smith, Woolf's troubled, tragic veteran, the words are illegible as language, and yet their form still gleams with meaning. He watches the words "languishing and melting in the sky and bestowing upon him in their inexhaustible charity and laughing goodness one shape after another of unimaginable beauty."

I have tried to learn what words were imprinted on the banner of the plane that crashed at Kew in 1938, wishing to catch a glimpse of its possible meanings, hoping to perceive a multitude like Woolf's, but the banner is hidden completely in photographs, its message unmentioned in newspapers. It remains a long blank strip, a secret message. It is a piece of my mother's imaginary silence.

Birthday Hill

BEFORE OUR TRIP TO England I ordered a map of Richmond—which sits on the southwest side of Greater London—from 1914, hoping to catch a glimpse of ways Virginia Woolf would have walked, and while I felt slightly uncomfortable with the expense of having it printed, I loved to touch its smooth surface. I put one finger on 34 Paradise Road, Woolf's house, and the other on my mother's. If the two of them were planning to meet, a fair halfway point would be the Great Pagoda at the far south end of the gardens. I moved my fingers until they touched, but my mother wouldn't be born until 1946 and Woolf couldn't wait that long.

What to know about the Pagoda: it has the wrong number of floors. Chinese pagodas are built with an uneven number of levels, for good luck. William Chambers built his with ten.

Woolf mocked his folly indirectly in her first novel, *The Voyage*

Out, calling a villa in Santa Marina "absurdly frivolous . . . like a pagoda in a tea-garden." During World War II, engineers saw its height as a useful resource and cut holes through the floor so they could test smoke bombs by dropping them through the Pagoda's center. In 1762, Chambers had workers install wooden dragons at its top. At some point they came down and vanished. Briefly in 2014, people thought one of them may have been found, as "[i]t had the hopeful initials WC—thought to stand for William Chambers," but "further research had revealed the dragon was part of the sign for a public lavatory."

Sometimes I imagine the future war or storm or abandonment that awaits the Pagoda and its surrounding grounds. The beautiful map ripped to bits. And then, one day, a sign to tell the story. All that was, gone, cast into words asking readers to imagine.

Does one trust the sign? Does it correspond to events in the world? At what angle? The danger of signs is that they can tell readers the past has been settled, contained in a reasonable narrative, and they need not look back to find a meaning of their own. In *My Garden (Book)*, when she goes to visit England, Jamaica Kincaid writes:

> I was in a country whose inhabitants (they call themselves subjects, not citizens) do not know how to live in the present and cannot imagine living in the future, they can only live in the past, because it, the past, has a clear outcome, a winning outcome. A subdued nature is part of this worldview in which everything looks beautiful.

In my childhood, the story of Kew Gardens was beautiful and was over. When we visited, we entered through the past, regarding newer buildings with practiced suspicion. The site in my mind that remains most heavily subject to the past is King William's Temple, which in my family is called Birthday Hill, as it was the traditional spot for celebratory picnics when they lived nearby. They brought me there as a baby, taught me the private name.

My mother, who loves to make art in almost every imaginable medium, once inked a drawing of the temple onto the chest of drawers where she kept her clothes, and so to visit her bedroom was also to visit Kew. The Gardens were, as they had been in her childhood, a daily presence in our lives, a reminder of her first home. When I walked through the Gardens with my mother and sister, it seemed almost impossible for the drawing to have sprung forth from its two-dimensional black lines into this actual space. Birthday Hill was the place I felt most populated with ghosts, sitting on blankets and eating bad British ice cream, scenes I borrowed from my mother's photo album. Everyone was white and sunburned and spoke in accents my infant ears knew were other than those I heard at home.

So many of my statements to my mother on this trip began *I wanted to ask you*, as if it were the final opportunity to understand her and her country. I wanted to pin it all down to the map, wanted to carry it home.

"I wanted to ask you," I said, as we walked the path to Birthday Hill, "about robins. What's the story of robins? I feel like I remember some kind of connection to Nannie?"

"No," said my mother. The robins were her own, have always shown up when she needed them, when she felt afraid or alone. I didn't ask her for more details; my mind reached toward the moment, hesitated and held back.

The world arranged a different sort of answer to my unspoken questions: when we sat on the bench outside the temple atop Birthday Hill to have our photo taken and layered into the place, a robin duly appeared. Behind us, on the bench, a child's sweater waited to be reclaimed.

AMONG MY MOST FREQUENTLY indulged hypocrisies stands my attitude toward my mother and coincidence. *My* coincidences, which are full of beauty and meaning, stem from my interest in the world, while *her* coincidences stem from her interest in herself. It is this part of me that wants to clip the robins of my mother's meaning, or to set it in a story I fashion on my own. I want to perceive the robins' significance, not inherit it.

The sun's magnetic field is about twice as strong as Earth's, and in the darkness of sunspots several thousand times more so. When sunspots are numerous, the rise in solar activity can lead to the release of a solar flare, a burst of energy that—when it reaches our planet—can cause disruptions to Earth's magnetic fields. Compasses go askew, power grids fail. Birds who rely upon magnetic fields to aid in their migration become disoriented.

Though a link had been proposed between migration and magnetic fields as early as the nineteenth century, it is only recently that scientists developed a plausible explanation for the mechanics of the relationship, with a particular focus on the case of the European robin (*Erithacus rubecula*), a slightly different species from the British robin (*Erithacus rubecula melophilus*).[1] Beginning a little over a decade ago, some proposed that the link between the birds' movements and the earth's magnetic fields can be traced to a protein at the back of the robin's eye, which is stimulated by blue light. Within an atom of that protein, a pair of electrons exists in a quantum state, always spinning in opposite directions. When light photons enter the bird's retina, one of these electrons is relocated to another atom nearby, but its spin remains coordinated with the electron in its original atomic home. Because electrons carry a negative charge, the two atoms are shifted out of a neutral electromagnetic state; one is now positive, the other negative, and the electrons form what's called a "radical pair."

According to the physicist Jim Al-Khalili, this quantum entanglement means that, though the pair no longer share the same space, "their fates remain intertwined." What does this mean for the robin? As the bird moves in relation to the magnetic field, the two charged atoms react, thereby changing the chemical reactions of the molecule they inhabit, and the signals it can produce. In effect, those signals permit the robin to "see" where it is in relation to the magnetic field, and use this information in its migratory navigation.

Asked in 1802 about the reason for his frequent attendance at scientific lectures at the Royal Institution, the poet Samuel Taylor Coleridge is said to have replied it was "to renew his stock of metaphors." Some in the sciences cringe at such use, fearing— often with good reason—the misapplication or misunderstanding of their work. Quantum entanglement is especially vulnerable

---

1   Incidentally, the British robin and the American robin are related by nothing but language and color.

to poetic exploitation, as it both upsets an understanding of the world in which things can exist in only one state or place at a time, and confirms a common wish for a bond with that which is at a distance. Though space keeps us apart, our minds or lives may yet be linked.

I try to hold my bond with my mother steady, try to navigate our relationship with care, but it is subject to frequent flares and storms.

When she was in labor with me, my mother says, she had a vision: a circle of faces looking down at me coming into the world, mysterious guardians, and then I was born, with a piece of the amniotic caul still over my face. Among the beliefs associated with such births: that the child will be lucky, or cursed, or capable of supernatural vision, or that the caul itself can protect its owner from drowning. Recently, knowing of my growing obsession with Virginia Woolf, my mother told me she thought one of the faces watching over me might have been the author. Though I smiled, I struggled to believe her. It was too convenient a link to a life I wanted to keep to myself. Later, mind wandering back toward my mother's story, I stumbled over a sudden and very loud question: if Virginia fucking Woolf had watched over my birth, then shouldn't someone have thought to save the caul?

A FEW MONTHS AFTER our trip, on Christmas—the last we'd celebrate in New Hampshire, as my parents were preparing to sell the house and move to a smaller place near my sister in Maine—my mother and I exchanged books. We do want to understand one another. We do want to be understood. My gift to her: two editions of *Robin Redbreast*, an anthology of poems, images, quotes, and fragments through which the bird makes its way, often stopping by jails and prisons. The first edition was compiled by the evolutionary biologist David Lack. The second was the work of Lack's son, Andrew. It is as if the book were a hereditary trait.

My mother's gifts to me: a copy of Woolf's *Kew Gardens* with the Pagoda imprinted on the cover, and the account of her childhood home she'd offered during our September trip. The recollections were handwritten in a dark blue diary with a postcard of the Pagoda glued to its front. At the end of the day—after stockings, gifts, Christmas crackers with paper crowns and ridiculous jokes, everyone taking turns to hold Chelly's new baby, sledding, custard, mince pies, and Christmas cake—I took the blue diary up the steep white staircase to my mother's art studio, which Chris and I were using as a bedroom for the week. She'd composed her sentences in 1992, when she was forty-six, but had written in the voice of herself as a child, calling her parents *Mummy* and *Daddy*.

Christmas, she'd written, "was a fun time—socks full of nuts, tangerines & little presents, gifts to be sorted & opened, a great big meal, turkey, ham, pork, pudding & mince pies, followed by a day of sitting around attacking the various bowls of sweets, nuts, figs, & dates, not forgetting the Christmas cake of course."

When she or her siblings were sick, she said, her father would cover them with his army greatcoat to keep them warm; the bedroom they shared was often cold, but:

You can hear the birds
singing in the garden & if
the window is open sometimes
they will fly into the bedroom.
One time a robin flew in when

I was sick & I just knew
that it came in to make
me feel better. Occasionally we
will find baby birds or birds
that have been injured in the
garden & we take them into
the house & put them in
a shoe box but they
usually die because they
are frightened.

In my mother's childhood bedroom, the light from the paraffin heaters "accentuated the multitude of shadows in all the corners which had a habit of turning into frightening shapes when you were trying to go to sleep."

"Everything," she went on, "seemed ok when Daddy tucked you up in bed . . . but somehow the room had a habit of growing when you were on your own."

Holding my mother's blue book, I gazed through the window without seeing evening's blue shadows on the snow. Instead, my mind brought forth a scene from Woolf's 1927 novel, *To the Lighthouse*, in which the family's youngest daughter, Cam, has trouble falling asleep because of the presence of a boar's skull in the children's bedroom. Mrs. Ramsay—a character very much drawn from Woolf's recollections of her own mother—soothes her child by draping a shawl over the skull, hiding it from sight, and then lulling her to sleep by transforming it further with words. With the shawl wrapped softly around it, the skull:

was like a bird's nest; it was like a beautiful mountain such as she had seen abroad, with valleys and flowers and bells

ringing and birds singing and little goats and antelopes . . .
and Cam was repeating after her how it was like a mountain,
a bird's nest, a garden, and there were little antelopes . . .
until [Mrs. Ramsay] sat upright and saw that Cam was
asleep.

Returning to the more immediate world, from where I sat I
could see, at the top of the steep white stairs, a doorway leading
from my mother's studio to the U-shaped room where Chelly and
I slept as children, one of us on either side. We each had a night-
light, a small ceramic house whose windows were illuminated by
a bulb within. Chelly's was squat and orange, a single story. Mine
was two stories and white. In the night, when I would wake, on
my own and afraid, my little house seemed not to be a house at all,
but a great gleaming skull, windows transformed to eye sockets
blazing a terrible light.

The next morning, in preparation for their move to Maine,
my mother had my father bring down boxes from the attic, full of
documents and detritus related to Chelly and myself. He placed
them on the floor of the family room, between the Christmas tree
and the woodstove. She asked us to sort through them; anything
we did not wish to take home would be thrown away. She sat
on the sofa and watched. After a time, Chelly had to go tend to
her baby. I kept at it. Our mother had saved so much. The drawings and worksheets from elementary school were easy enough
to look through while under her surveillance, but when I reached
the shoebox holding my middle school years I felt her gaze shift.
I moved more rapidly through the box: dreadful poems, angry
notes from friends, pencil drawings of Kurt Cobain. I had been
so wildly unhappy that it felt physically painful to touch the era's
artifacts. A diary entry recounted the mandatory family therapy

session that followed an attempt I'd made at killing myself one awful drunk night.

"This is really hard," I said. "I don't think I want any of this."

I picked up the box and carried it into the kitchen. I threw it away. My mother nodded her approval from the sofa, through the doorway.

"It *was* hard," she called out. "You know, I always loved you, but sometimes I didn't like you very much."

Virginia Woolf was thirteen when her mother died, and for years after she thought of her obsessively, with frantic, desperate love. It was through writing *To the Lighthouse*, with its vivid depiction of Mrs. Ramsay, that Woolf finally unbound herself from her mother's ghost. Standing in my parents' kitchen in the silence following my mother's declaration, I looked down at my empty hands. I felt a thought land there, unbidden: what form would the haunting have taken if my mother had died before I became so difficult to like? Quicker than reason could gather its devastating answer, fantasy proposed a shimmering line of speculation. Perhaps she would have been a tender ghost. A ghost with a shawl or a greatcoat. With murmured words. The bird's nest, the garden. A song to ease one to sleep.

IN THE SPRING I was offered a job teaching poetry at a private university in Atlanta, and Chris was able to keep his own university position in a switch to teaching online, which gave us the unprecedented wealth of two regular salaries, plus a research fund. We sold the house, abandoned the mural, began again. We had lived in Atlanta once before, ten years earlier, and now we would live near old friends from that era, plus others who had moved there in the meantime. Everyone was a poet, a writer, an artist. I could buy so many books.

My joy grew complicated when I learned that one of those friends, Molly, had also applied for the job. There are so few steady positions in our field that it's hard to explain the scarcity to people outside of academia. The competition is miserable. Molly lashed out, sent me a hurt and furious email. Then her husband Blake's mother died. In May, when I came down to Atlanta to look for a house to rent, I went to the funeral, sitting next to our friends Nick and Carrie, who looked so normal I felt momentarily confused, until I realized it was because of how accustomed I am to seeing poet friends dressed in all black. After, in the reception room, Molly approached me. She thanked me for coming. I raised wary arms to hug, to tell her how sorry I was at the loss. I wanted to apologize for getting the job too, for what felt like a great blow to our friendship, but before I could find the words she began to tell me that she was leaving teaching for good. Higher education, she said, was a disaster. She couldn't imagine going on in it. Too unethical. I didn't know what to say and so I just nodded, stiff arms back by my side, hoping I had somehow misunderstood.

I flew home, packed up our belongings. In June, for the first time in my life, I forgot my mother's birthday. She texted to ask if I was okay. I said sorry. I said yes. I was okay, mostly. Our furniture would reach Atlanta before us. Blake oversaw its arrival. The house was small and awkward, but we would, we said, live there for just a year.

By October enough time had passed that it seemed possible to try to reconnect with Molly. She and Blake had us over for dinner with Nick and Carrie. We ate in the dining room among their shelves of books. In the passageway lined with china cabinets, Molly had hung the gorgeous wallpaper herself, matching the repeating pattern seamlessly. She wore a dress made from an old silk map. She had forgiven me, I hoped. I was overwhelmed by all the newness—job, house, my book about to come out—but thought maybe we could go for a walk some time. She said that sounded nice. I felt my arms soften. She recommended her hairdresser, her therapist. We will have, I thought, everything we need. A genius at baking as well as language, Molly brought out a pavlova she'd prepared, a dessert my English godmother used to make, too, and which my grandmother used to buy from the frozen section of Marks & Spencer. Molly worried the meringue part was wrong.

THE EVENING BEFORE MY thirty-ninth birthday, just over a year after I visited Kew with my mother and sister, I traveled back to England alone, flying through the night to meet the day across the Atlantic. My new research fund from the university meant I could afford such journeys; they were work and I would make from them a book. The oval windows on the plane filled up with orange sunrise, like juice in a cereal advertisement. I played alternating American and English pronunciations of the word in my head. AdVERTisement. ADvertisement.

I dropped my bags at the Kew Gardens Hotel and made my way to Saint Anne's on Kew Green, stopping in the churchyard to visit my grandmother's ashes buried beneath the soil, and then walked on to Birthday Hill. I had never been the subject of the hill before, and didn't know what to do. I sat down on the grass and felt embarrassed. In company the decision to sit on the ground has an immediate story, one person's desire for rest and the reassuring agreement of another. Alone, with no distribution of responsibility, the weight of that decision is a lot for one person to carry. I felt my consciousness exposed. I took a picture and sent it to my mother. She will like that, I thought. I was at once an adult in a raincoat and a baby in a Liberty print dress eating sticky mouth-fuls of bad ice cream, or I was not even born; my mother was the child turning from one year to the next. My grandmother was both sitting behind me and mingling with the soil of the Green. I wanted to lie with my face pressed against the ground until the grass had written itself into my cheek, but I was too beholden to the unspoken rules of the place, its invisible signs. I lacked the courage to misbehave.

Instead I walked to the Pagoda and climbed its interior, spiral-ing staircase. I was exhausted from the journey and frightened that jet lag might send my mind into one of its more dangerous plum-mets. *Cyclothymia*, the disorder is called, swinging one's mood in uncomfortable circles, through euphoria, despair. Mine seems gentler than the illness from which Woolf suffered—I have never hallucinated, as she once did during the breakdown following her mother's death, that the king was yelling curses from the azaleas (a subgenus of rhododendron)—but I tread through days with care, relying on routine to keep myself steady. The spinning route up the Pagoda stairs and an increasing sense of vertigo made one half of me nervous, while the other half scolded that I could not have come all this way and spent all this money to stop without reaching the view. I looked out in the direction of the house where Virginia and Leonard Woolf founded the Hogarth Press, where they first printed *Kew Gardens*. I tried to make my gaze a thread, but airplanes kept snapping it in two. On my way back down the stairs I moved slowly, clutching the handrail. The helpful guide below had given me a hint that the fourth floor would reward greater attention, so I stopped there, found graffiti scratched into a windowpane. It was difficult to decipher until a cloud passed behind and against the white the words came clear:

J. Piper March 16th 1883
It is Snowing[2]

Time collapsed; it was surely not snowing that fine October afternoon, but I was transported. Piper's words—the insistence on that one moment, that snow, that "I am still alive"—so moved me that the fine day dissolved and I found myself looking out not through the window, but the lines of a poem by Wallace Stevens:

It was evening all afternoon.
It was snowing
And it was going to snow.

Had I reached out my hand, I thought later, the glass of the window would have softened. It would have let me pass right through.

---

2   *The Times* confirms the window's report, saying on this date that "The weather to-day has been generally unsettled, with showers of snow, hail, or cold rain in all parts of the kingdom."

Wall

++

THE DAY AFTER MY birthday, in the reading room of the library and archive at Kew, I touched a knot, a slim blue thread Virginia Woolf tied to hold the binding of the first edition of *Kew Gardens* together. The institution put me through the usual rituals of entry: I surrendered my belongings to a locker downstairs, wrote my name in their book, swore to treat the papers with care. Still, despite the ceremony that permitted me access to the library, I felt emotionally unprepared. The little book, which I flew across an ocean to see—no, to touch—was sitting like any other in a grey box on a gray cart. Nobody stopped me from opening it. I felt like a fraud, an intruder. How was it possible for my position in space to coincide so closely with Woolf's? To touch the thread, to feel the knot (how tightly she tied it!) press against the soft pad of my finger?

The feeling I experienced did not quite align with Woolf's moments of being, but more closely resembled C. S. Lewis's description of joy, a word he capitalizes. "All Joy," he writes, "reminds. It is never a possession, always a desire for something longer ago or further away or still 'about to be.'" Like Woolf, he recalls a few early instances of the feeling in his life, remembering how his brother Warnie decorated a biscuit tin with moss, and "twigs and flowers so as to make it a toy garden or toy forest. That was the first beauty I ever knew. What the real garden had failed to do, the toy garden did. . . . As long as I live my imagination of Paradise will retain something of my brother's toy garden."

This brings Jamaica Kincaid back to my mind, her well-formed scorn. Why must this country's imagination be so captivated by a yearning for the long ago? Why must the world be reduced to a toy or a map redrawn to suit the cartographer's stories? Why do these objects please me, against my better judgment? They do. I have to say this. I despise monarchy and British nostalgia, but when I think of Queen Mary's dollhouse at Windsor Castle, I awake in me a child in awe and full of longing, pressing her nose up against the glass to peer at the little rooms. The child's mother crouches down to whisper, "Isn't it *lovely*?" and the pair of them are on the verge of shrinking to wander the dollhouse together when Woolf walks past, scoffing.

Asked by the dollhouse committee to write something that could be printed in miniature form for their library, Woolf refused. She laughed aloud. I love that sound, its joyous announcement that she would let no such space collect her. I want to step into the shape it leaves in the air.

In the life-size library at Kew, as I turned a page of Woolf's words, a minuscule speck of paper flaked off onto the table. I stared at it. I hungered. If I had a tiny envelope, I thought, I could perform the smallest theft. A crime at the scale of a dollhouse. It remained a thought. I kept reading. Later, I told my friend Robyn, a poet, about the speck and my desire. She is American and immediate. *Oh!* she said, *but you should have eaten it.*

ON SUNDAY THE ARCHIVES were closed, so I went to church, to the service at Saint Anne's on Kew Green. I wanted to be inconspicuous and clothed myself in a calf-length dress, beneath a rose-pink coat I bought from Marks & Spencer. In the churchyard it occurred to me that I had unwittingly disguised myself as my mother in photographs from the 1970s. In silence it was an effective costume, but speech would give me away. I walked in, settled into a pew, and greeted my closest seatmate with only a nod.

When I had traveled with my sister the year before, I heard her occasionally shift into an English accent, I thought as a way of deflecting attention from herself. At the time I was surprised by her choice, but at Saint Anne's among the stained glass and cross-stitched kneeler covers I felt an understanding. The parishioners were reciting the Lord's Prayer, "Our Father, who art in heaven," among the first rhythmic language I ever memorized, and without my mind's permission, my body gave over to the softness, the unison, as if I'd fallen into a river of speech and the current would carry me home.

"And forgive us our trespasses, as we forgive those who trespass against us."

I knew it was my mouth moving, but it was my mother's voice spilling out. It felt like trance, like surrender. As if I were a doll being moved about by a child's giant hand, I found myself lining up to take communion, an act I'd not participated in for years. By the time I reached the altar I had managed to break out of the trance, but could not will myself back to my seat, could not bear the thought of the attention my behavior would draw. I distracted myself by silently reciting lines from a poem by Jack Spicer:

> when you've tried the blessed water long
> Enough to want to start backward
> That's when the fun starts
> Unless you're a poet or an otter or something supernatural
> You'll drown, dear. You'll drown

I learned early to be afraid that, like Woolf, I would drown. Myself, I mean, though drowning is only a manner of speaking. My ideation prefers other means. It joined me before I was fourteen, before I felt my back against the wall in Camden Town. The wall is not the source of my ideation—I feel compelled to make that clear—but I can't say it isn't a tributary.

BEFORE CHURCH, IN MY hotel room that morning, I'd been scrolling through images of Woolf—laughing and smoking in her garden, playing cricket with her sister in matching dresses, heavy and dark—when one photograph arrested me: Woolf as a small child in the arms of her mother, Julia. I knew, I thought, that shape. From where? I watched the matching image float up from the depths of memory until it fully surfaced: a photograph from my own family albums. I sat in my mother's arms, the straight part of her hair a precise echo of Julia's, the same corner of her face obscured by a daughter. I'd scanned the photo years ago, I remembered, and grabbed my phone to look for it, suspecting I'd find the pair less similar than I was imagining. I was wrong. The composition was so alike it was as if my mother and I had staged a re-enactment.

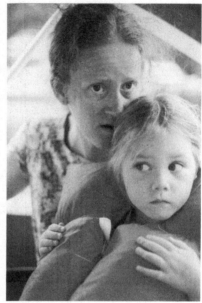

And yes, I see the life vest. It's so on the nose that I almost think the gods must be playing one of their little jokes. They mean well. They are trying to help. *Don't worry!* I tell them and wave. I remained—remain—afloat.

AFTER CHURCH I WALKED over to Richmond to meet family for lunch, through incessant rain. I followed Hooker's wall until it ended, then called up the map on my phone. I was a blue dot creeping ever closer to Water Lane. Some of the dots to whom I am related—Scott, Kate, their niece Sophia—arrived at the pub soon after me, but the others—aunt, uncle, cousin Alison, her son Ethan—were caught for hours in traffic or weather or the wrong side of the river. I ordered a Bloody Mary and settled in for a wait. I spoke brightly when spoken to. When I was young, I was permitted to bring a book to occasions such as these. In the distance, I saw a panic, the hour at which I would become so frantic to be alone that my manners would disintegrate—my footmen shrinking down to mice.

Half my mind was in this room; the other half was watching the river through the window and remembering from Woolf's diaries that these streets sometimes flooded and redirected her walk. Kate joked that the water would trap us here.

When at last the others arrived, my aunt and Kate smiled and chattered. Sophia was sorting out where to go to university. Ethan, impatient with the family's turns between appeasement and teasing, gladdened when Kate brought out a bag of paper, pen, and games. A teacher of young children, she understood his struggles. My uncle sat in silence until with sudden decision he asked, "So how are book sales, then?" My book was about crying. My book was not out yet.

The food, said everyone, was lovely, though there was some worry about indigestion. I could not tell whether I was hungry or full. My plate contained steamed zucchini, which the menu called vegetable marrow. Hiding my phone under the table, I looked up the term's origin and learned that while in England the word refers to long summer squashes, in Scotland *marrow* means *one of a pair*.

When the food was mostly gone a decision was made—through a conversational process at once tentative and inevitable—to go for a walk. Desperate to focus, to contain, I suggested we head toward Richmond Green to find the house where Leonard and Virginia Woolf lived briefly when they first moved to the area. My aunt added her own vague aim to locate Maids of Honor Row, the Georgian houses where ladies-in-waiting once lived, or she allowed herself at least the quiet suggestion that such a structure existed, probably nearby.

Umbrellas up, we clumped into an amorphous cell that contracted itself when other people needed to pass on the sidewalk, while still sending communicative signals within its membrane: the weather is unpleasant, the house is to the south. When we reached number 17 on the Green, we found it under construction, hidden behind painted plywood boards adorned with signs advertising Woolf's former presence, alongside a history of the building's life in the eighteenth century (coffeehouse) and nineteenth century (cooking school). After Woolf, it was a storeroom for the local pharmacy.

Next to Maids of Honor Row, to the west, stands a gatehouse, the only remaining part of Richmond Palace. Henry VIII died here. So did Elizabeth I. I was taught their deaths as a child, through a timeline of monarchs marked on a blue ruler my grandparents bought for me from the gift shop at the Museum of London. It felt like the ruler itself had been left inserted in my head. I wanted to shake it loose. I wanted to run through the arch and down to the river to walk its length home while there was still light in the sky, but first the family had to say our goodbyes. We held our umbrellas away from each other to hug. It emerged that the goodbyes were incomplete; Scott and Kate were staying. They were going to H&M and I was going with them. The second floor light was white and the floor was white and every item of clothing was covered in flippable sequins that children touched one way and then the other, like they were stuck in a perpetual GIF.

"It's a shame your mother couldn't come with you this time," said Kate. "We always have such fun with her. And she cleans our plants, which I never remember to do."

"You're really lucky," added Scott. "Your mum's so cool."

"Maybe next time," I said, and lifted up a fluorescent shirt, pretending I was considering whether to bring it home as a gift for Hattie.

It is through Scott that my mother remains most connected to England and her family. I try, and mostly succeed, in not begrudging her the relationship, but sometimes it causes confusion. When Hattie was born, Chris and I had to declare who would become their guardians were we both to die. Talking through the matter with my mother on the phone one day, she idly asked, "What about Scott? It would be nice for Hattie to stay connected with the English side of the family." I ended the call as quickly as I could.

Through the window of H&M I could see the sky deepening to indigo from the scarrow of twilight, and I reached down into my body to pull forth the words with which I could finally conjure departure.

By some miracle it worked. Stunned by my success I wrenched myself away with such force that it felt like I had catapulted through the window to land in the dark street. I didn't even stop to pee, despite the fullness of my bladder. I had to walk. I had to walk to the river, toward Kew and the blue knot and the wall, and I had to do it alone, by which I mean with no one but Woolf for company.

Model

IN 1769 GEORGE III sent James Cook and the botanist
Joseph Banks (Kew Gardens' unofficial first director) on a voyage
to Tahiti so that they might observe the transit of Venus from a
point at a great remove from England, and the king would make
his own observations from a specially built observatory at Kew.
They were under some pressure; the transit would not be observ-
able again for more than a century. In triangulating their data,
thought scientists across Europe, they would be able to determine
the distance to the sun, which would enable a simpler way to cal-
culate longitude. At the time they relied on a complicated system
of charts that tracked the precise phases of the moon. To improve
upon their imaginary grid would increase their nations' ability to
transport their cargo across the seas: indigo, cotton, sugar. People.

Venus's edges are difficult to discern with precision, and
Cook's observations differed enough from his partner's that their

numbers proved virtually unusable. Meanwhile, back at the Kew Observatory, it was recorded that the king "was the first who saw the Penumbra of Venus touching the Edge of the Sun's disk." He was attended in his observations by the keeper of the observatory, who stocked the place with a wealth of scientific equipment, including an orrery, a not-to-scale model of the solar system whose bodies, represented by balls, can be moved by clockwork. These grand movements, these massive expanses of time, writ small. The instrument was absorbed into the royal collection, and is now held by the Science Museum at Kensington. I let my mind dwell there to imagine the king, a human granted genocidal powers, peering down at a solar system sized for his use, watching it turn and pause according to the rate at which he spins a little handle of brass and oak, because it is within this disoriented scale I feel most able to sense the pattern and motion of the country's history.

When teachers want to introduce students to planetary movements, they have to decide whether to first show them an orrery, which simplifies the solar system by compressing the distance between celestial objects, or a more complicated, realistic model, which might overwhelm its audience. Researchers who have studied the matter point out that people "often forget that all models are metaphors," which means that we can "over-extrapolate" meanings that make sense within the model, but do not correspond with reality. We may be further apart than the model tells us to think.

AS I WALKED AWAY from Richmond along the towpath by the river, my headphones played me a podcast featuring Woolf's great-niece, Virginia. (These names, like comets, recur.) She was recollecting how her father, Quentin (Woolf's first biographer), used to get his children to "make paper cities," how they'd spend a week creating the city's "churches and bridges and houses and palaces," and then "take it out onto the terrace in front of the house and set fire to it."

The first I heard of the Great Fire of London was at an exhibit at the Museum of London, a tiny replica of the seventeenth-century city in a dark room, slowly lit by a path of flickering electrical flames representing the fire's four-day progression from the baker's shop where it began to its consumption of more than 13,000 houses. In the miniature form in front of me the little buildings remained impervious. You had to imagine them gone. A nearby room was constructed as a replica of a Blitz-era bomb shelter; above us burned imaginary flames. Or perhaps this was in the Imperial War Museum. Or the Royal Air Force Museum. I received so much instruction.

I have a stronger memory of visiting Bekonscot Model Village, "the world's oldest and original model village," a half hour drive from my grandparents' flat. We encountered the village as the scholar Yael Padan argues tourists often do, as a representation of the nation in which—like an orrery—time and space are condensed. Bekonscot was first opened to the public in 1929, and while some of the modelscape still dated from that era, my marvel stemmed from the many years folded into one place, as workers had continued to build new constructions, keeping the village a reflection of the present world, so that tiny brutalist concrete structures lived alongside the Tudor cottages.

Chris grew up loving miniatures too. Before Hattie was born, we visited Miniature World in Victoria, just across the Canadian border, a city named for its distant, imperial ruler. I remember nearly nothing of the space itself, but recall with a kind of horrified glee a certain postcard image from the gift shop, of a giant white woman with a perm and a royal blue shirt peering down at a chest-level carnival. She was monstrous and gleaming, a huge smiling sun rising over a scene it planned to devour.

Miniatures require visitors from the larger world to reveal their secret. To regard a postcard of Bekonscot with nothing but models in view is to remove scale. It's not that the postcard pretends the scene's tininess is reality, but rather every postcard looks through a standard window into a scene that could be any size, at any distance. The land of elsewhere. Wish you were here.

IN 1996 BEKONSCOT DECIDED that its newer buildings were no longer pleasing; they tore down the models that would have looked out of place in an imaginary 1930s. Their website now describes the setting as a place that is "forever England," quoting Rupert Brooke's 1914 poem in the voice of a soldier heading off to war: "If I should die, think only this of me: / That there's some corner of a foreign field / That is for ever England." This was not their intention, but with these words in my head and my eyes on a photograph of the little village, for a moment I cannot help seeing Bekonscot as a large English grave.

In my childhood, on the day my family visited Bekonscot, a camera crew was filming. They needed people in the background, so before we entered certain parts of the village we signed a release form and were paid "a shilling, or something like that," according to my mother. The director was pleased by our looks, "perfect little English girls," he said, and I preened in my cardigan, my white socks, my leather sandals, clothing my mother had scoured thrift stores to find. She never had enough money to buy the new clothes Chelly and I wanted, but she also disapproved of their look. I remember a pinafore she sewed for me, from fabric bought on sale, dark blue thread pulling its smocking tight across my chest. I despised it. I still have it. Hattie wore it until it grew too small. Now it is in a box in a closet, awaiting whoever comes next.

But Bekonscot. It was 1989. Chelly's ruffle-shouldered sweat-shirt gave her and the year away, but I could have cut myself from the scene and pasted my image into the 1930s without causing much uproar, and I knew this was desirable, that the adult world loved old-fashioned children. I had read *A Little Princess*, with its approving description of the young heroine, Sara Crewe, whose father was a British Army officer stationed in colonial India, a heavy investor in diamond mining. The book taught me to note the value of the "old-fashioned thoughtfulness in her big eyes," her "old-fashioned speech," her "old-fashioned air." I did not note the "ayah who worshipped her," nor the unspoken violence with which Sara's father extracted their wealth. I did not understand exactly how she and her father ended up in India. I only knew it was to England she had to return.

I never suffered the fantasy that I was secretly of royal blood, but I liked the way our nuclear family rhymed with the queen's in her childhood: mother, father, two girls. When then-Princess Elizabeth first visited Bekonscot it was on the eve of her eighth birthday, and the visit went unphotographed. She returned with her sister when she was ten, still not yet heir apparent to the throne, but when I look at the image of her touching the roof of a little house, I see an element of possession, of dominion. I see the hand of her third great-grandfather contentedly spinning the planets.

THE PODCAST WAS OVER and I still had to pee. I told myself I would cross back to the main road through the Old Deer Park, as Woolf used to do, before the tow path reached Kew, but when I looked to my right I could see nothing but ditches, a scraggle of trees, and darkness. I took off my headphones. The King's Observatory, I knew, was just over there, but the route was blocked, and in any case the building had become a private residence. Streetlamps had vanished. A few lights from the other side of the river gave dim outlines to the trees and bushes, but the ground and its soft mud were in utter obscurity. I took out my phone to use as a flashlight. I could have turned back, but a stubbornness in me refused, or else the force with which I wrenched myself from family into solitude created such momentum that I could not resist stamping onward.

A human figure with an enormous backpack shuffled out of the bushes on the park side of the path, and my pace—already brisk— grew quicker. I was too tired and in too much discomfort to argue with my fear. In daylight, people marvel that a stretch of urban river could so suddenly give way to the sense of rural isolation. It opens over them, but caught in the night I felt it bearing down. The trees grew taller. The darkness deepened. Enough time and distance went by without seeing another person that I considered veering off the path to pee in the woods, but then a jogger loomed up and I lost my nerve.

When eventually I reached Kew Palace—the smallest of all the royal palaces, built at the edge of Kew Gardens—I fantasized about climbing the wall into the privacy of the well-kept bushes to relieve myself there. I couldn't help thinking of a correspondent scene from *The Madness of King George*. The king, who would go on to be imprisoned at Kew, is in the throes of a manic episode. He wakes at dawn and demands that his attendants follow him outdoors, where they recite the Lord's Prayer together. Possessed by seemingly endless reserves of energy, the king stalks back to the palace, where—struck by a sudden and urgent need—he bursts into the room of an unidentified woman, uttering "Piss-pot, piss-pot!" and with his desired object in hand, pauses to offer himself encouraging words: "Do it England, do it," before at last he empties the royal bladder and exhales in blissful release.

Bibliomancy

AS SOON AS I returned home to Atlanta, I began planning my next trip, a summer visit this time, so I could inhabit the kind of hot July day in which Woolf set *Kew Gardens*. I looked forward to it, the promise of future work, a useful place to put my mind when the noise of publication of *The Crying Book* grew overwhelming. All the books I'd written before had been poetry collections, which the world tends to receive more quietly. Feeling overly exposed, I hid in other people's pages, preparing to understand more of the country to which I would return. I gathered together Woolf's diaries, her letters, her essays critiquing the empire. I read Jamaica Kincaid's *A Small Place*, where she writes of her disdain for tourists in Antigua, her home country, and of her fury with the crimes of British colonizers: "[W]hen I say, 'I am filled with rage,' the criminal says, 'But why?' And when I blow things up and make life generally unlivable for the criminal (is my life not unlivable too?) the criminal is shocked, surprised."

It's astonishing how offended, how *sad*, the English can be. Take, for example, the words of the art critic, Alastair Sooke, who sighs that "these days it's unfashionable to aspire to be a 'citizen of the world,'" and goes on to insist that "the greatest masterpieces," such as the Parthenon Marbles, "transcend national boundaries." "Transcendence" keeps reappearing in the sentences of those who do not want to give the marbles back; it is apparently one of the statues' most important responsibilities. In any case, they don't belong to Greece, says Sooke, "They belong to us all." I couldn't help sensing the unspoken limits of Sooke's "us," and the people one would happen to find at its center.

Idly I clicked around to learn more about him, and discovered— my blink of surprise quickly giving way to a nod and a shrug—that at the age of fourteen Sooke played the role of Kay Harker, the main character in a BBC radio adaptation of the children's fantasy book *The Box of Delights.* Earlier, the BBC had produced a televised version of the same story, which Chelly and I watched obsessively in childhood, gathering scraps from which we built up our sense of how to be English. It helps, we learned, if it's Christmas. It helps if you inhabit an imaginary version of the 1930s. If everyone is white. We were taking notes. We recited lines to each other. Some of them still break periodically into my consciousness: "The English haven't got tails!" scoffs Kay when he travels back in time to argue with a stranded sorcerer, who's convinced otherwise.

THAT DECEMBER WE FLEW up to Maine for Christmas with my parents, Chelly, and her family. I was exhausted. All the travel to promote the book, the disordered hours, the telling and retelling of tears, they accumulated until I felt I had no mind from which to speak. I slept through most of the visit. When we returned to Atlanta, I started seeing Molly's therapist, as well as a psychiatrist who would—at last—prescribe medication to ease the plummets and surges of my mood. I worked to focus on my students, to perform my new role at the university. I asked Chris to tell me everything would be okay. I felt my energy return, saw him grow hopeful. I watched Hattie draw portrait after portrait and taped them to the wall. I hung a little bottle of hand sanitizer from my backpack, concerned about reports of a new virus spreading through Wuhan.

"I'll see you soon," I told the students on the last day before spring break, unsure of what *soon* might mean.

We filled the freezer with food, just in case.

One Monday afternoon, as he drove me back from a preparatory conversation for a radio show interview about my book, Chris glanced at me in the passenger seat and said, "I have to tell you something really sad." I didn't want him to. I wanted to already know, to get outside the moment. Impossible. I felt fury. He kept going.

"I got a phone call while you were talking."

He paused for too long before saying that Molly was dead.

"No," I told him, and in my mind she died a thousand different ways at once, though I already knew what he would say next.

"She killed herself yesterday."

I lifted my legs up onto the seat and pushed my shoulder against the closed car door, trying to get as far from the news as possible, while a voice spilled words out of my mouth.

"Why are you still driving? Why are you telling me this? Stop the car. Stop the car."

I thought if he stopped the car then it would also stop time, stop speech, stop understanding. It didn't work. We called Nick and Carrie, then went over to Blake's house. I brought disinfecting wipes. Someone was cleaning the kitchen. Blake was on the sofa. When I leaned down to hug him his body felt incongruously solid and strong.

Back at home we grew scared. We stared at our screens, trying to determine what was safe. Chris said we should not go to the funeral, worried about the risk of exposure for Hattie, who has asthma. He could tell that I still wanted to attend and added that he would not stop me. I stopped myself. It felt like betrayal. I was coming unmoored. Who would die now? How was it that Molly already did not know this strange time? Carrie posted photos from the funeral, relics of Molly's life arranged in a small and beautiful way. Her baking. Her books. They glowed up from my phone, casting blue light on my hands.

Bereft, I went looking for Woolf. In her diary for July 2, 1918, she wrote "Influenza, which rages all over the place, has come next door." Two days later she added "We had a great bout of people yesterday, as we tend to do nowadays." I wanted to run in and shake her. *They have to stay home, Virginia.* I wanted to keep everyone safe, but they were inching toward the moment when the epidemic turned deadly. I could flip the pages and bring them there, to October, when she wrote that "we are, by the way, in the midst of a plague unmatched since the Black Death, according to the *Times*."

I went to the *Times* digitized archive and found their tone to be milder than Woolf described, but then, she did love to tell a good story, was tethered only lightly to facts as others might report them. The newspaper suggested, as preventative measures, "fresh air, cleanliness, and constant disinfection."

I wanted the fresh air at Kew, as if—could I only get there—I'd be in a different timeline. Molly still alive. Virus unspread. I wanted none of what would happen to happen. In the garden I harrowed the soil.

At Rikers they offered prisoners six dollars an hour to dig mass graves. I thought back to another line from Kincaid: "Only the impossible can make me still." They could have released the prisoners; this was not impossible. The jailers named it so to halt imagination. It was as if they thought of their captives as already dead.

My mind caught itself in a loop: What will happen. What will happen. I would not have minded losing that present to a reading from the future, no matter which glancing qualities were lost. Let it be a story, I thought, in type, over there, instructing me in how to act. In an act of desperate bibliomancy I opened Woolf's *The Years*. The first sentence: "It was an uncertain spring."

PART TWO

"She glanced over the walls covered with
books, as if for a second she had forgotten the
position of the door."

—WOOLF, *Night & Day*

Bridge

I RETREATED TO SLEEP and read and write in a closet. In January, we had discovered it was large enough to contain a twin mattress, and I moved in, determined to reduce the sleep deprivation tilting me again toward suicidal ideation. It helped, but Molly's death made the danger return and feel more real. Sometimes in those weeks, when I took a walk—performing the complicated ballet of keeping distance from others—I could only go so far before I turned myself around, because it was too easy to imagine a slip off the curb and into the street. Traffic was much lighter, but there was enough.

The closet felt safe. Out there, in the space of the house and the garden, time relentlessly spat out its present events: hard and loud and large. In the closet, time and space reconfigured, fluid as waves. I wandered through Kew in videos, a parallel life, one in which I could think beyond fear and grief, the autocaptions' haphazard transcriptions opening tiny windows into a garden grown wild:

> *they often have spectacular flowers they know how to exist*
> *historic follies guttered through our cube landscape*
> *world with ferocious Victorian collectors*
> *unobstructed space for the spreading crown*

I took notes. I practiced new methods. I ordered an object called Google Cardboard, a corrugated box equipped with stereoscopic lenses. When it arrived I slid my phone in and it told me to look at the fox. I turned my head and looked at the fox. It cocked its head and jumped. I tried to wander Kew but the closest the box would permit me was near the London Eye. I walked this path with Kaveh, Paige, and Raewyn the day we rode the ferry down the Thames and I tried to will the executioner's sword from reaching Anne Boleyn's neck. I looked left and right, trying to see who was here now. There was no identifying these people. Their faces were blurred out, featureless, as smooth as a doll's crotch. When I set the box down I was still in my closet.

TO THE NORTHEAST OF the gardens stands Kew Bridge, the third of that name, a straight line laid over the wavier route of a vanished ferry. From the summer of 2009 to the late spring of 2010 a group of activists created the Kew Bridge Ecovillage nearby, squatting in a space of derelict land slated for the erection of luxury flats. The ecovillagers built structures from discarded materials and gathered their food from what supermarkets threw away. The activists' foe, a development company called St. George, would eventually have activists forcibly evicted, despite opposition from many of their neighbors in local council housing, who had long worked to petition against the site's development. In one painful scene from a documentary about the group, men trying to empty the village of its inhabitants have stripped an ecovillager of his pants. He stands atop a remaining hut, holding out against St. George alone, bare-assed and trying to protect his genitals from view, while the men who will carry him away holler and jeer from below.

The company's name might be seen to overlap with a figure and flag beloved by English nationalists, but St. George himself is hard to assign to a single place. In some traditions he is a Greek or Roman soldier, killed for refusing to renounce his Christianity. He comes from Palestine, or Ethiopia, or Coventry. The earliest versions of his story focus on his martyrdom, but over time he became additionally revered for slaying a voracious, plague-breathing dragon who terrorized a village into sacrificing first their sheep, and then, when all the sheep were dead, their young people. In some iterations of the story George declares he will kill the dragon only after the villagers have promised to convert to Christianity, which—unsurprisingly, under such duress—they do.

Our days of isolation seemed to endlessly repeat, generating little material for conversation with my mother when I called her on long walks around the neighborhood, wanting to keep her company through the dual strictures of viral containment and Maine's cold days. I began to use my closet research as a way to give form to our talking. I was not yet ready to face the moments in which I'd felt abandoned in England—the present was hard enough already—but we could, I thought, explore something on the subject's perimeter. Maybe it would make some future path feel smoother, oil a rusted gate.

"Tell me about St. George," I said, stepping into the street to avoid a family walking in the opposite direction.

"For St. George and England!" she exclaimed, pretending to seriousness, quoting Shakespeare.

"No really, do you have any kind of personal attachment to him?"

"Well, you know how when I went to Sunday School I was in the Girl Crusaders?"

"What on earth are the Girl Crusaders?"

"My Sunday School was called the Crusaders, appeared to be harmless at the time, but who knows. And they had the flag of St. George as their symbol. I'll send you a picture of my Bible leaf, which I won for perfect attendance at the age of six." She laughed. It was a good sound.

"What do you know of the story of St. George?" I asked.

"I just think of the story of St. George and the dragon."

"And what happened?"

"Just that he killed a dragon. So he was a hero!" She imitated a fanfare of little trumpets.

"And your statue?" I pictured it, carved from ebony, with a removable spear in St. George's hand, ready to strike the dragon cowering below.

"Now that *was* interesting, because I bought it in a little shop in North Conway that sold African imports, and I really *shouldn't* have bought it, because we really didn't have the money, but I was friendly with the owner, so I talked her down a bit on the price and then when I got home I found out it was St. George's Day!"

"What a coincidence!"

OTHER NATIONS BESIDES ENGLAND have also named St. George as their patron, including Ethiopia and Georgia (the country, not the state where I live), and he's often spoken of as coming from wherever his supplicants call home. His global popularity means that relics associated with him were, and are, held in several different locations. His encased arm, for instance, is on display in Venice, alongside some blood of Christ and a skull of John the Baptist. St. George's own skull (or most of it, minus the jaw) was possessed by a church at Livadia in Greece, from which in 1393 a failed attempt was made to sell it to England's king. A medievalist, Kenneth Setton, spoke of tracking this particular relic at a 1972 gathering of the Medieval Academy held at the Beverly Hills Hotel, a location whose incongruity—even in the dark of the closet—brought me delight.

In his speech, Setton pointed out that "St. George appears to have had more than one head," but this did not diminish their power for believers. Reading further, seeking deeper understanding, I slowly grew overwhelmed by saintly reproduction. It began to feel monstrous, grotesque, and contagious. Like his several heads, the meanings behind St. George's name also tend toward multiplication: work, earth, struggle, pilgrim . . .

My mind swarmed with Georges. I wanted to contain the spread of their stories and body parts, maintain a safe distance, but despite the isolation of the closet I felt the effects of their ongoing transmission. The words strained to join with George III across the river at Kew, the mad king who was also a farmer, his dragons atop the pagoda, the sheep he bred below. It was as if vines grew through the closet in such a tangle that I could not move. I struggled. I tugged. But the roots were stubborn, spidery, and deep. I picked up an entirely unrelated volume, seeking relief: W. G. Sebald's first book, *After Nature*, not the prose amalgamation of fact and fiction for which he'd later become famous, but a work of poetry. As soon as I read its opening lines I had to throw the infested thing against the wall:

Whoever closes the wings
of the altar in the Lindenhardt
parish church and locks up
the carved figures in their casing
on the left-hand panel
will be met by St. George.

I FELT MYSELF BECOMING unreachable, drifting deeper into the closet as spring, strangely, bloomed in its usual way. Hattie and Chris cast messages under the door, in hope of making contact. One afternoon, while I visited the kitchen, Chris gave me a small book containing a version of Woolf's short story "The Mark on the Wall" as it was first printed by the Hogarth Press in 1917, "retaining words and phrases removed from later editions." The book and I scuttled back to the closet, where I read with pleasure through the familiar sentences, in which the narrator notices a mark on the wall that puzzles her, and then performs a feat of associative thought so as to avoid getting up to discover what the mark might actually be. At the story's end, the narrator's companion gets up to go buy a newspaper, and in his accompanying remarks reveals that the mark is a snail, to which the narrator responds not aloud, but in her ongoing narration, "Ah, the mark on the wall! For it was a snail." The pleasure this work delivered to me came not only from its flights of fancy and nimble leaps from thought to thought, but that final instant of recognition, long-delayed, and of such small importance that it seemed almost empty of content, as if it were made entirely of the sensation of realization itself.

The moment of my pleasure kept lasting, strangely, as if a bell had rung and then—instead of dying away as one would expect—grown louder. I sailed around my brain to find the reason for this and discovered it was in fact the ringing of another bell, a sister sentence, the famous conclusion to Woolf's 1925 novel *Mrs. Dalloway*, in which Clarissa Dalloway's old flame, Peter, who has been waiting for a moment to speak with her at her party, wonders to himself:

> What is this terror? What is this ecstasy? [. . .] What is it that fills me with extraordinary excitement?
> It is Clarissa, he said.
> For there she was.

Later versions of "The Mark on the Wall" left out the word *for*, and the omission kept me from seeing the correspondence between these closing moments, which—once it became apparent—felt too precisely alike to ever have missed.

For there she was.	For it was a snail.

The *for* operated in my mind as the fixation point (often a small black square) that researchers use to anchor the centers of images to help them investigate the visual phenomenon of what they call "binocular rivalry." Binocular vision—sight as it exists in creatures with two eyes—permits people to experience the sensation of depth when they look through a View-Master, or stereoscope, when each eye is presented with a slightly different angle of the same scene. (It was a variation on this optical trick I had in mind when earlier—how long ago it felt now!—I imagined the simultaneous perception of the two images of the Crystal Palace: one newly built, one in flames.) Binocular vision is stealthy, but there are ways to pull it out of hiding. If you hold your index finger up a few inches from your face, focus on a point that's further away, close one eye, and then open it while closing the other, switching back and forth between the two points of perception, you'll see your finger hop from side to side. The two views are different, but close enough that binocular vision can resolve them into the single, integrated view that most people experience in daily life.

On the other hand, if you pick up a stereoscope and look not at *slightly* varied images that reproduce the familiar work of binocular vision, but rather *irreconcilably* different ones, strange things happen. Occasionally, a person will experience "piecemeal rivalry," when a patchwork image appears, the brain assembling bits and pieces of both images into its best attempt at coherence. In the paper I found to explain this to myself, piecemeal rivalry is demonstrated with a surreal picture that is at once a woman's face and a house. In the center of the separated images, a small black square instructs the brain that it must put them together.

This word of Woolf's, this *for*, this small and central black square was enough for me to hold both sentences in my mind at once—"For there she was," "For it was a snail"—and feel their piecemeal combination of snail and woman, or rather of the moments the sentences record, moments when the snail and Clarissa Dalloway are perceived, recognized, maybe even loved.

Left Eye   ## Right Eye

 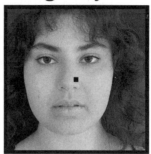

Conscious Percept

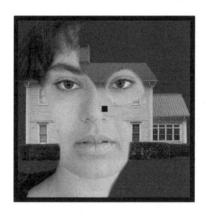

In the closet, I experienced such instants as a sign of life, a sign that the pleasure it gave me might stay. I prayed that it might stay. I lapped it up like I'd been lost for days at sea. The joy I felt in that measure of time occurred not only because of the recognition of similarity, but because of all the difference that surrounded it, and the awe of recognizing the great distance that small word, *for*, had to bridge. Maybe, I thought, this was the key that could unlock the garden gate, that would let my mother's past and mine be perceived, recognized. (I could not bring myself to say *loved*.)

Or, to put it another way, to record another of my attempts at bridging across such apparent divides: my moment of touching the knot Woolf tied to hold her *Kew Gardens* together is different from the moment when worshippers reach their hands toward a saint's skeletal remains, but I could find a fixation point to connect them, and through which a flash of perception could occur. There is a difference between bones and a book, but both have at their center a spine.

On Fire

‡‡

POETS LOVE WALTER BENJAMIN. He often wrote criticism and philosophy as if they were poetry, gathering strange assemblances, making associative leaps, and turning his attention to objects others may have viewed as of little significance. Born to Jewish parents in Germany in 1892, he had a comfortable childhood, thrived in his studies, was thwarted in his attempt at an academic career, and wrote so profusely that were his collected works to be written out in one unbroken line they would stretch from where you sit to the sun and back again.

He was also a father. His child, Stefan Benjamin, was born to Walter and his wife, Dora, in 1918. The marriage did not last, and even before it ended Benjamin was often away from his family, but when he was not he delighted in recording Stefan's developing language and play. In 1921, when Stefan was just three years old, Benjamin noted that his son "was addicted to imitating objects, the beating of a clock, the form of a pear, by coiling himself up on the floor." Echoes of his fatherly observations sometimes show up in his work on the cultural history of toys. In 1928, for example, Benjamin postulated that it would be an error to "assume the imaginative content of a child's toy is what determines his playing," when in fact it is quite the opposite: "A child wants to pull something, and so he becomes a horse; he wants to play with sand, and so he turns into a baker; he wants to hide, and so he turns into a robber or policeman."

I cannot say what desire Stefan sought to satisfy in becoming a clock or a pear, but I do know that during the months when I kept flying away to talk to people about *The Crying Book*, Hattie (now five) was addicted to imitating an egg by coiling themself up in my lap. They wished to be small and held and for me not to go away.

Stefan and his mother were able to escape the advancing Nazi threat, emigrating to London in the 1930s. Walter was less fortunate. In September of 1940, he attempted to cross the border from occupied France to Spain, but—believing himself about to fall into the hands of the Nazis—he took an overdose of morphine and died. He had with him a suitcase containing a manuscript his traveling companions said he valued above his own life. It was never recovered.

Stefan's initial refuge in London did not last long. In July of 1940, when he was twenty-two, British authorities had him deported as an enemy alien and taken to be detained in Australia. More than a year later, realizing their error, they authorized his return to Britain. As an adult, until his death in 1972, Stefan ran a used and antiquarian bookshop at 28 Museum Street, around the corner from the British Museum. Records of his life between release and working at the bookshop are difficult to find, but he did marry several times, fathering two daughters not long before his death.

The ship that carried Stefan Benjamin from England to Australia, the *Dunera*, later became notorious for its guards' cruelty and abuse of deportees: a haphazard mix of Italian fascists, Nazis, and Austrian and German refugees, most of whom were Jewish. Another refugee, Georg Chodziesner, wrote an account of the *Dunera*'s voyage, offering detailed testimony of the torments he and his fellows were made to endure. At the outset of their journey, soldiers ransacked the prisoners' suitcases, tossing their belongings into a single pile. Below deck, they forced prisoners to surrender "all cigarettes, matches, lighters, razor blades, knives . . . and documents." The prisoners put these objects onto a table and soldiers gathered them into a bucket for inspection. Fearing the loss of the most precious documents—the means by which they could hold the British to their promise to reunite them with their families—some prisoners kept those papers hidden beneath their clothes. Suspecting such protective acts, soldiers conducted body searches, and when they found these hidden papers, they tore them into fragments. Later, Chodziesner writes, the prisoners worked through the night to reconstruct individual documents "from the paper heap."

The *Dunera* was so overcrowded that very few prisoners were able to sleep in beds. It was impossible to wash, or—given their lack of access to their belongings—change into fresh clothes. The stench below deck, where the prisoners were confined except for brief interludes of compulsory jogging, grew so unbearable that they developed a system in which each of them was permitted a ration of ten minutes at a time breathing next to a ventilation port. When guards discovered this they sealed the port shut.

When the Great Storm of 1987 struck (the one that knocked over hundreds of historic trees at Kew), a group of Sri Lankan refugees were being held on a ferry that had been converted to a prison ship. Margaret Thatcher had refused to grant them entry to the UK. Among the many privations to which they were subjected, "the cabins were small, cramped and badly ventilated . . . the food was inedible, the water undrinkable, medical attention inadequate and the women even denied sanitary towels." Of all these cruelties, recorded by Tamsin Treverton Jones in her book on the storm, *Windblown*, my eyes hovered in grim recognition above one in particular: "the port-holes were permanently sealed."

These acts of structural violence, which recur with horrific precision, were absent from the vision of England I received as a child. Though so was the passengers' work of piecing documents together, the communal care people can offer one another.

Perhaps, if we had lived there, my mother would have felt comfortable with a deeper critique. I know she left the country in part because she wanted to get away from its stiff hierarchies, to begin a new life. And yet, when she reached the US, England became a crucial backdrop for the self she'd present. The two grew entwined. I did not know how to love my mother without also loving her country. Neither seemed to take kindly to being questioned. Conflict was impolite, possibly intolerable. If there was trouble, then it must be in myself.

READING CHRISTINA SHARPE THAT summer, I came across a reference to Mieke Bal's writings on museums, and her description of "the blinding effects of sameness in repetition." Bal explores this effect in particular through the presence of Rothko's paintings in museum after museum, and how "by the repeated encounter with the same style or concept, the public is bound to get used to the idea which the particular work represents." *Lack* means *robin*. *Benjamin* means *book*.

Family albums and private collections can build these repetitions too. On leave from fighting in the Second World War, my uniformed grandfather took his young son to Trafalgar Square, where they were photographed together, my uncle on my grandfather's knee. Years later, my mother told me, my uncle returned to the site with his own young son, my cousin Scott. They struck the same pose, made the image recur.

I wanted to step outside repetition, or to find a way to perceive it differently, closer to Gertrude Stein's questioning: "Is there repetition or is there insistence." For Stein, nothing can be repeated exactly by a living person; the emphasis will differ, transforming repetition to insistence. She learned this, she says, by observing the conversations of her "group of lively little aunts," whose speech might have recurrent patterns, but was marked by difference in emphasis, meaning it was not repetition, but *insistence*. It was only when one of the aunts stopped listening to another that the words fell from insistence into repetition. "Nothing makes any difference," says Stein, "as long as some one is listening while they are talking."

On one of my walks around our neighborhood, talking to my mother on the phone, I mentioned a visit we once made to Trafalgar Square, and she asked if I remembered the pigeon who shit on my head. I did, I said. Her voice held the idea that this was a funny story, one she might have penned onto a postcard. Curious about how close memory and story really were—or what, in my mother's telling, I might hear as insistence, rather than repetition—I had her pass the phone to my father so I could ask him to digitize and send me the home video footage from the trip. A few days later, I clicked on his reply and watched the blue line progress across the screen like a tiny creeping flood.

We made the journey to England in 1990 to celebrate my grandparents' fiftieth wedding anniversary, a rare family reunion with branches flying in from Pretoria and Boston, driving from Reading, taking the train from London, rewinding ourselves back to Richmond. Somehow I'd forgotten that during the trip we'd made two separate visits to Kew, but when I pulled the cursor forward to find my bird-bedecked self, the familiar water lilies stopped me. There we are again in the Gardens. I am holding out my hand and waiting for a robin. My uncle and great-uncle smoke their matching pipes. I dragged the cursor elsewhere.

Now everyone is in my grandparents' room at the Richmond Hill Hotel. My sister and I are dressed in matching peach brides-maid's dresses, filling in the wedding party my grandmother always wanted, but—as a wartime bride—could not have. Someone has decided we must sing, and so we stand side by side and perform a single verse of, for some reason, "Itsy Bitsy Teenie Weenie Yellow Polka Dot Bikini." When we finish there's silence and then my grandfather's voice asks the question I had too: "Is that all?"

At last I reached Trafalgar Square and saw my nine-year-old self looking back at the camera in desperate appeal, covered in birds and fear. She does not know how to shake them off and stands in panicked stillness, as if posing for a Victorian portrait photograph, waiting for the light to do its work. Nothing moves except her lips, which part around a nervous laugh, and her eyes, which I stared back at in futility, unable to meet.

It turned out that the pigeon shit on Chelly's head, not mine. With Trafalgar's tallest monument, Nelson's Column, looming up behind us, I watched her watch the young me, her face a reflection of my unease with the talons gripping my scalp and shirt, her hunched shoulders echoing mine. When the birds flock over to her, when shit falls onto Chelly's hair, my young mouth falls open in horror. I watched my mouth. It can't believe this is happening. I sent my sister the clip. "I remember it as something that happened to US," she texted back. "We invented mirror neurons."

She's right, I thought. So many events felt this way as they unfolded in our childhood, the two of us close and in joint understanding.

When I looked at my mother on this screen I felt like she was already dead. She was that beautiful, that far away.

ONE WAY PEOPLE TRY to fix others into permanent place is to gather official documents and call the history they write *definitive*, but paper's easy to burn. When the British departed from colonies who'd at last won independence, they often marked their leaving with fire, destroying what records they could of the lives they had marred and stolen.

In a review of recent books on the British Empire, the historian Maya Jasanoff observes that "'Erasing history' is a charge invariably lobbed at those who want to remove the statues of contentious figures. But taking down a statue isn't erasing history; it's revising cultural priorities. . . . Burning documents: now *that's* erasing history." That erasure and its consequences are ongoing, says Jasanoff:

In 2018, it emerged that dozens of immigrants of the "Windrush generation" (named for a ship, the Empire Windrush, which brought Caribbean migrants to the U.K.

in 1948), who had legally settled in Britain between 1948 and 1973, had recently been deported by the Home Office because they couldn't prove their status. Their landing cards—often the only record of their legal arrival—had been destroyed in a procedural culling of the archives in 2010.

One distinct difference between my mother and her country: she has made no such culling, set no such fires. I am the one who threw away the box I could not bear. What would I find in the pages that remained? I knew she had written accounts of moments from inside our years of drifting apart. It began to feel necessary to read them, though the prospect rattled me. It would be impossible, I thought, to begin with Camden Town. Instead, I'd return to a different night, of which we rarely spoke. My mother texted me scans of the diary pages I asked for, from 1995, along with a note of warning. "It's not easy reading," she said.

"Where to begin?" she began. "It is Memorial Day weekend, a weekend that I would rather not remember." Strange, then, to choose to write it down. Perhaps her purpose was not memory, but something closer to what Woolf described when she wrote, in "A Sketch of the Past," that "it is only by putting it into words that I make it whole; this wholeness means that it has lost its power to hurt me."

Where to begin? Given: my father was at sea. I was fourteen, Chelly thirteen. My mother had recently taken me to a sale at the Banana Republic outlet to buy clothes that would meet the dress code at my new school, an expense, she reminded me, my scholarship would not cover. I was lonely. My grandfather was dying. My mother was on her own. Chelly had a friend coming to sleep

over. I had been trying all week to convince someone—anyone—
to come over, to no avail. My unpopularity, it seemed, frustrated
my mother.

"I have tried to help her to be a normal fourteen-year-old,"
she wrote, "encouraging her to invite friends over, but they never
invite her to their houses."

Then, by miracle, my friend Stacy suddenly agreed to come
over. She brought a forty-ounce bottle of vodka with her. When
my mother went to bed we drank it all. I felt more relaxed than I
had thought possible, until our noise grew loud enough to draw
my mother's annoyed return. When she came in and saw the
empty bottle she thought at first it was a joke. When she saw it was
real she grew very angry. I remember lying down on Chelly's bed,
feigning sleep, playing dead. Stacy refused to tell my mother her
phone number, making it impossible to send her home. Furious,
my mother said that if Stacy wouldn't tell her the number "then
the police would have to do it for her." Seeing my friend's resistance to my mother, and furious at the threat to call the police, I
found myself emboldened. I had had enough.

My mother's account said, "Heather started to get angry and
calling me a fucking bitch and telling me how much she hated
me and that she was not going to take my crap anymore and was
going to kill herself." It was, I remember thinking, the only sensi-
ble solution.

"She went to the bathroom," my mother went on, "and grabbed
a razor, which I took from her." Frightened of what her friends
would say if she called them for help, for "Who can be a true
friend & help & not go blabbing the story all over town to be gos-
siped about?" she instead made good on her word and called the
police. I tried to hit her. This frightened her too.

I looked for, but could not find on the page, a sense that she was frightened *for* me. Only of.

It was over, I thought, everything was over, what was the use in holding back now, and I cracked a dining room windowpane with my head. The policeman arrived while I was in the bathroom, where I halfway undressed and climbed into the tub, grasping drunkenly around for a razor and screaming (I've always hated that word, its melodrama, how neither the term nor the sound it names ever sound wholly real) *I want to die, I just want to die.* Chelly, my mother wrote, was crying, thinking me already dead.

The walls around the bath were covered in white vinyl with a splotchy gold pattern, not meant to represent anything, but just to the left of the faucet the golden marks formed what I had always thought looked like a sheep—an accidental, secret meaning—and I remember thinking how funny it was that the same animal who'd watched me play and splash and soap my face was now going to watch me die, though it was proving more difficult than I'd thought. So many interruptions.

I told the policeman he was stupid. My mother marveled at his calm while I went on—her word—screaming: "Heather screaming, screaming—saying that she had tried to tell me what she was feeling before, but all that I could do was tell her about my nervous breakdown—she said that she did not want to go to Brewster, that everyone expects too much of her, that she is no good, that she hated me," and then, as if realizing that these words were inadequately conveying my awfulness, she added that I was "vicious and snarling, totally gone." *Vicious* and *snarling* I may have been, but *gone* I was not. This was precisely the problem.

Nothing makes any difference if some one is listening while they are talking.

The police—there were two of them now—took me away in handcuffs. At the hospital they removed them, but put them back on again when I refused to let them take a blood sample. They needed it, wrote my mother, to determine whether I was too drunk to be committed to a psychiatric institution. As it turned out, I was, and so I remained in the hospital where I had been born.

My mother fretted about whether to tell my father what had happened, fearing how expensive such an action might be were he to abandon ship and buy a ticket to fly home. She decided not to risk it. "I just hope to God," she wrote, "that I make correct decisions."

Years later, for Christmas, my father gave my sister and me each a brick from the hospital's maternity wing, which had been recently demolished. I wonder if Chelly still has hers. I don't know where mine is. I think I lost it.

WALTER BENJAMIN LOVED SNOW globes, collected them. They can be dangerous; just as irregularities in glass house panels once scorched plants at Kew, snow globes have been known to concentrate beams of light so intensely that buildings have burned down. Christmas is a dangerous season. I learned this because I was trying to find out if anyone had ever made a snow globe containing a tiny house on fire. I can't remember why.

In the shorthand Chris and I use for my mental state we agreed that I had been "having a hard time," that summer in the closet. I increased the dose of my medication. We hoped that it would help.

Molly's book of poems came out. I blurbed it. She had asked me to before she died. I said yes, but she died before I could make good on my word. I hated my slowness. The word *now* in the poems hurt:

Now pines creak like phones
in the park, all day. Be glad

if you ever meet your ugliness.
Some can't. They stay

at the foot of a range
that only appears insufferable.

We clean
their monuments. Ugly music

is all over us.

I wished she had not died. I wished she could have seen the monuments fall. I knew it would not have stopped her turn to death but still I wished it.

One night I dreamt she made me kill her by shoving a lit flashlight down her throat. *Be glad* she said. I woke afraid.

I put Molly's book away and picked up Priya Satia's *Time's Monster: How History Makes History*, in which she observes that "at a basic level, what we perceive as time's passage *forward* is in fact the cyclical movement of our planet in a loop, repeated revolutions in space that entail continual return to the same *place*." It's not that she's resigned to violent repetition, but neither does she subscribe to visions of a utopian future, consigned by linear time to an always retreating horizon. Instead, she warns that when "utopia takes the form of a possible future, as opposed to a way of being *now*, when it presumes the linear flow of time, it cramps the space for ethical maneuver."

Now I mouthed, almost out loud.

I was surprised when the book turned its attention to poems. Satia says poems "[ask] the reader to let go of the comfortable, automatic assumption of linear time" and finds, in that letting go, patches of sunlight breaking through, illuminating other ways of being. "Liberation is not," she writes, "a condition we achieve at the end of linear time but something we experience in fits and starts in the very pursuit of liberation."

AT ONE CORNER OF the diary page on which my mother wrote her account of the night I was taken to the hospital, there's an excerpt from a poem by E. E. Cummings. She must not, I think, have perceived it as she wrote, its printed presence merely decorative and irrelevant to her frantic composition—it came with the diary. When I scrolled through the scan she sent me, the lines gave me a start. "This is the garden," said the poem, innocent of its surroundings, instead watching

> . . . colours come and go,
> frail azures fluttering from night's outer wing
> strong silent greens serenely lingering,
> absolute lights like baths of golden snow.

It was there, I thought, *the garden was right there*, the past now opening a gate where my mother had written a wall. I could walk through it into the green, unhandcuffed, while golden snow settled around me. All I had to do was shake the pages.

Some day that summer a postcard arrived from 1912. I thumbtacked it to the closet wall. In it, visitors to Kew sit at little outdoor tables by the Refreshment Pavilion. A waiter stands in a stiff suit with a bow tie, the Great Pagoda looms up in the distance, and a woman in white walks from the righthand margin. She has been walking for more than a hundred years and she has never reached her table. The Pavilion looks sturdy and permanent. A year later it burned to the ground.

Night and Day

HATTIE AND I WERE sitting in bright midday sun by a man-made lake watching a heron catch fish when we heard the official news of Trump's electoral defeat. It arrived through my phone, first a ripple of notifications, then a text and call from Chris. I scanned the park to see if others were also receiving the news. A person in jogging clothes pushing a stroller paused at one corner to tap something into her phone. Another passed on the sidewalk behind us and though a mask hid his mouth, his eyes revealed his grin. Beyond the park the news made its way deeper through the city and cars honked in rising waves.

In one of Virginia Woolf's notebooks, there are pages and pages of a chapter she cut from *The Years*, at a point when the novel was still named *The Pargiters*, after the family whose lives it records, beginning in the 1880s and continuing through to Woolf's present in the 1930s, with history making its marks along the way. One of the cut scenes floated into my mind, as Hattie and I walked around to the other side of the lake. Crosby, the Pargiter's servant, is walking through Richmond with two of the family's small children, on their way to Kew. She catches sight of a placard that reads "Three British Cruisers Sunk," news that marks the cost of the country's entry into the First World War. In the gardens, Crosby and the children settle by the manmade lake. The news has rippled out to other visitors there, like a man and woman sitting on a bench who scoot down to make room for them. The man looks for further details in his paper, but "there's nothing more about it." A goose opens its wings and frightens the children, but here the echo of the scene through which Hattie and I were walking faded. Woolf left us behind to follow a salesman out of the Gardens, down a villa-lined street to the train station.

Woolf's books and life were full of rides on public transportation: trains, omnibuses, trams; they were vehicles I found I could use when I wanted to feel connected across the time and space that held us apart. Building up a chain of touch, I imagined that my great-grandfather, who worked in the early twentieth century as a trolley-bus conductor, on some unremarkable day collected Woolf's ticket, and those same hands would on that same ordinary day collect his lunch from his daughter, my grandmother, when she brought it to him at the public cattle trough and drinking fountain by Kew Bridge. Years later, my grandmother would hold my hand as I learned how to walk. Later still I would hold hers as she worked to remember. I stared at my palm as if Woolf's ticket was about to materialize upon it.

My chain was, I knew, a fantasy, and when I reached out this way, I inevitably found myself bumping up against the class divide between Woolf and my great-grandparents. After the critic

J. B. Priestley published a condescending review of one of her books, and his subsequent screed against "the highbrow," Woolf wrote an essay in which she argued that "in so far as I am a highbrow (and my imperfections in that line are well known to me) I love lowbrows; I study them; I always sit next to the conductor in an omnibus and try to get him to tell me what it is like—being a conductor." Her tongue was in her cheek, but still I wondered what my great-grandfather might have told her. I wondered if he might have been wanting to get on with his work.

His wife, my great-grandmother, was in service when she was young, beginning as a scullery maid, later promoted to the parlor. In my kitchen drawer I had seven bone-handled knives her employer passed on to her when they were no longer wanted. One morning, as I picked one up to butter my toast, I listened to the sound of Woolf's voice in the only recording of it that exists, a short radio lecture, posh beyond measure, so that while she may have been speaking of the nature of words—and I ought to have felt her company in this meaning-making—the rhythm and tone could communicate nothing but dismissal.[1]

Toward the end of my grandmother's life, when her dementia set her circling in swift conversational repetitions, my mother liked to walk with her through Kew when she flew over for a visit. The glassmaker Dale Chihuly's massive sculptures are periodically installed throughout the grounds, huge and colorful echoes of the shapes of the plants around them. Personally, I can't stand his work, but it brought my grandmother joy, over and over again. Each time they came upon one of the glass sculptures, my grandmother would marvel at its size and ask, "But how did it *get* here?"

---

[1]   In truth, were Woolf to somehow catch wind of my particular existence, I suspect her dismissal would be driven by her disdain for—heaven help me—*the middlebrow,* not to mention the poor taste of my Americanness.

When I open my drawer and take out one of her mother's knives, I hear her laugh the same question into my ear.

Americans often mistake Englishness for an indication of a high class position. In the post office of my small hometown, clerks referred to my mother as "her majesty" when she came to the window to pick up a package—which she loved—but her family's move from working class to lower middle occurred in her lifetime. Her education culminated in a two-year technical degree, the business of fashion.

She sometimes wonders what art and life she might have made had she received the education provided to my sister and me. I do too. I remember once gathering with friends of hers in the converted barn gallery where they exhibited their work. One friend proposed a question: What did everyone hope to learn in the coming year? What were our ambitions? I cringed at my mother's answer: *I just want to continue to help people with my art.* That's not what it's *for*, I wanted to say. The smoothness of the idea made me recoil. What, I wanted to ask, might she have been capable of if she could bear to risk putting something greater on the line and failing? If she had—whether in school or elsewhere—been challenged to plumb greater depths, other feelings? Instead, she flitted from one medium to the next, remaining determinedly cheerful. This sounds, I recognize, to be less a matter of material or cultural resources, than psychological ones. I still wonder what it would cost her to admit to anything like shadow. What it costs to run back unceasingly into light.

She did have access to more education than her own parents. My grandfather left school when he was thirteen, "due to illness," according to a document my mother texted to me. When he was younger he had suffered from rheumatic fever and in 1929 was sent for a time to live at a Dr. Barnardo's home, a charity founded in the Victorian era to care for "Destitute Waif Children." My mother says he spoke fondly of the place. She thinks he enjoyed having a whole bed to himself, regular meals, clean clothes, luxuries hard to come by at home with his eight siblings.

In *Night and Day*—the magazine Thomas Barnardo published to raise awareness and funds for his work—he cast himself as a rescuer, wandering slums at night to save children from starvation and depravity. He also sold photographic cards, pairs of images that displayed children first in rags and misery, then in tidy clothes and industrious activity.

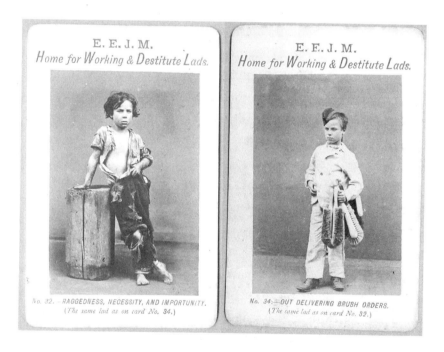

The scholar Susan Ash argues that central to Dr. Barnardo's conception of himself was the idea of an "open door," meaning that his homes were open to all, and that the children were free to leave whenever they wished, but in truth, their movements were highly constrained. They were often surrendered to Barnardo's by parents whose poverty gave them few other options. They were photographed not only for the sake of fundraising, but so that police and future employers would have an easy way to recognize children who were accused of crimes, or who tried to run away.

Mindful of popular fears that his city was being flooded by immigrants and paupers, Barnardo reassured his supporters that he produced citizens whose work would be as "farmers and settlers" in the countryside and colonies. On ships carrying them to the latter of these futures, the children were dressed according to direction again, not in rags, but in traveling costumes that made the girls look "like a company of Red Riding Hoods." They would start over in lands whose histories—as far as the imperial imagination was concerned—began at the moment of European invasion. Of the many ways in which the children's movements were controlled, the one that most chills me is Barnardo's instruction that they never allow their thoughts to drift into the past. They must be taught, he said, to forget.

By the time my grandfather entered the Barnardo's Home, its founder was long dead. I wonder if they still taught the art of forgetting, or if it just runs in our family. In my childhood, next to the Lilliput Lane cottages on the mantel in our house in New Hampshire, my mother set one of her yard sale finds: a miniature ceramic house with DR. BARNARDO's painted on its side. There was a slot for coins in the roof. They fall, I pretend, on my grandfather's head. They knock the memories right out.

ONE DAY NEAR THE end of the nineteenth century, out on a walk with her young daughter, Virginia, Julia Stephen clapped her hands in delight and said, "That was where it was!" pointing at the place where Little Holland House once stood. Constructed as the dower house to the nearby Holland House, for over two decades it was home to Julia's aunt and uncle. They hosted a regular salon through the 1850s and 60s, and the young Julia had been a frequent visitor, along with another of her aunts—the photographer Julia Margaret Cameron—as well as many members of the Pre-Raphaelite Brotherhood. A beauty, "'a vision,' as they once said"—as Woolf would later write—Julia modeled for many of the artists in Little Holland House's circle. Cameron made dozens of portraits of her, over years in which the name serving as caption beneath the image transformed as Julia married, was widowed, and married again.

The Pre-Raphaelite Brotherhood became, in the 1990s, a particular interest of my own mother, an interest she believes and insists is particular to herself, and which I in my cynicism view through the haze of the market. These were years of a Pre-Raphaelite merchandising boom: notebooks, curtains, wrapping paper. Stores filled with coffee table books. When the books were remaindered enough for my mother to afford their purchase and bring them home, I stared. These women! Beauty, I learned, was to be found in full lips, long noses, and above all a cascade of undulant (preferably red) hair. Elizabeth Siddal, the artist, model, and wife of Dante Gabriel Rossetti, so fully understood the importance of her hair that she continued to let it grow after her death, much to the joy of her husband, who saw it when he exhumed her body to retrieve the poems he'd buried with her, having changed—beneath his hair—his mind.

My sister and I grew up under the gaze of another of Rossetti's beauties, *The Blessed Damozel*, who hung on our living room wall as a black-and-white photogravure in a gold-painted wooden frame. My mother bought her at an antiques fair in my hometown, in New Hampshire, at a discount, she texted, "because it looked a bit like me." I will explain my mother's hair. It is red and abundant and streams about her shoulders in the waves Rossetti required. Not anymore: over time it has paled, and she keeps it trimmed not far past her chin, but photos spanning decades keep her former color pressed into place. In one from the late nineteen-sixties she stands in a tree looking down, her dress and tresses long. Among the treasures of her personal archive: a note in which the singer-songwriter Donovan called her "firehair." Her redheadedness inhabits the present tense. It persists in how she perceives herself and how I in turn perceive her.

The power of a mother's clothes! One morning I was in the closet staring at a photograph of Woolf as an adult, wearing her dead mother's dress for a photoshoot with *Vogue*,[2] when Hattie came in wearing the peach bridesmaid's gown I'd worn for my grandparents' fiftieth wedding anniversary.

"Isn't it *beautiful*?" they asked.

"*Yes*," I said. I was dead!

ANOTHER DAY, IN DIFFERENT clothes, Hattie and their best friend, a boy with whose family we had formed what people were calling a bubble, were digging a hole in the backyard. The dirt in Georgia is rust-colored, and pretty lines of it streaked the children's faces. Hattie was thrilled, kept running over to me with bits of rock and roots. "Look, Mama! Ancient debris!" They pronounced it "debriss," lifting the word up from the page where they found it. This is my favorite moment in language, when I get to witness the journey

---

2 In the years since this moment, Charlie Porter has published an intriguing argument that the dress was not Woolf's mother's, but belonged instead to Ottoline Morrell.

of a person's relationship with a word from the quiet embrace of paper to the experimental promenade of public speech.

I had been carrying on my own relationship with the word in the closet, reading Walter Benjamin's "Theses on the Philosophy of History" in which he watches the "Angel of History" weather a storm "blowing in from Paradise," which "irresistibly propels him into the future to which his back is turned, while the pile of debris before him grows skyward." When I looked around I saw I was surrounded by the accumulated debris of my months of reading and hiding. The closet had barely any more room in which to think.

On September 27, 1940, the day after Walter Benjamin died, Nazis dropped a bomb on Holland House.[3] I first learned of this link from an essay by the critic Eduardo Cadava (whose pages I'd printed, annotated, and left scattered about the closet floor), whose first sentence declares: "There can be no image that is not about destruction and survival, and this is especially the case in the image of ruin." Many weeks after the bombing, a photographer took a picture of three men browsing the unceilinged library. It told a story of resilience, or unflappability, or a taunting at death: *You can't catch me.*

---

3   Not Little Holland House, where Woolf's mother and the Pre-Raphaelites gathered, but the larger building from which the dower house took its name.

Some remnants of the house remained and were adapted into other purposes in the now-public Holland Park. In the 1970s, my mother lived in the neighborhood and liked to walk through the park when she was not pouring drinks at the Ladbroke Arms, a pub she managed at the time. I sent her the pair of photos, curious about what she'd notice. "The X!" she replied, and when I looked again to the ruins to see for myself the letter came clear.

Tides

‡‡‡

WE HAD NOT LEFT our city for nine months when we finally drove four hours to the coast, where we would spend a week at a house we rented. It was the first real vacation for the three of us; all our previous travels were to see relatives or to give readings. Only so much time, only so much money. The year we were in—the year of two salaries and the peril of meeting with our beloveds—changed the equation. We drove along a rising line chart of disposable household income and found ourselves at the beach.

It was December and the town where we stayed, built for visiting crowds, was empty enough that we could walk without worry of coming too close to others. We brought takeout to the beach and watched not the sunset, but the deep fog that obscured it. Soon, said administrators at Chris's university, they would announce which professors they planned to fire. The prospect felt like a boat moored near the shore that we could mostly not see.

We made a plan to visit the lighthouse the next day if the weather was fine, and when the day arrived and we failed to go I joked that now I was—like Mrs. Ramsay in Woolf's *To the Lighthouse*—doomed to die in a subordinate clause.

Woolf's novel begins with a child's request to his mother to visit the lighthouse the next day, but the weather gets in the way. Mrs. Ramsay, often seen as an avatar for Woolf's mother, whose death so devastated the young Virginia, is a vital, central character in the story, which means that the book's offhand mention of her death in the second section—"Time Passes"—moves many readers all the more strongly: "Mr. Ramsay, stumbling along a passage one dark morning, stretched his arms out, but Mrs. Ramsay having died rather suddenly the night before, his arms, though stretched out, remained empty."

To the Lighthouse draws heavily on Woolf's memories of the seaside house in St. Ives where she and her large blended family spent idyllic summers before her mother's death in 1895. (She transposed the story from St. Ives to the Hebrides, causing all sorts of inaccuracies in the book's flora and fauna.) A version of her father, Leslie Stephen, appears as Mr. Ramsay, always struggling to progress in his knowledge, which he imagines being like the alphabet.[1] His mind has "no sort of difficulty in running over those letters one by one, firmly and accurately, until it had reached, say, the letter Q. He reached Q. Very few people in the whole of England ever reach Q." Mr. Ramsay is disappointed at not being the "one in a generation" to reach Z, but he, at least, does get to the lighthouse

---

[1]   Leslie Stephen was the founding editor of the *Dictionary of National Biography*, volumes of which were published in alphabetical order. After the appearance of volume 26, which brought him to the letter H, he grew exhausted and retired.

in the end, along with two of his adult children who managed to survive "Time Passes," through which deaths roll like waves.

While Mr. Ramsay lives through the end of the book, the real Leslie Stephen died in 1904. Woolf also suffered the loss of two siblings, as well as her mother; one of her half-sisters died not long after her mother, while typhoid killed her older brother in 1906. George and Gerald survived, as did Virginia, Vanessa, and Adrian. Their other half-sister, Laura, whose disability is uncertain, had been institutionalized since at least 1893. The large, blended family of eight children and two parents dwindled shockingly down.

When Woolf's sister Vanessa Bell read *To the Lighthouse* for the first time, she wrote to Woolf from her country house, Charleston Farm, to say she thought it a remarkable portrait of their mother and that she found it "almost painful to have her so raised from the dead."

How afraid I was of my own mother's death, how frightened that the year of distance would be the one to kill her. I say "year," but I think I meant "book." It was getting harder to tell the difference between things; such was the fog. But look, I was out of my closet bedroom and back in real weather! I went for a run at low tide and discovered a pelican stiff, headfirst in the sand. With Hattie I gathered shells. Signs instructed us on the difference between living and deceased sand dollars, which we could safely pick up. Signs instructed us on the danger of tides.

ONCE, IMAGINING LIFE A century on from their vantage in 1936, Vanessa and Clive Bell's adult sons Quentin and Julian wrote a play in which visitors to their family home at Charleston Farm are led through the house by a misinformed guide who tells them about Bloomsbury's notable figures. The house stands, but it's grown full of comic fog. Time bends events and people into funny shapes.

In time as I knew it, from my screen-bound vantage in the beach house, the people who ran Charleston in the actual present displayed an enchanting obsession with historical accuracy. The gardener, for instance, chose to plant flowers based on those that appeared in Bell's and Grant's paintings. Off the canvas they went, back into the soil.

Once we knew whether Chris would be fired we would understand if we could buy a house. Or a portion of a house. A condo, a townhouse, a flat. Wherever we would end up I wanted to paint every surface. Could not go to Charleston, could not reach Kew, could not return to the unfinished mural in Ohio. I was tired of uncertainty and impermanence and the closet's horrible brown walls. Perhaps, I thought, if when we moved I found a wall and painted a garden all the way to conclusion then the fates would let us stay.

To the south, a small container ship. On my left, a seagull perched on a rotting watermelon. In the waves, dual fins rounded out of and into the water as if they were attached to a rotating View-Master disc. I thought they were sharks. I could have been mistaken. After reading *To the Lighthouse*, one acquaintance wrote to Woolf to say that "[her] sparrows are wrong." It pleased me to imagine the wrong sparrows, their mistakes.

Woolf laughed at her mistakes too. At the close of her rather wonderfully over-the-top preface to *Orlando*, she went so far as to say "Finally, I would thank, had I not lost his name and address, a gentleman in America, who has generously and gratuitously corrected the punctuation, the botany, the entomology, the geography, and the chronology of previous works of mine and will, I hope, not spare his services on the present occasion." It was *Orlando* I brought with me to the beach, not *To the Lighthouse*, even though the latter was on my mind. People call *Orlando* "a romp" and it was a romp—not a resurrection of loved ones lost—that I needed.

THE MAIL, ALREADY A reliable source of small novelties upon which I had grown to depend that year, had grown to a plump stack while we were away. Among the Christmas cards and bank statements I found an envelope from my mother. She had filled out the form to request information on her father's time at Barnardo's home. In the section that asked for "Any further details you consider helpful," in the block capitals the form required, she wrote— "HAROLD SUFFERED FROM RHEUMATIC FEVER AND WAS TENDERLY CARED FOR AT DR. BARNARDO'S—HE REMEMBERED THAT CARE UNTIL HIS DYING DAY."

Beneath the form I found a photocopy she'd made of her diary entry recounting her father's funeral. When I looked at the date, my mind delivered a calculation I did not want to receive: just eight weeks stood between the night the police took me to the hospital and the night in Camden Town. If she had been less ashamed, I wondered, would she have told Scott and his girl-friend, Melanie, of the danger of giving me alcohol? I remembered them joking with her about taking me out for a drink. Why did she not intervene? I knew her grief must have played a role, but still, when I thought back to everything I'd shouted at her that night, I couldn't see how I could have expressed my level of dis-tress more clearly.

Her father's funeral, she wrote, was attended by over three hundred people, and the family could "feel the love, comfort and peace all around [them]." The night before, a friend stopped by to express his sorrow. "It may seem strange," wrote my mother, but she and my grandmother felt stronger after he left. "By comforting others," she explained, "we gained strength, & what would have been a long evening turned into a time of fortitude, which we needed for the next day." In the morning, Scott and Melanie brought me over. I was, she wrote, "sporting a new hairdo courtesy of Melanie, it looked good, less of a thatch than she had left here with." I think this must have been after Camden Town, though I'm not sure. She does not mention me again. We rode to the funeral in separate cars.

Her own dying was another subject of this mail. She was not doing so any faster than usual, but the year did raise the subject. She wrote out wishes for what was to be done with her body, her clothes, her art. She imagined her cremated remains traveling across the seas: "Maybe I will become the base of a shell or two for someone to find & treasure years in the future, maybe some part of me will wash up in the waves on a Cornish beach or in Malta (I have always wanted to visit Malta)."[2]

We unpacked from our seaside trip, though a clear plastic bag of shells remained on the counter. I didn't know where it should go. Our house had so little room. Chris put Hattie to bed and went out walking, eager to stretch his legs after our long day in the car. Sitting at the kitchen table, I placed one hand on the form, the other on the letter, closed my eyes and breathed in. I cried, not much, a few brief lines down either cheek.

---

2   Chelly thinks it is unethical for me to include my mother's plans for her remains unless I am willing to also share my own. I want my body to be magically preserved for eternity, but I realize that even if that were possible it would probably be very expensive, so I am settling for burial.

AS CHRISTMAS APPROACHED, HATTIE grew sad at our ongoing distance from loved ones. We tried to distract and entertain them. We decorated a tree. I told them we'd make mince pies. I couldn't find mincemeat anywhere and had to make it from scratch. The recipe called for candied peel, also unavailable, and so I peeled the citrus fruit myself, setting the bright pieces to boil down in sugared water. Hattie helped to stir. The process was almost unbearably slow. They suggested a prank: we'd disguise ourselves in old-fashioned clothes, sneak out, and knock on the front door. When Chris answered, he wouldn't recognize us; he'd think we were Christmas carolers transported from the past. I tucked Hattie's hair into my mother's old beret, their hands into a muff. We stood on the dark porch and sang our tidings of comfort and joy.

I wished, for Hattie's sake, that we had been able to travel up to Maine, but another part of me felt relief. True, we were missing my mother's mince pies, but we were also missing the annual ritual of trying to align everyone's needs and routines into a calendar that obeyed the laws of time and space, and—to be honest—I was too angry with my mother to trust myself to behave. The questions her diaries raised were roiling in me. I feared they'd spill from my mouth and sour everyone's mood. My mother and I had a difficult track record around such conversations.

When Hattie was a baby, we flew north from Ohio to spend her first Christmas with my family. They came down with an ear infection, waking and crying night after night until I was raw with fatigue, uttering terse commands for help so I could nap. Chris had to go back to Ohio as planned—the cat-sitter could not stay any longer—while I stayed to keep nursing Hattie, until they could fly without agony. On New Year's Eve, my parents went out to a party, and the next day I asked my mother for details, hungry for thoughts of anything beyond fever and milk.

"Oh, it was lovely," she said. "Such a big house, with a band playing up in the balcony, and they have so many interesting friends."

"Anyone I know?"

"Joan was there—she asked after you, actually—you know she loves your poems." I clung to this.

"Does she?" I wanted more. My mother laughed.

"She pretended to be quite angry with me for not bringing you. She said she'd been dying to meet you." *I'm famous!* I thought. *People at parties want to meet me! How proud my mother must be.*

"Of course," she continued, "I had to tell her *Not right now you don't.*"

I didn't understand.

"I don't understand?"

"Well, she wouldn't have much fun meeting you right now, would she?" I looked at my lap. I was still in my pajamas. Neither the baby nor I had bathed for some time.

"Oh," I said, "right."

Days passed. Hattie's ear improved, but I could not patch my own wound. While Hattie napped I told my mother I needed to talk to her. She looked afraid. We sat on the sofa in her studio, surrounded by her self-portraits. You hurt me, I told her. It was a joke, she said. But it hurt me, I repeated. I wanted her to look. I wanted her to see. She cried.

"Why are you being so mean to me?"

I'm not, I told her, and though I felt my fatigue return to me like a snowstorm obscuring the windshield I kept driving onward, the road too slippery for brakes.

"I just think you should know you can hurt people." I only realized, as I said it, that she did not know this, that such knowledge was unbearable to her, that she could not orient herself in relation to it. How terrifying, I thought, these things we hide from ourselves, scanning my mind for the faults I'd kept obscured, trying to sort between the convenient fictions anxiety offers and those that are real: my selfishness, my vanity, my obstinance, my (but here I clouded over).

"Is this about when you were a teenager?" she asked. I sighed and inclined my head to shake it no, but she was already speaking again, and crying, and anyway, my no would have been a lie.

"I'm sorry," she said. "I tried to be a good mother. You would have done whatever you wanted to anyway, wouldn't you?"

"I don't know."

"I didn't do too badly, did I?"

I could not bear the need in her eyes.

"No," I said. "You were fine."

CHRISTMAS PASSED AND THE new year began. Hattie and I planned our next costumes: wildlife biologists, a family team. We'd convince Chris to let us observe a new species of squirrel we suspected was in the backyard. I woke early each morning, so that while my family slept I could play my way through time. Marveling that I could flip so lightly from scenes of Woolf living on Richmond Green, to her afternoon walks around Monk's House—from the First World War to the Second—it struck me that a biographer such as Hermione Lee is permitted an understanding of her subject that is always denied to the subject herself, an understanding born of the ability to perceive the entirety of a life, all the way to the end and after. Even Woolf, who investigated herself with such keen curiosity, could not see, as she once did with that flower at St. Ives, the whole—*part earth, part flower*—and so while half of me wished to align itself with Lee's declaration that the biographer should read her subject's death as "just the next fact in a series of facts," a perspective that would suggest a talent for a cool and unsentimental surveying of the world, I could not help but feel a hot sharp desire to defend the significance of death as the event that encloses a life, gives it the shape that permits an understanding of the whole, and to sense a pulsing fury that I am permitted no such understanding of my own life, the shape I inhabit and from which I look out at the world, so that even if I were to follow Woolf to the river and bend the arc of my life toward conclusion, I would be able to know only one fuzzy side of the encircling border, while those who outlived me—how I want to stamp my feet at them!—could look all the way through and beyond.

Autobiography was, I decided, impossible. In truth, in those months, I struggled to compose the life itself. Then I had a thought. I could choose—when I wrote my next chapter—to leave my mother wholly out.

Portraits

〰〰〰〰〰〰〰〰〰〰〰〰〰〰〰〰〰〰〰〰〰〰〰〰〰〰〰〰〰〰〰〰〰〰〰〰〰〰〰

"'I LIVED THE FIRST SIX years of my life in the small eighteenth-century house at No. 6 The Grove, Highgate. This garden is still for me the imagined background for almost any garden scene that I read of in books'—thus Roger Fry began a fragment of autobiography."

Thus Virginia Woolf began her biography of the art critic, whose affair with her sister, Vanessa, Fry's family forced her to leave out. The composition was arduous. Famously, it led her to write to her friend and former lover Vita Sackville-West, exclaiming, "My god, how does one write a biography?"[1] Becoming more specific, she went on, "How can one deal with facts—so many and so many and so many? Or ought one, as I incline, to be purely

---

[1]   Hermione Lee borrowed the sentence to begin her own biography of Woolf.

fictitious? And what is a life?" She must have had somewhere in mind her late friend Lytton Strachey's observation that "it is perhaps as difficult to write a good life as to live one," which he included in his introduction to his collection of four biographical portraits, the wildly popular *Eminent Victorians*. Of course, the problems of biography grow thornier and weedier when the author's own family is involved. One dons gloves, builds a trellis, grabs a knife.

Biographies of the Honourable Vita Sackville-West must begin where she grew up, in the enormous and ancient countryside estate of Knole House, which she loved, and which she knew from childhood that her sex would prevent her from inheriting. In her lifetime, Vita was known for her writing—essays, poetry, novels—some of which the Woolfs published at the Hogarth Press. A passionate gardener, she spent hours designing, digging, and planting at Long Barn and later Sissinghurst Castle, her homes after Knole. She was married to the diplomat Harold Nicolson, who—like Vita—had many queer love affairs, an arrangement which generally suited them both, and provided a central thread of the joint biography their son would later write: *Portrait of a Marriage*. The most tumultuous of Vita's romantic relationships was with Violet Trefusis, which began when they were adolescents and continued for years. They periodically ran away together, and during these escapes Sackville-West was free to inhabit life as Julian, a wounded soldier, until at last, in 1920, both their husbands flew from England to France to demand a permanent return home.

It was the dual threads of Vita's attachment to her noble ancestral home and her multifarious gender that inspired Woolf to translate her lover's life into the mock-biography, *Orlando*, complete with the genre's requisite portraits. She borrowed paintings hung at Knole, contemporary images of Vita, and photographs of Woolf's niece, Angelica Bell, who dressed up as the young Russian princess (a character based on Violet Trefusis) with whom Orlando falls in love as a youth. The book is also a depiction of English history, particularly its literary history, and Orlando composes through its pages a long poem called "The Oak Tree," beginning the work as a young man in Tudor England, publishing it as a Victorian woman, and deciding at last, in the twentieth century, that its public success (seven printings!) matters very little. Long thought of as a symbol of England, the oak tree first appears in the novel as a place for Orlando to lean and dream up lines. Little in the young Orlando's poetic consciousness is permitted to remain simply or only itself. The oak, for instance, is not only a tree; it is also "the earth's spine." (Or "for image followed image, it was the back of a great horse that he was riding, or the deck of a tumbling ship—it was anything indeed, so long as it was hard.")

I love *Orlando*, with all Woolf's exuberant acts of imagination as she plays with the conventions of biography, stretching her subject's life out across centuries, but I cannot make myself care that Vita could not own Knole. Locked out of her family's estate, she and Harold bought Sissinghurst Castle instead, where they tended—and she wrote of—her gardens. She let the public in for a fee, calling the visitors "shillingses," and she rather despised them.[2] (She rather despised a great many people.) (She would have despised me, but she did not live to meet me so I get to despise her first.)

When she was alive, Vita swore she would never let the National Trust get its hands on her castle, but both Sissinghurst and Knole are now owned by the organization, and are open to daily public

---

2   Though she wrote warmly of them in her columns, privately she revealed other feelings. When a bus route was proposed to run near her castle, she complained that she "hate[d] *la populace*," and wished they had not been educated out of their "rightful place."

tours. Hunched over my laptop on the closet floor, I wrote to the manager of Knole to inquire whether they might allow me to stay on the grounds of the estate until midnight on October 11, the moment when Woolf chose to end *Orlando*, aligning its final pages with its 1928 date of publication. (I was born on October 10, and though I did not mention this, I imagined the night at Knole as a birthday gift to myself.) The manager replied with cold politeness that such a request was impossible, and I felt Vita's dismissive hand wave me away, but it only made me more determined. I was sick of confinement, of behaving. I scouted the grounds on Google Maps. If travel ever again felt possible, I decided, I would not just visit. I would break in.

IN THE 1930S, AS fascist organizing spread throughout Britain, led by Oswald Mosley and his British Union of Fascists (also known as Blackshirts), anti-fascists fought back, disrupting their rallies, demonstrating outside their headquarters, and countering their propaganda. In September of 1934, as Mosley planned a march in London's Hyde Park, a tailor and a laborer painted words in white on the plinth of Nelson's column in Trafalgar Square:

All Out on September 9 to fight Fascism
Down with Fascism
Fight Fascism

The tailor, a nineteen-year-old Jewish Irish anti-fascist organizer named Max Levitas, was caught by police with a wet paintbrush in his coat pocket. The laborer arrested with him, according to *The Times*, said that "this was the only means they had of 'protesting against Mosley.'" The paper reported Levitas said "their object was to demonstrate against Fascism, which meant mass murder for Jews and Gentiles, as had been shown by Fascists in Germany." The headline reads "NELSON MONUMENT DEFACED." The term was a legal one, reduced from "willfully damaged."

When I went looking for how the event was covered in *The Blackshirt*, the monthly newspaper for members of the BUF, I thought at first I must have been confused, or fallen into a moment of déjà vu. The very same article appeared word-for-word, but with a different headline: "JEWS DESECRATE NELSON'S COLUMN." (That word, *desecrate*, would recur when Trump reacted to the toppling of white supremacist monuments by saying, "The unhinged left wing mob is trying to vandalize our history, desecrate our monuments, our beautiful monuments.")

In 1936, Max Levitas took part in the "Battle of Cable Street," during which residents of the East End—including "Jews . . . Irish Catholics . . . and Somali seamen"—prevented the BUF (and the police who sought to clear their path) from marching through their neighborhoods, which had endured antisemitic Blackshirt attacks for months. Two days after Cable Street, Oswald Mosley got married in Germany, at Joseph Goebbels's house. Hitler was a guest.

In 1931, before founding the BUF, Mosley led in the creation of "The New Party," joined by Vita Sackville-West's husband, Harold Nicolson, who stood for—but failed to obtain—a seat in Parliament. It's hard to say precisely when Mosley's shift into overt fascism occurred, but reading through even the earliest iteration of *Action*, the newspaper Nicolson edited during the New Party's brief existence, alarming rhetoric abounds. In response to a prescient accusation of fascism by the Communist Party of Great Britain, Nicolson wrote, "Being modelled themselves upon foreign conceptions, they imagine that others also take their ideas from abroad." He followed this xenophobic (and, given the links between Jewish Londoners and the CPGB, antisemitic) line by offering up a familiar performance of reasonable open-mindedness, a self-satisfied belief in his publication's dedication to being *fair and balanced*. Nicolson wrote:

> We are perfectly prepared to study the methods and the ideals of Fascism. We are also prepared to learn from the Nazi movement in Germany, from the Vienna Socialists, from the admirable planning of the Soviet, from the less admirable expedients of Pilsudski, and even from the strange dynamics of the Ghazi Pasha.

On November 12, an unsigned *Action* article, presumably by Nicolson, included the observation that "Hitler, who only a few months ago was regarded as an adventurer devoid of political judgment, is hailed as the sole remaining hope of financial and social stability," and was accompanied by an illustration of a Nazi poster of a hulking white man surrounded by swastika flags, the sharp points of their staffs sticking up like arrows.[3]

IN BETWEEN THE PAGES of *Action* in which her husband and Mosley's words appeared, Vita Sackville-West wrote a column about gardens. (Mosley gave her "the creeps," but not enough to stop her contributions.) The week after the issue with the Nazi poster, for instance, she noted the delights of miniature gardens—she once made a gift of one to Woolf—and suggested that, should one

---

3   In the interest of being fair and balanced, I should add that—after accompanying Mosley on a journey to Mussolini's Italy—Nicolson left the New Party and came to oppose fascism, though he remained deeply racist and antisemitic.

require inspiration or instruction, "a visit to the Alpine house at Kew will give you many suggestions."

One day, years before this column's appearance, Woolf and Sackville-West went to Kew together. I followed them there on my laptop on a rainy February morning, watching *Vita and Virginia*, a film adapted from a play adapted from their letters. It was a month in which I heard many speak of hitting a "pandemic wall," and I do not know if it was that shared structure or my own interior rooms acting upon me, but I was falling apart with regular, atomic precision. All scale vanished. It did not matter how religiously I napped, or exercised, or took my medication; I could not find my sense of proportion.

I gathered what strength I could to teach. I was guiding the students through James Schuyler's Payne Whitney Poems, written during his 1975 stay at the psychiatric hospital. I have always loved the last lines of his poem from February 13, his plaintive declaration of desire for the impossible, in small and concrete terms: "I wish I could press / snowflakes in a book like flowers."

A few lines earlier, he expresses relief that he's not yet reduced to watching morning television. I did not tell the students that I was myself so reduced, and anyway, I told myself, *it's for research.* Still, when I reached *Vita and Virginia*'s scene at Kew , the research took an emotional, personal turn, and disappointment bit at me, sharp. Though in my mind I cycled through every angle I could recall from the actual place, none of them aligned with the glass architecture on screen. *Where are you?* I asked the women, who pretended they could not hear me, went on pretending that they were at Kew. I tracked down the film's location manager, who told me they had shot the scene in Dublin's Botanic Gardens. It was a smart substitution; Dublin's glass house, like Kew's, was engineered by Richard Turner, but their curvilinear resemblance only made Kew's absence more acutely felt. What a mean trick, to let me dream up this other path to Kew, only to find in its place another wall.

Later, after their day at Kew, Woolf would bring Vita back in the guise of Orlando. How do we know Orlando is at Kew? Woolf's narrator—Orlando's biographer—points the way: "Do you recognize the Green and in the middle the steeple, and the gate with a lion couchant on either side? Oh yes, it is Kew! Well, Kew will do." It would do, nicely, I thought, could I only reach a different time, one in which a person could fly over the Atlantic and ride to the Gardens without first quarantining in solitude at a hotel. I could not make it work; the math of absence from my family as we lived on without childcare, the ratio of days I'd have to spend in isolation to days in which I could travel freely. There was no path to Kew in the present and the future had been canceled. England took on a supernatural glow. If I could get there, I told myself, I would understand . . . everything. The word *everything* was for now a closed gate and I could not see behind it, but that did not matter. When I arrived the gate would open and tell me where to go.

We were coming around again to the moment when the pandemic began, the moment when Molly died, like we were riding the sweeping green line a submarine's radar leaves on the black circle until it touches the event, awful and bright. The last day before we retreated to our house I drove Blake, deep in his grief, to therapy. He told me Molly was angry with the way I moved through the public world, my job, the success of my book. Her scorn aligned with my fear: I deserved none of what I had, was shallow, a fraud. I was not unique in drawing her ire; her fury with people touched many. Touched Blake himself. I waited for him on a bench near an artificial lake. That was the last public thing. I went home and pulled the door shut.

FOR REASONS I DO not understand, my dreams remained, until this late moment, located in a time outside of the pandemic and its catastrophes, neither before nor after, but altogether apart. And then one morning I woke into recollecting the terrors I'd dreamt the night before: the house full of unmasked strangers and news arriving that coordinated fascist attacks were occurring across the country. I did not want to be shot. The strangers could not or would not tell me what I wished to know, and when I tried to locate my phone to learn more, to reach Chris and Hattie, whose whereabouts were unclear, I discovered my bag contained every phone I'd ever owned and discarded over the past two decades, none of them able to connect in or with the present.

I understand some people consider it poor form to go on about one's dreams, and so I will stop. Instead, I will tell you about my friend, who for decades has dreamt a parallel existence, a place she returns to each night, where she has another house, job, lover, life. I wondered whether the virus had arrived in this other space. In waking life, her university was firing people too. She, an English professor, was on their list, while those who dreamt up the university's luxurious new sports center were not.

We were still waiting to hear what form the list would take at Chris's university. Now, they said, the names would be revealed in June. We were on a ship sailing through fog toward a retreating horizon. Come June it would either continue retreating or we would be directed to the lifeboat. The mood in the grid of digital meetings with their university president was bleak. Sometimes it leaked into our house. We cooked, we worked, we waited. One morning in the closet, our cat knocked a book off a shelf over-head, and it hit me on its way down.

"Ouch," I said, and then looked at the floor to see what it was. "Not funny," I told the cat, picking up *A Room of One's Own*.

A PACKAGE ARRIVED, A copy of Vita Sackville-West's story writ-ten for the queen's dollhouse. That house, filled with miniatures created by artists and craftspeople across the country, was a gift for Queen Mary's birthday in 1924. Vita's story was shelved at one-twelfth scale alongside others in the dollhouse library. Woolf was also invited to contribute a manuscript, but she refused. Vita pushed her to change her mind, and Woolf mocked her for it in a letter to her sister's husband, Clive Bell. "The poor girl," she says, "has lost her way and don't know which light to turn on next." She composes a conversation, taking on Vita's voice: "Why won't you contribute to the Queen's dolls House, Virginia?' and then replies "Is there a W.C. in it, Vita?"[4]

This new edition of Vita's dollhouse story was published it at standard picture book size. Removed from the space whose story it purports to tell and blown up to a scale exceeding its meaning, the book felt false and hollow, an object made to hold another and yet with nothing inside. It is called *A Note of Explanation*. I dislike it. When I first learned of its existence, I felt a stir of excitement, reading of its potential connections to *Orlando*. Vita's main character is a sprite who has lived a very long time, who is enchanted by the dollhouse's modern conveniences. Some see in this time-traversing figure a possible inspiration for Woolf's mock-biography, but when I read it for myself the idea fell flat.

---

4   In fact, there is, and the room is equipped with working plumbing. The faucets run; the toilets flush.

History's shifting atmospheres—so crucial to Woolf's work and her understanding of the world—were absent.

Once, speculating about her distaste for Sackville-West's gardening articles, Jamaica Kincaid mused that "the source of [her] antipathy . . . is to be found in [Sackville-West's] observations of the garden, in the way she manages to be oblivious of the world. For the fact is that the world cannot be left out of the garden." Vita's obliviousness was not limited to prose; in her poetry she actively worked to wall the world out:

> Yet shall the garden with the state of war
> Aptly contrast, a miniature endeavour
> To hold the graces and the courtesies
> Against a horrid wilderness.

Both of Vita's long pastoral poems: "The Land" (which Woolf reimagined into Orlando's "The Oak Tree") and "The Garden" (in which the above lines appear) attempt to anchor time not in the rhythms of the city or history or politics, but in the seasonal movement through moments: of the blossom, the egg, the harvest. "I tried to hold the courage of my ways," wrote the aristocrat, "In that which might endure / Daring to find a world in a lost world, / A little world, a little perfect world."

I ordered a used copy of *The Garden*, and when it arrived I stood in the kitchen to unwrap the package, opening by chance to the section titled "Winter," from which—I could hardly believe it as it happened—cut-paper snowflakes fell, weather from a previous reader, some white, some silver. In at least this one element of Vita's garden, I thought, I could rejoice. The wish Schuyler made in 1975, "I wish I could press / snowflakes in a book like flowers," had finally come true.

"What would you wish for right now?" I texted Chelly, "if you could wish for anything in the world?"

"HELP," she replied. "A BABYSITTER."

I tapped the message to laugh react.

She texted again later to say our parents had dropped by briefly to deliver a gift: a rose bush.

A rose bush, I thought, *is nice.* Then, *a rose bush is not a babysitter.* Then "*Rose is a rose is a rose is a rose is a . . .*"

My mother told my sister she chose this particular rose because of its cultivar name, because she wanted to make Chelly happy. "Look," she said, and pointed at the label. It was called "Hope for Humanity."

I had to let her in. She is my mother.

Correction

MY OLDEST FRIEND, HANNAH, remembers everything. She is a whole archive, a repository of days and details which others—I—have forgotten. She loves silk and punk and plants and tiny things. In the photographs she posts of the tiny things, she holds them in her gloved hand so as to reveal their scale. We have known each other since preschool, through a thousand transformations. She collects old paperback books, including a copy of *Orlando* that is split in two, across one sentence, like this:

Instantly—such is its   took a human shape—such
impetuosity—love   is its pride.

One morning Hannah's copy of *Orlando* arrived in the mail, an unexpected gift. She had fastened it together with a dark red velvet ribbon tied in a bow, which I undid. Because I had grown into the sense that I had not seen any pair—of anything—fully unless I gazed at it through my cardboard stereoscope, I aligned images of the split pages on my phone, slipped it into the box, and tried to read my way through the lines in which Orlando sails across the Channel back to England. It was slow work, the piecemeal combination almost incomprehensible and certainly impossible to remember long enough to examine in depth. The only way to understand was to record myself reading aloud, halted as a newly literate child. Then I played the sound back, listening to the scraps of meaning that emerged—

she had to be a moth for now . . .
praise god I'm a woman and cried . . .
the exploded folly . . .

until I heard my voice grow fluent and these lines fell out of my mouth in one long and silken string—

The crept-in horizon of the last sentence.
"Love—love," said Orlando.
"The cliffs of England, ma'am," said the captain.

His words, I thought, sounded like a correction.

YEARS AGO, WHEN I was still living in Ohio, my mother and I sat in a windowless café, making a timeline of her life with Post-it notes. When we reached the summer of 1995 she paused to ask me a question. She wanted to know why I didn't tell her about what happened in Camden Town sooner.

"I thought you knew," I told her, and thought of Scott and Melanie. "I thought they told you."

"No," she said. "They told me you had food poisoning. And when I found out the truth later I was so angry. They left you alone and came to eat dinner with us like nothing was wrong." Her voice nearly broke, but she went on. "I thought about that for a long time. I hated the thought of you alone."[1]

Her anger reassured me at the time, but in the years since an unease returned. Why had she not shared her anger with me then? Why had she pulled away? Her collection of family photos sputters out in 1995 and doesn't pick up again until 2006, when Chelly and I threw a large party for her sixtieth birthday.

I went into the closet to call her, while Chris was putting Hattie to bed. I had been thinking, I said, that she must have felt unprotected as a child, and that probably made it hard for her when I went through my own assault. Maybe, I said, that was why she withdrew.

"But I didn't know," she said. "You didn't tell me about it."

"Not while we were in England," I said, "But I did tell you."

She was quiet, thinking, confused.

"When?" she asked.

"It must have been some time that fall," I said, "because I know you had me start on the pill. We were sitting on the white stairs, remember?"

A slow thought sunk through me. She hadn't realized, when I was fourteen and sitting with her on the staircase, that I was describing an assault. Just sex. Just getting drunk. Just admitting

---

[1]   My mother and I remember my being left alone; my cousin and his ex do not. The discrepancy makes me think of Roy Pascal's statement in *Design and Truth in Autobiography* that in such works "we find indeed open admissions of the conflict between two truths," offering an example of how André Gide "appends to his book a letter from his cousin which corrects some statements of his." I have no such letter to append. I have only the obligation to repeat what it seems all memoirists must: memories differ, sometimes to the point of irreconcilability.

that I had again misbehaved. It must have been later, toward the end of high school, when I let myself use the word *rape* that she finally understood the significance, that she finally became angry.

"I don't remember," she said. "Maybe you're right. I'm sorry."

"It's just hard," I said, pressing on through murky waters, "when you talk about me being horrible as a teenager, because I know it wasn't easy for you, but I was going through a lot, and I really needed you, and it felt like you weren't there. You know, you have this thing you say about how 'you always loved me, but sometimes you didn't like me very much,' and I *knew* that. It's really hard when you can tell your mother doesn't like you."

"Well, maybe I did pull away," she said, choking up. "But if I did, it was for self-protection."

I rested my head against the brown wall.

"Let me put it this way, Heather. Would *you* have liked you then?"

I closed my eyes.

"If Hattie acted like you, if they told you they hated you, you would still like them?"

"Yes," I said. *"Because that's my job."*

"Well I'm sorry, but what do you want me to do? I can't go back and change the past." She sounded panicked.

"I just want you to stop saying I was horrible."

"Okay," she said, and blew her nose. "I can do that."

I GOT MY FIRST shot. After the second I went back to my office to retrieve my map of Kew and hung it up in the closet. I apologized to the potted plant I abandoned a year ago, and then I threw it away.

My cousins Scott and Alison and I gathered in my laptop's grid, in preparation for another trip to England I hoped I would at last be able to make. Covid precautions had shifted and the country would

let me in. I leaned away from my mother and toward my family
in the UK. Maybe, I thought, they would know things my mother
did—or could—not. I would fill in my map from other angles. Tell
me, I said, about Kew, or Bekonscot Model Village, or the garden
behind our grandparents' flat. I was overexcited, greedy to know
everything at once, but my cousins smiled and humored me.

On the day they buried our grandmother's ashes at Saint
Anne's, Alison said, her husband took their daughter, Sophia, into
Kew Gardens. (Their son, Ethan, had not yet been born.) Now
grown and visiting home from university, Sophia came in when
her mother called for her, showed me her scrapbook of photos
from that day that Chelly and I had missed—her small self next to
a plant beneath which she'd penned *Massive Leaf.* Her handwrit-
ing reminded me of Hattie's.

Days later, Alison sent me a message: inspired by our conversation, Scott had taken Ethan to visit Bekonscot, the model
village now reopened. Scott texted a picture from their outing, a
group of archaeologists digging through the earth to find a Roman
mosaic—a scene that could have been at any scale, though his
words shrank it down to inches.

I smiled, but felt my mouth drift downward when I performed
the expression in texted reply. Always, when I knocked on my
words to Scott I heard a hollowness. I could not tell if he shared
the sensation, but in our conversations I felt a nagging awareness
of my own tiny shovel hidden behind my back, unsure whether I
should ask questions closer to Camden Town, whether his answers
would be like my mother's, whether I should dig, and where. (But
the ground was so far away.)

Kept for now at a distance from the place I wanted to understand, my access took the form through which Woolf once
imagined she might hear the past: "I shall fit a plug into a wall;

and listen." This might happen, she mused "in time," by which she meant the future. It made me happy to watch Woolf play with time and devices, a good place to put my thoughts when feelings threatened to overwhelm. You *can* go back and change the past, I thought, arguing silently with my mother. You just have to look. You have to look again. Looking changes what you see.

Once, in "Flying Over London" (a short story dressed up in essay form), Woolf pretended to be in an airplane looking down through Zeiss binoculars at tiny buildings vanishing into an ancient landscape: so that she was seeing the Thames "as paleolithic man saw it, at dawn from a hill shaggy with wood, with the rhinoceros digging his horn into the roots of rhododendrons." This was an imaginary flight, a flight of fancy. Woolf herself—I mean *corporeal* Woolf—never once flew.

The imaginary plane in which Woolf flew over London was a Moth, a model popular at the time, and whose name must have particularly appealed to her. She and her siblings grew up practicing lepidoptery like the good Victorians they were taught to be. Woolf's head was full of moths, and when she was in need of an appellation or image she found them within easy reach. She even wrote of words as moths, noting how in daily life "[W]e refuse words their liberty. We pin them down to one meaning, their useful meaning, the meaning which makes us catch the train, the meaning which makes us pass the examination. And when words are pinned down they fold their wings and die."

WHEN WOOLF DIED, SHE left behind drafts and notes for her two final essays, which were intended to form the beginning of her next book, a history of English literature. She would start with the ancient figure of "Anon," who is "sometimes a man, sometimes a woman . . . the common voice singing out of doors . . . a simple singer, lifting a song or story from other people's lips, and letting the audience join in the chorus." Anon is a wanderer, who "lives a roaming life crossing the fields, mounting the hills, lying under the hawthorn to listen to the nightingale." As she wrote her way beyond Anon, Woolf struggled to find a way to transition between eras, between social and literary histories. The scholar Brenda R. Silver speculates that "the text reveals the search for a link between past and future that would bridge the emptiness of the present." That present—the first years of the war, the last years of her life—began to feel hollow to Woolf. She had a "curious feeling," she wrote in her diary, "that the writing 'I' has vanished. No audience. No echo."

In this, the second pandemic summer, the present was filling in again, aided by our vaccinations. I heard Hattie and Chris at play in the kitchen through the closet wall. *He lives*, I thought. *They live.* I cast my eyes less frequently to a future I struggled to imagine. The ideas I found in my thoughts each had a weight I could comprehend, and around them were perceptible edges. The paths between moments felt sturdier. I booked my ticket to fly back to London. I would roam a path whose pages my mother did not see. I would not need her and I would not behave. I would look until I changed the past and the past, in turn, changed me. The plane, I told myself, would be real.

HOW BRIEF WAS THE hopeful summer. Our landlord, a doctor, texted us, "Y'all stay safe and don't need an ER or anything. Next few weeks seem like they're going to be tough." He was right. Delta tore through the state. The intensive care units filled. Emergency rooms turned people away. Hattie returned to school in person for the first time in a year and a half. The children ate lunch out-side. They were not supposed to talk. My fears were like brake pads worn down to the metal. We followed all the protocols: masks, distance, hand-washing, but something in me had broken. Surrendered.

I kept waiting for news that travel would no longer be permit-ted between the US and UK, but in its absence I continued my preparations. I placed pins in maps, marking sites of which I'd read in Woolf's pages, places my mother had described, buildings I knew I had been to as a child but could not now remember. I did not differentiate between them. The pins were all one color.

Hattie was angry that I was going to England, angry that in the meantime I was so often plotting out my journey in the closet of debris. Bedtime grew complicated.

"Do you love the book more than me?" they asked.

"No."

"Then why are you going?"

"It's the only way I can finish the book."

"I kind of want to kick the book."

"I know."

"I kind of want to burn it."

I knew I needed to find a way to fully return to a life beyond the page, but I struggled to see past the heap at the closet's door. There was an exit, but I had to take the long way around—through England—to reach it.

One rainy afternoon back in my solo October journey to England, just before the pandemic, I had walked from Kew to Richmond by myself. I peered at Woolf's house on Paradise Road, but could see little of its dim interior. Through tiny spaces between the fence in back I caught glimpses of an unremarkable garden. Later, eating dinner in comfortable solitude, I looked out the window and saw a construction sign leaning against a building across the street, its words familiar to passersby, but to me a strange way of saying END DETOUR, the phrase we use in the US. The sign was a warning or a reminder or an omen. In England they say DIVERSION ENDS.

PART THREE

"I will take my mind out of its iron cage and let it swim—this fine October."

—WOOLF, *Diaries, Vol. 3*

Hither

AS IF THEY TOO had little social subtlety left after this year-and-a-half of pandemic, the gulls conduct their conversation in screams. I am on the high footpath alongside the River Ouse, a trail I chose for the sake of its broad view of the soft green hills called the Downs rolling up and down to my left, and to my right fields, smattered trees. My path will take me from Lewes, where I am staying for a few days, to Monk's House, Woolf's country home nearby, though I've chosen to delay my arrival, have plotted a circuitous route. A group of cyclists passes below me on the lower path, and at the end of their pack I hear a father call out to his child riding behind him.

"Come round."

"What?"

"Come around."

"I can't hear you."

"Come around so you're not at the back."

"Why?"

"Because if you're at the back I can't see you; you might drop off."

Across the river a sign says DANGER. *I know*, I tell it, pretending to less concern than I possess, and then turn my head to face forward, walking back into my truer, more tenuous thoughts. Am I trying to prove the river cannot tempt me? That despite the danger I will not drop off?

When I reach the point where the path from Monk's House meets the river, the river where Woolf left her life, two teenagers are chatting up on the embankment, while a third, who stands down on the rocky shore the low tide has revealed, plays with a dog happily swimming after every stone the boy tosses into the water. I do not turn; I follow the river. I want the walk to last.

The day is damp enough that I almost chastise myself for not wearing my raincoat, but then the air dries and all that remains of the threatened precipitation is the wetness of the grass beneath me, and the exquisite drops arranged on every spiderweb I pass. *Cobweb*, I think. *Spiderweb*. I prefer the former, but it's not the word I (or others in the US) most readily use. I want to take a picture of one—web, not word—and then realize there's no point, that what I want to share with others is not the look of the thing, beautiful though it may be. I want to share the sensation that I could touch, could disturb this perfection, and am choosing not to. Then I wonder why on earth I'm throwing myself into the great pit of veneration for the untouched, the unspoilt, the virgin. Why must touch mean ruin?

I have never felt sure of which words to place around the night in Camden Town. I am still angry that my mother needed me to say *rape*, a pinned-down word that somehow leaves everything out. Something occurred that had not before. From my present moment, that is the closest to the event I can get, a sentence bending itself into a circle that holds the indescribable within. Is this why I hate to speak during sex, that I cannot do so without feeling I am telling a lie? That seems too tidy an explanation. Wordlessness feels like boundless joy, as if I've finally moved outside of language altogether and can there find relief.

A man and a woman in clothing designed to passionately specific weather standards are standing by a fence lining this section of the path, gathering wild raspberries. I slow my walking, imperceptibly, I hope, so that I can hear a bit of their conversation as I pass.

"Somewhere the other day I heard a word, from Norway maybe? A container you keep with you in case you find anything you want to forage."

I stick my hands in my pocket, let one tap my notebook. DANGER is already gathered within. The last sign I forage on my walk is by a house not far from the Woolfs'. It gives the house's name, and it gives more: a smile on my face it did not mean to elicit, but I am struck with perverse delight to find LITTLE EASE. Each of these moments is a relief—a broadening of my journey's purpose—and thus a protection against Woolf's disdain, of which I go in fear.[1]

"I do not know," Woolf once began a *Guardian*[2] article on a visit to Charlotte Brontë's house at Haworth, "whether pilgrimages to the shrines of famous men ought not to be condemned as

---

1 When I feel this, I hear also the voice of the writer and artist Renee Gladman, who traces lines between the words of women she reads and then says, "We were suspended in time. Still talking to Virginia Woolf, still searching for Zora Neale Hurston, wanting to empty Woolf's words of their racism, wanting to be loved by Stein."

2 Not *The Guardian* newspaper, but a clerical publication of the same name.

sentimental journeys," but she wrote this so long ago, so young, newly freed by the death of her father into life as a writer in public, a moment when she lived perhaps in fear of being condemned as merely sentimental herself, and thus by famous men dismissed. She knew too—knows, if I am to use the strange conventional tense, suspending her in time—the joys of moving one's body into a space heretofore much imagined, "as though we were to meet some long-separated friend, who might have changed in the interval—so clear an image of Haworth had we from print and picture."

Not long after this 1904 article she wrote another, "Literary Geography," in which she elaborates on the nature of such pilgrimages: "We are either pilgrims from sentiment, who find something stimulating to the imagination in the fact that Thackeray rang this very door bell or that Dickens shaved behind that identical window" (and I do indeed recognize my own sentimental journey in these lines). "Or," she continues, "we are scientific in our pilgrimage and visit the country where a great novelist lived in order to see to what extent he was influenced by his surroundings," and while *scientific* might be a stretch, I do believe I'm seeking correspondence between page and land, paragraph and room, my life and others', though I measure nothing, but listen for echoes and rhymes. If I gather enough, I think, if I line up the right pairs, then the past will come clear, and so will my place within it.

Outside Monk's House two women wait in hopes that the National Trust will let them in, despite their lack of pre-booked tickets. The house is small, and visitors are limited to six each hour, slots that rapidly fill. The older woman used to live in this village, she tells me, in Rodmell, and for a moment she flickers from three-dimensionality to a paper cutout of a person, snipped from the pages of Woolf's last book, *Between the Acts*, which is set in a place much like this, and I watch the words spilling and shifting to accommodate their new margins when she moves her body slightly toward her daughter.

"We used to see him around sometimes," she says.

"Who?" asks her daughter.

"Leonard."

"Did you ever speak to him?" I ask.

"No, he kept himself to himself," she explains, relying on the phrase that British people always use in mysteries when asked about the murderer, or the missing person. Not two months ago a man was arrested under suspicion of spying for Russia, and *The Guardian*[3] reported that "a woman sitting in her garden terrace reading, a couple of doors away from his flat, only said he had 'kept himself to himself.'" This land! The solitude! The books!

Another couple (I am the only person here alone) consists of a man who hardly speaks and a tall thin woman in a pale green brocade coat. She looks thematically linked with historical sofas and is immensely kind. She works—it emerges, as we practice building up the tales of ourselves we will tell through these next few hours—for a museum, alongside a man whose recent book arguing for the repatriation of looted objects has elicited an intense wave of publicity.

"But if we give back everything we stole we won't have anything left!" laughs the daughter, and behind my mask I open my mouth, wanting to intervene in the recitation of this talking point, but though I feel my throat close on the threshold of speech, before I can release my breath forth into the definite shaping of words the National Trust volunteer arrives. She tells the daughter and mother that all slots are filled for the day, so they walk off to the

---

3   Not the clerical publication, but the newspaper of the same name.

pub up the road, while the rest of us go into the garden. The tour begins in Leonard's conservatory, she says—everyone here refers to the Woolfs by their first names, and I am surprised by how uncomfortable it makes me (too intimate, too close)—but as the space is so small, she asks us to enter in staggered pairs, not all at once, and in the meantime to wander the grounds.

I exhale in happy relief, wanting, now that I have arrived at last in the place so long imagined, not to rush in, not to crash through the door and devour the rooms too quickly. I follow the path through flowerbeds, the green of everything so vivid beneath the sky's weird bright clouds that I think I might not be able to bear it. It does not, I do not, cohere. I jangle loosely. My body ceases to make sense, or rather, it makes too much. I must, I think, find a way to turn it down. I walk on to the orchard, whose trees are abundant with apples. My desire is instantaneous, as is my fear. I want to pick one, I want to eat it, and I am afraid of being caught and thrown out before I am let into the house. This is not, I tell the world, the book I'm looking for. I stare. I take a picture. I have the sense that if I were to eat it I would transform, maybe dissolve into the earth, but my fear, I learn, is stronger than my desire. I leave the tree untouched.

Inside the house I go wild with questions. What is the seed packet at the bottom of the stack on the desk? (Dahlias, from Bees' "SEEDS THAT GROW.") (Is not this the implicit promise of all commercial seed packets?) (This question I ask silently.) The Sri Lankan woman painted on the cabinet, is her image based on a photograph? (They don't know; they don't think so, no.) Are the books on the shelves from the Woolfs' actual collection? (No.) (This last answer pleases me as it means someone has placed one book with cover exposed on playful purpose, like dressing a set for a show: *Gladioli and the Miniatures* by Roy Genders. I laugh. I feel myself aglow.) The chair they say matches one of

Vanessa Bell's at Charleston Farm, where would I find its twin? (At Charleston they will know.) I linger too long in the living room and miss half the story of the next, the dining room, which— is this correct?, I ask—once served as a guestroom whose door Vita had difficulty unlocking when she came to visit, nearly found herself stuck. (Yes, this is correct.) (How petty my satisfaction!) From another visitor: how long has the house been managed by the National Trust? (Let's see, it was in 1980 they bought it, so sixty-one years, that makes it?) (The guide's math is incorrect but for a moment I believe her, that the year of my birth does indeed sit at that distance, that two more decades have gone by— hidden within the pandemic's disorientation—without my notice.) In Woolf's bedroom, when did she switch from writing here to working in the shed? (The binder is consulted. Lots of writers are like that, aren't they? They need to get out of their house, into a different space.) (What can I do but nod?) Then my most pressing question.

"Ah, the apples. We usually—we used to—have a day, a big event, where everyone comes and picks apples, but this year . . ." She takes a half-breath and makes a gesture with her hand toward all that can be understood without being said. My hope must be blazing from my face; when her gaze turns back to me she smiles.

"You should pick some," she says. "Help yourself."

Some seems too many—why am I still so afraid?—but I permit myself one, circle round the tree, find the right fruit to pluck. I cannot eat it in front of these strangers and so tuck it into my backpack for later. I walk on. In one side of the shed (or lodge, as it is called here), a video plays on a loop: experts discuss *A Room of One's Own*, the first Woolf I ever read. Lucy Day comes on and reads an excerpt containing the phrase "hither and thither," one of Woolf's linguistic tics, and I ride its current from that page to one from *Orlando*, a passage I love:

Memory is the seamstress, and a capricious one at that. Memory runs her needle in and out, up and down, hither and thither. We know not what comes next, or what follows after. Thus, the most ordinary movement in the world, such as sitting down at a table and pulling the inkstand towards one, may agitate a thousand odd, disconnected fragments, now bright, now dim, hanging and bobbing and dipping and flaunting, like the underlinen of a family of fourteen on a line in a gale of wind.

This passage gets cut off in one track of Max Richter's music composed for *Woolf Works*, Wayne McGregor's ballet, which I otherwise adore. The passage begins with a dreamy voice saying, "Memory is the seamstress," but stops at "dipping and flaunting," leaving out Woolf's comic final clause, consigning her to a smaller tonal range than the varied moods in which she wrote and lived. Why not let her get to the underwear? It is dishonest—cruel—to stop her from reaching her laugh.

It's because she so often gets cut off at such moments that her life dwindles down to her depression, as if she'd walked through each day with stones in her coat pockets. Inside the house, when a guide spoke of her suicide, another visitor turned to a portrait hanging beside her and sighed, "She does look sad, doesn't she," when a moment earlier she might have been allowed to look like she was *thinking*. I wanted to step between the painting and the sigher and growl. I did not; I channeled the growl through my notebook and pen, as if my scribbling could make the visitor feel Woolf rolling her painted eyes. I am a ridiculous person, a bag of geese in a human costume, jangling about in anger and wanting and fear. The costume feels precarious, having been hung up for so long in the closet, and though I do not mind laughing at myself

I still fear the laughter of others. I am worried someone will notice the geese.

But I am back outside now, on the steps of Woolf's shed, sitting in sunlight and watching visitors wander the gardens. She worked on *Orlando* here. She must have laughed aloud. Leonard used the loft above to store apples and she complained of the noise of their tumbling. In 1941, as her life came to its close, she watched that of the garden continue. When I think of the words she wrote in her final days, I want to distribute my attention fairly, across the different pages. Woolf penned her farewell notes to her husband and sister, but she took time to make note of ordinary moments too. Life is, after all, largely composed of the daily, of the ongoing, even when few of one's own days remain. Her diary's last entry concludes with an ellipsis, with Leonard, with care for this garden where I stand: "L. is doing the rhododendrons . . ."

THE DOORS TO HER writing space are locked, but I can peer through the window at the inkstand, the armchair, the view out the French doors on the room's other side, where stands a thick chestnut tree. The window reflects my body too, a dark outline silhouetted against the green, playing at transparence.

The thin woman in the historical coat pauses near me. She finds such inspiration here; she hopes I will too. She is so kind and I am so full of geese. How fascinating, I say, to meet someone from the museum. Yes. I can feel her reach for a metal detector, working to locate the buried scraps and shards of my beliefs.

"It's difficult," she says, "because I can see it from both sides. Of course I understand what the museum is trying to do, and it's very necessary—I don't know if you know we took the—I can't remember the correct term." (I can't either; it's *tsantas*.) "We used to call them shrunken heads—we removed them from the display, and it had been quite disrespectful, but then I understand the public's view as well, that they are losing something."[4] *Whom do you mean by the public, though,* I wonder, and almost ask her, before calculating the time that would be lost to such a question and thrusting my beaks beneath the water, out of sight.

I wander round the outskirts of the garden. I press my hands against the trunks of two trees and am briefly imprinted with their bark. These are not the elms beneath which the Woolfs' ashes were scattered. A storm took Virginia's down swiftly in 1943, while disease took Leonard's more slowly, in 1985. Closer to the house, on a low wall, I read a plaque:

The ashes of LEONARD and VIRGINIA WOOLF
who lived in this house from 1919 until their
deaths were scattered under the great elm tree.
In 1972 the plaque in Virginia's memory which
Leonard had placed there was moved from
the elm to this more permanent position. At the
same time the bust of Leonard Woolf and the
plaque in his memory were placed here.

I do not ask anyone where the elms would have been. I find my wanting embarrassing, sentimental, but I crouch a long time by the wall, parsing the plaque, whose letters in some places are nearly worn away, and which nowhere makes mention of the other

---

4   The scene from *Orlando* that most unsettles me also makes use of such a display, the young man play-fighting the head of "a Moor" that his "father, or perhaps his grandfather, had struck . . . from the shoulders of a vast Pagan who had started up under the moon in the barbarian fields of Africa; and [which] now . . . swung, gently, perpetually, in the breeze which never ceased blowing through the attic rooms of the gigantic house of the lord who had slain him."

elm, nor of either tree's death. It is a stretch to say they "lived in this house" that whole time, from the year of Woolf writing "Kew Gardens," through the year of her writing "Anon." They did often come to stay, but it was only when war threatened London—with bombs that would eventually destroy their city home—that they moved here permanently. Leonard's life here was longer, his hands full of years, seeds, and soil.

When I stand, the garden darkens. Deep brown enters the edges of my vision and crowds to the center like a filtered photograph, a shrinking vignette. I sway, I stop myself from falling down. I have walked too far without food. I should go. I should go and eat.

My route here had taken me south of the house, down to Southease before turning and rounding up to Rodmell, to the northwest. The footpath the Woolfs would have walked from the house to the river I have not yet touched. In the shortness of my time this is a moment I work to prolong. My desires and fears are intertwined. I do not want the path to narrow down to meaning only her death (she would have walked it with her dogs, with friends, with the solitary company of her books' composition), and yet I also do not want to force and flatten her into a happy shape for my pleasure or use.

The sky, river, and fields are at first obscured by walls, houses, and trees. Through a gap in the canopy I glimpse Lewes Castle, gray and thick and medieval on its hill—a view Woolf would have glanced at in her own time—while directly beneath the historic building, in the more immediate scene of the backyard, sits a plastic Little Tikes play castle whose closeness makes it larger than the structure it represents. It is a good joke, seemingly authorless, and I am reassured. I walk on. At the edge of the more overgrown part of the footpath I struggle to open a gate. I've unfastened many today, each a little different, some broken and replaced with bits of rope, and they've come to feel like a sequence of small puzzles one must solve before being permitted to move on to the next page of a myth.

Having finally succeeded, I turn for the first time to the open view, uninterrupted by trees or gates or people on the path. The fields, green and gold, stretch to either side, while in front of me the embankment rises up grassy, following the river's curve.

When I look up, the sky is replete with a dozen paragliders, and the sight of them opens my mouth into an involuntary O. Each sail is a different shade, some solid, some parti-color, none pale, all bright. Their curves cast on the Downs a flock of parentheses, shadows who wait through the night in the dark to be drawn by what interrupts the sun.

Again a force beyond my control takes hold of my mouth; when three paragliders float behind the lines of electrical wires strung between posts, the figures transform and pluck speech from me: *Like notes!* I have forgotten how to read music, but it does not matter. My very blood is a song. I think of Woolf's teasing words from *Orlando*: "Trees were withered hags, and sheep were grey boulders. Everything, in fact, was something else."

Woolf is laughing and feeding my geese and I do not mind their being discovered. I walk on; she stays in the field.

At the top of the embankment a gate marks the place where earlier I observed the teenagers and the dog, but when I climb up to it I see the river has changed, the tide has risen, so that the stones with which they played are now hidden far below. I can crouch and reach down and touch the water. Can wash my apple in it. Can dry the fruit on my sleeve. Can breathe. Can take a bite.

Thither

‡‡

THE NEXT DAY, ON the other side of the river, I pass through the outskirts of the town, up over the first hills and into a valley, where—in the intervals when the sky grows empty of planes—I hear no human sounds. Sheep arrange themselves among the yarrow on the slopes and down into the level space my phone map tells me is called Bible Bottom. I spin myself slowly around, happy to be alone and here, with ample hours rolling before me on my way to Charleston Farm, home of Woolf's sister, Vanessa Bell, and her teeming family. Woolf loved to wander the Downs, to walk to see her sister, and I want my feeling for her life to branch out beyond Monk's House and the river.

My climb brings me to the hill to which yesterday's paragliders have returned, close up now, with visible bodies and faces. When they step from the edge of the land and float into the sky, the paragliders look, from here, like children on swings the wind has untethered from the earth, but no, they cannot have come from the earth; the earth here, on Mount Caburn, bears the marks of an Iron Age hillfort and Bronze Age bowl barrow, a great grassy ring, while the paragliders are carried by bright synthetic parabolas in seats attached with nearly invisible strings. Land and sky seem segmented, two wholly different times. I belong to neither. I feel like an alien observer. Paragliding is an instance of human behavior, I think. Like building forts and barrows.

I follow the path down toward a village rung round with sheep. Yesterday it was cows. I place them on a little scale in my head so I do not forget. Cows, Woolf; Sheep, Bell. Stray handfuls of wool stipple the fields. I pick one up and take a photo of it in my hand.

When I was six, and the whole family journeyed north to a house in Penrith for a Lake District vacation, we spent the days walking and gathering wool like this. My mother's photo album holds pages of pictures in which we duckbill our mouths to hold a tuft up beneath our noses, making it a puffy yellowed mustache, we its grumpy men. Feeling light and loose, I send my mother my new picture, pretend it is a postcard. *Thinking of ewe.* She types back right away. *Make it a moustache!* I do not want to. We've done that already. My path and my hands are my own. The wool belongs with yesterday's apple. A mistake, I think, to have shown her. I try to shake off the album. I do not reply.

The houses here all have names: Rose Cottage, Orchard House, Wisdoms, Welsted. Some wear them on small oval signs, others I learn by zooming in close on my map. Across from Wharf Cottage, on a street called The Street, children arrive at a little hall for a birthday party in Peter Pan costumes. I get nervous; none of them are in masks. Pulled into the moment, I miss my turn, go back, walk the other way, realize my first path was correct, retreat, start again. The buildings are too close up and too closed in. My looseness tightens. I'm supposed to go down Spring Ditch, but it runs through a private field, and the way is blocked off with an unopenable gate. I stare at my phone and inch forward, reluctant to go where I must, to cross the A27 with lane upon lane of cars speeding past. I have not wholly adjusted to their driving on the left side of the road and do not quite trust myself to know where to look. It would be funny if I died here, I think. It would be funny if I died anywhere on this trip; I am putting my body only in places thick with significance and were my life to end here a biographer would be hard-pressed to write it as "just another fact in a series of facts."

I stand there, stuck, until a man in serious gear with serious calves walks up and casts his gaze back and forth until, with such determination that he becomes a ship and I a fish in its wake, he crosses and we arrive on the other side.

"Bit dodgy, innit?" he says, and strides onward, while I try to determine which of these side paths is the one I'm meant to choose. I step toward a turn, but another gate I think should be open is locked. I give up and climb over it. I trespass through cows—some pregnant, some farrow—past rolls of cylindrical hay, onto the grounds of a manor house where people are having a wedding. I do not like manor house weddings. I am afraid I will have to trespass through the event, but the path veers off in another direction and I enter the woods.

A loop of synthetic blue rope holds the final gate shut, its threads frayed and wild. How good, I think, for it to be this way, distractedly shaping the pliable image into a pleasant meaning, and walk on, only to find that gate was penultimate. This one is final. The latch is smooth and easy, lately oiled, but when I pass through and turn to slide it back into place, my hand brushes against a nettle and my finger swells up, stung. The existence of some leaf that could relieve me swims up from memory, always grows nearby, but I won't let myself look up its name or text my mother. She would be too pleased to help and I do not want to need her. The day is mine and mine alone. I carry on with my sting.

Inside the house, I learn, the solution to every problem was to paint, using a mix of pigments, rabbit skin glue, and chalk they gathered from the surrounding earth. When, mid-century, the work of Vanessa Bell and Duncan Grant fell out of fashion and money ran short, they sold a Picasso or two, first painting copies so the walls would not sense the loss. When Vanessa's young son Quentin placed an oil lamp in front of a mirror, which heated to the point of cracking, Grant painted one in its place, its reflection unchanging, though days and seasons passed. Years. They weren't precious, says a guide, pointing at the lowest panel of a door in Clive Bell's study, whose original ornamentation fell victim to the children's reenactment of the sacking of Rome. In the dining room, pointing at errors in the wallpaper pattern—a purpled black covered in hand-painted white squares and gold chevrons—another guide presents them as evidence of nonchalance: "They didn't think that in a hundred years we'd be traipsing through here."

"But they did," I hear myself stage whisper inside my skull's dark auditorium, where I've whipped out the manuscript for Quentin and Julian Bell's 1936 play, "A Hundred Years After, or, Ladies and Gentlemen," set here, in Charleston's studio, a century into its imagined future. It's a raucous muddle of Bloomsbury facts, in which a guide takes a group of tourists—including a loud and misinformed American—around the site. The play both satirizes and participates in Bloomsbury's habits of self-mythologizing, and was performed before those selves in Vanessa Bell's London studio, with a velvet rope separating players from audience, whose bodies the actors treated as parts of the set. Taking an archaeological turn, the guide—played by Lytton Strachey's nephew—notes that some believe "Woolves" had once lived in Sussex, citing an ancient umbrella dug up nearby as evidence. One tourist, seeking to supplement the narration, pulls out her Baedeker guidebook and learns that Charleston attracted literary luminaries, including Virginia Sackville West. (It's as if she's looking at Vita's and Virginia's names through a stereoscope, and binocular vision pronounces them wed.)

The play closes with the guide's revelation of Charleston's pièce de résistance: a sign with an arrow pointing in the direction of the imaginary offstage toilet the tourist characters desperately require. At least one recent visitor to Charleston, ashdown2011, who reviewed the site on TripAdvisor, would find such binary signage pleasing, dissatisfied as they were with Charleston's real-life, gender-neutral toilets, "a supposedly progressive device which reminds me of going in toilets in French cafes years ago." In the Bells' script, the Baedeker guide gives Charleston three stars; ashdown2011 gives it four, calling it "a lovely place to visit," but complains that—in addition to the apparent toilet deficiencies—they could not find the café's menu and were not told where to queue.

Though the Bells' script makes me laugh, some other part of me winces at the younger generation's repetition of the older's flattened lives. In the gift shop at Charleston, mugs and scarves and cutting boards designed by Quentin's daughter echo the circles his mother brushed throughout the house, obsession giving way to recitation. My wincing is touched by recognition, by my own intermittent fear that the path my mother had trodden is one I am compelled to walk too.

In the myths that hung about her—some draped there by others, some by herself—most brightly I saw she was wild. As a teenager, every weekend she'd go to see the Rolling Stones, first at Richmond's Station Hotel, later at Eel Pie Island. Her headmistress despaired of her hair, red and untamed. She knew Ian McLagan from the Small Faces. Men loved her; she drove men wild. The night in Camden Town when I was fourteen was my clumsy performance of this myth. My costume purchased for the occasion: pink minidress in fuzzy synthetic, white knee socks, plastic glittery platform shoes, newly shorn hair dyed red. Whose idea the hairstyle was I do not know. But *look at me* I thought, and they did, men did, men called out to me from the street in the voices my mother would once have heard. Inside the costume I knew my own flatness, walked in terror I would be found out, they would see me a child. I did not want to be returned to that lonely state.

Standing in Charleston's library, I again wonder whether the man who took me into the alley and reached beneath the costume noticed the underwear that gave me away. I think he probably did not, not in the dark, not soaked as he was in drink. I want to pull a book from a shelf for protection, but as it's not allowed I have to search my mind instead. Would Gertrude Stein call my obsessive return to this image—the underwear—an act of repetition or insistence? It feels closer, I think, to the former, no variation in emphasis. Flat. Whatever happened left the cotton marked with blood. I will ask Scott. I will have to ask Scott. Scott is the one who will know.

When Woolf visited Charlotte Brontë's home, she thought "the most touching case" was that which contained "little personal relics, the dresses and shoes of the dead woman." Woolf describes gazing upon them, how in doing so Brontë, the writer, vanishes, but "Brontë, the woman comes to life." She puzzles through her interest and her discomfort: "An effort ought to be made to keep these things out of these mausoleums," by which she means museums, "but the choice often lies between them and destruction." She admits a certain gratitude for the clothes' preservation, and a simultaneous unease with the thought that "the natural fate of such things is to die before the body that wore them," but "her shoes and her thin muslin dress have outlived her."

The youth I was is buried so deep I find it hard to bring her to life, but the conservator in my head has preserved with meticulous expertise the "trifling and transient" clothes she wore. I can register to visit them. Am even allowed to touch.

Though touching is not permitted here, at Charleston, there's far more freedom of movement than at Monk's House. The rooms are without velvet ropes. I can wander and peer close. Someone has placed Bell's broad straw hat on the bed where she died. A replica hangs on the gift shop wall. I want to take it down and hide it, but am too scared. My phone is dying. I ask a gift shop worker if I can charge it in one of their outlets, feeling oddly embarrassed by the unwieldy size of my travel adaptor. I buy postcards, and ceramic buttons for my mother. I will give them to her for Christmas. They look *expensive*, she will say, and I will nod, and we will both be pleased.

I'm tired and the day is dimming. Luckily, I've planned ahead, booking a cab to drive me back to Lewes. Miles into the return journey I suddenly realize I can't find my phone. The driver turns around and we go back to the gift shop, just about to close. Frantic, I ask a worker whether anyone's found a phone. They have not, she says, but I can take a quick look around. She's quite sure I had it here, she adds, because she remembers how enormous the charger was. I want to disappear. The phone is sitting on a table of books, vanishing into the dark cover behind it.

"Oh thank god," I say, and pick it up. The screen comes on, offering its stack of missed notifications. At the top, a text from my mother: *Seen any robins yet?*

Tourist

‡‡‡

I STAYED DRY ALL the way through my days of wandering the Downs, so it is only fair that the ten-minute walk from my Airbnb to the railway station leaves me and my suitcase soaked. The train carries us to London, Victoria Station, where I drag the case damply to a taxi, which ferries us to my hotel in Covent Garden. It feels as if the far side of the car's floor is lifting us up and dumping us—the suitcase and me—onto the sidewalk, into a new phase. The automation continues within, a conveyor belt (imaginary) ferrying me from reception to the elevator (real) and on into my room, to my bed, where the floor tilts up again and drops me flat. The television screen has my name on it. If I need anything, just ask.

After a magnificent nap on the bed's vast expanse, I wake into a sense of purpose. I dress myself up as a scholar, ready to walk to the various Bloomsbury Squares where Woolf and her circle lived.

I'm in *London*. I'm staying in a *hotel*. It's for my *job*. I feel fancy, a self-conceit I do not want to have inherited from my mother, but the association doesn't stop my inward brag. It's only halted when my route takes me past the old St. Martin's School of Art building, when Jarvis Cocker's voice singing "Common People" pops into my head, reminding me how everyone feels about tourists (a sentiment that would cost $1,300 to quote).

That rhythm carries me all the way to my first destination, Gordon Square, where the Stephen siblings lived after their father's death, where they began their evening gatherings with Thoby's Cambridge friends. After Thoby's death, in 1907, when Vanessa agreed to marry Clive Bell, it was decided the couple would remain in the house, while Adrian and Virginia moved a mile away, to Fitzroy Square. This is my second stop, which makes my route somewhat inefficient, but I am trying to match the chronological order of my movements to Woolf's. Duncan Grant and Maynard Keynes lived nearby as well. It was from here, in 1910, that Duncan, Adrian, and Virginia departed to take part in a prank that became known as Dreadnought Hoax. Disguised as a royal diplomatic delegation from Abyssinia,[1] they bluffed their way onto the HMS *Dreadnought*, a naval battleship. Their success caused a scandal, and the story was picked up in newspapers across the country. A photograph of the group shows the twenty-eight-year-old Woolf costumed and made up in blackface as an "Abyssinian prince," an image I have learned to hold in my mind next to a photograph her great-aunt, Julia Margaret Cameron, took of an actual Ethiopian prince, whose story, or rather a truncated version of it, Woolf would have grown up hearing.

Cameron photographed Prince Alemayehu in 1868, soon after

---

1   Abyssinia was their name for Ethiopia.

his arrival in England, at Freshwater, her home on the Isle of Wight.[2] The prince was brought there from his home in Maqdala, after the British invaded his father's kingdom, led by General Napier. Having lost all hope of victory, Alemayehu's father, Tewodros, took his own life. Alemayehu and his mother, the Empress Tiruwork, were swept up in the march of the British as the troops retraced their steps, carrying the precious objects they'd looted, some of which are now listed on the website of the British Museum, who refuse to return them despite years of requests. In a remarkable act of projection, in 1953 the British colonial administrator and Orientalist John M. Gullick wrote that the Ethiopians' "natural inclination to plunder the foreigner made Napier's withdrawal much more difficult than his advance had been." He does not mention that Napier had been assigned an archaeologist from the British Museum for the invasion, to supervise and catalogue the pillage.

On the march, Alemayehu's mother died of tuberculosis. The British kept her dress and her jewelry; they keep them still. Orphaned, Alemayehu fell into the care of Captain Tristram Speedy, a British mercenary soldier who could speak Amharic. For a time, Alemayehu lived with Speedy and his wife in India, but when the captain was reassigned to a colonial post in Penang, the Chancellor of the Exchequer decided the couple were no longer fit to care for him. Thus, against his wishes, Alemayehu was sent to the first in a punishing sequence of English public schools.

At some point Alemayehu's grandmother wrote to him, saying his compatriots looked forward to his return. It's unclear whether

---

2   *Freshwater* was also the title of a comic play Woolf wrote about her aunt and her social circle, including Alfred Tennyson, and the artist G. F. Watts. It was performed privately by actors including Leonard Woolf, Vanessa Bell, Duncan Grant, and their daughter, Angelica Bell, in Vanessa's studio in 1935, a year before Julian and Quentin Bell put on their performance *One Hundred Years After*.

he ever was given this letter, but in any case he begged to be sent home. Told that this was "out of the question," Alemayehu was instead deposited in the home of Cyril Ransome, a tutor in Leeds.

Ransome would later write a book in which he called the Maqdala expedition, "a petty war which Lord Derby's government was forced to undertake against King Theodore [the anglicized version of Tewodros's name] of Abyssinia." In this public history, Ransome wrote "The British brought away King Theodore's only legitimate son . . . and he lived in England till his death in 1879." Privately, in his unpublished autobiography, Ransome said more of Alemayehu. In October, "by a foolish act (he went to sleep in the w.c. [an outhouse] in the middle of a cold night), he caught a violent cold which developed into pneumonia." Ill for weeks, and often refusing food, he died on November 14. He was eighteen years old.

In the 1990s, the scholar Panthea Reid suggested that while Adrian would have approached the *Dreadnought* hoax as a prank and nothing more, Woolf's costuming can be read as holding deeper, more pointed significance, referring back to Alemayehu's story, to puncture British colonial self-regard. More recently, Nadia Nurhussein added that "although Reid's view of Woolf's intentions is more generous than mine—it is difficult to ignore the mockery she makes of Abyssinian imperial culture—Woolf's desire to represent Abyssinianness specifically is indisputable." In the poet Kevin Young's analysis, "the '*Dreadnought* hoax" enacts a truth not just about those they fooled but about the hoaxers themselves." Their misspelling of Abyssinia, argues Young, "in a telegram to the commander of the Home Fleet, a clue the commander surely should've caught, also indicates that the country being conjured was only an idea—a backdrop, or a black one—an abyss."

However one reads the hoax—and I am inclined toward these

latter interpretations—I cannot place Woolf's flimsy costume here without perceiving, just beyond it, the child whose clothes and mother and life the British took. I do not know what was in Woolf's head at the time, but her later accounts of the hoax present the story as more of a comic romp than a political statement. In those pages, of Alemayehu she speaks not a word.

If I were to write of everything Woolf left out, this work would never end; why is it that Alemayehu's story stays with me so insistently? I think it is not, in fact, the connection to Woolf, but the deluded story Queen Victoria and her country would go on to tell themselves about their care for the boy, as if they bore no responsibility for his suffering. I think of him, too, alongside Walter Benjamin's son, Stefan, both of them torn from one home after another and left too long alone. I picture their ships crossing paths, and then watch a flock of Dr. Barnardo's Red Riding Hoods rush to the side of their own deck, not far off, sailing away from the pasts they were told to forget. I imagine the small waves everyone could have exchanged.

I walk on, through time, to Tavistock Square. The Woolfs' niece, Angelica, remembers visiting them there for tea, and how after the meal "Leonard [would descend] to the basement while Virginia and I retreated to the sitting-room at the top of the house, decorated by Vanessa and Duncan. It was this room which, bombed in 1940, flagrantly exhibited its coloured walls to the world at large, while the rest of the house lay collapsed in a pile of rubble." I have so frequently heard such bomb sites described as looking like dollhouses that even as I gaze upon the life-size hotel built in its place, a miniature takes shape in my head.

In the corner of the square's green, a bust of Virginia gazes out at the people passing through. Someone has left a plastic-wrapped bouquet of flowers where her feet would be if the bust did not end. Maybe, I think, her body is now made of that which passes through that space: dust, pollen, pigeons, the hands of admirers leaving their gifts. A bus churns past and a plane drones overhead. I look up and lift my fingertips briefly from my side, but I am too shy to wave.

My walk back to my hotel takes me past the British Museum, which I glare at, pointlessly, before remembering that it was here, around the corner on Museum Street, that Stefan Benjamin kept his bookshop. I know it is gone, he is gone, but I still want to look. I stand across the street and take pictures on my phone, catching the dismissive glances of the people eating at tables outside the present-day restaurant the once-bookshop has become. *Tourist* say the glances, and the word pushes me onward. A hand-painted sign down the block says CAMERA MUSEUM, tugging me through the door and toward the collection of a man now dead. The living man on the ground floor is at work repairing a camera. Entrance fee: one pound, the sole coin I have in my pocket. I try to hand it to him, but he shakes his head. I'm supposed to pay on the way out. He does not want to talk. He points to the stairs.

I descend into the basement crowded with cameras. Of people it is otherwise empty; I am the only tourist. From the corners, surveillance cameras watch me gaze into the cabinets of specimens, arranged by manufacturer and time. They are too new to have been aimed at Alemayehu, but too old—and filmless—to see me now. I find a fake pigeon with a camera strapped to her chest. Behind her, a photo of a real pigeon with the same camera. Neither of them can eat, but someone has strewn the glass floor of the cabinet with bread crumbs. My body feels too large, like it is in this space a protrusion. On my way out the man takes my coin, silent as Charon, and I do not look back.

The Distant Thames

NO BASEMENTS TODAY, I tell myself. I have been walking outside all morning, from my hotel through Trafalgar Square and onward to Hyde Park, where I'm standing now by the Serpentine, the long, artificial lake that runs on into Kensington Gardens, where its name changes to the Long Water. In their childhood, the Stephen children—Virginia and her siblings—used Kensington Gardens as my mother and her siblings used Kew, knew its hiding places, its patterns of people. Their father liked to roam the grounds, loudly reciting poems about admirals.

In 1814 miniature ships reenacted the Battle of Trafalgar in the Serpentine. (Britain won.) In paintings the ships seem to be the size of people. They are small ships. They are large miniatures. Were a replica of Admiral Nelson aboard one he'd be the size of a child. In place of cannons they used rockets. Down went the French.

Many decades after that reenactment, at the nearby Round Pond, the nine-year-old Virginia experienced the loss of a ship of her own. In *Hyde Park Gate News*—the family newspaper the children produced—she wrote of her grief when she lost a toy boat called *The Fairy*. The toy "nearly reached the other side of the pond when she was observed to get suddenly smaller and then disappeared from view." At forty-six, Woolf returned to the idea of the toy boat, though this time she lent it to Orlando, who—at the close of the original manuscript—swells up into a crest of ecstasy upon which rides "a toyboat on the Serpentine." (In the published version of the novel it disappiared from view.)

I make my way to the gate I imagine the Stephen family would have used and leave the park, turning toward Hyde Park Gate, their street, which is strewn with BMWs and blue plaques. Their house, at the end of the street, is bedecked in scaffolding, like a skirt cage that has lost its cover. Within the cage, in a vertical row next to the door, the house is buttoned together by three blue circles, plaques for Leslie Stephen, Vanessa Bell, and Virginia Woolf, sewn on from top to bottom in order of their birth. It was in this house that Woolf learned to read, to write; suffered the death of her mother, half-sister, and father; was sexually assaulted by her half-brothers; and eventually found herself free to enter the twentieth century, whose literature she would shape. If I could find a place to sit I might keep looking and in time develop a feeling, but it's all money here and no benches. Feeling slips away.

I tell my feet to take me westward, through waves of shoppers, until I reach Melbury Road and walk to its bend. Here stood Woolf, a child, and her mother, a beauty clapping her hands at Little Holland House, the building no longer there. I like to know I am in the place where Woolf looked at what was gone. I like to be alongside her a child, learning the figure of a mother. How much easier it is to perceive that figure through the place alone, without a body to stand in imagination's way.

She liked to walk in Holland Park, my mother, so I turn away from the bend and toward the green. Here in the park the bones of the Holland House and its hollowed-out library remain, but they too are hidden by scaffolding, fences, construction. I circle round and round, trying to get close enough that I could understand where the X once stood. Once this was the place where the last two letters of Alemayehu's father, Tewodros, were held, part of the house's collection. I do not know their route from Maqdala to this site, only that they survived the bombing. In his final written sentence—closing a letter attempting to make peace with the invaders—Tewodros told the British, "I am your friend, a lover of artifacts, so see to it that I am not lost to you for naught."

I am too shy to talk to the workers. I stare at the photo on my phone and try to align myself with its windows in the physical world. Tewodros is not here, but his words are imprinted in the air. The house is newly built. The house is on fire. Walter Benjamin has just died. His son Stefan does not know yet; he has only just stepped off the ship of deportees, but he will learn, and he will carry the loss with him back through London. At the front of the remains of Holland House, held back by the gates, I try to hold an image of the building as it once stood in completeness, before letting my eyes admit to the trees and the sky.

At the corner of my vision, a redheaded woman passes by, then disappears. How did my mother get so young? I walk to the flat she lived in in her late twenties. Two gardeners are tending to the slight grounds. She is not at home, but the pub where she worked is just around the corner. I linger with my lunch at a table out front. It's mid-afternoon and I don't really want a drink, but it feels like my visit would be incomplete or incorrect without one. In between sips of wine I write postcards to friends about where I am and where I have been.

When I run out of postcards I turn to my notebook. Tomorrow I will see my cousin Scott. We will meet by the river and I will learn what his memories hold. I practice the questions I want to ask by writing them on paper, flinching at their language, the words pinned down to their useful meaning. They look naked and I want to cover them up.

IN 1851, THE SCOTTISH inventor David Brewster demonstrated his new stereoscope to the public at the Great Exhibition at the Crystal Palace, alongside a panoply of goods and technologies extracted from or made by subjects of the British Empire, as well as other nations. Brewster's invention became a great commercial success, spurring the manufacture of thousands of stereoscopic cards, from erotica to military propaganda.

A century later, two brothers prepared to demonstrate stereoscopy again, this time in motion, at the 1951 Festival of Britain. While 3D films were not entirely new, they were rarely used for documentary purposes, which made the work of Raymond and Nigel Spottiswoode unusual. Their film was called *The Distant Thames*, and as I watch it the next morning, in stillness, in the library of the British Film Institute, I have the sense that the camera is an invisible boat I am riding, while tree and bridge and swan pass me by. It is a film about time. As the screen takes me down the Thames through the countryside and on toward Windsor, a voice addresses the river with *R*s rolling from his tongue like marbles down a long carpet:

Flow on, sweet Thames, between the pastures and the
   parishes,
the cities and valley villages, past the trim churches to the
   widening reaches.
Flow on from age to age, through this enduring, ever-
   changing English heritage.

Woolf would have laughed at the script's pomposity, its silly alliterations. I feel her company in this, but I also think she would have appreciated that the Spottiswoodes emphasized the artificiality of their creation, insisting that however much people might describe 3D film as replicating precisely the work of human eyes, the effect was in fact otherwise. The simulated sensation of a z-axis is not the same as being on the Thames.

As Raymond Spottiswoode wrote, objects in stereoscopic film "cannot be observed from all sides, like objects in the real world," and so "proposals have been put forth for throwing multiple images onto layers of fog," but such methods were unlikely to work until "far in the future." In any case, he argued, "it is the differences between film and life which give the medium its value."

Woolf anticipated this principle in "The Cinema," in 1926, where she moves from the initial sense of immediate reality that films offer into their actual distance: "We behold [things] as they are when we are not there. We see life as it is when we have no part in it. [. . .] The horse will not knock us down. The King will not grasp our hands. The wave will not wet our feet." She is right. I look down. My feet are dry and there is no river. Moreover, she adds, all these images come from years ago and so, "We are beholding a world which has gone beneath the waves."

The Festival of Britain took place on the site I am on now,

Southbank Centre, in concrete structures erected for the occasion, on riverside land leased from the Shell Corporation. Other films made for the occasion included *Forward a Century*, sponsored by the Petroleum Films Bureau, and *The Waters of Time*. Viewers of *The Distant Thames* sat inside the new cinema as the boat, the camera, traveled down the river from countryside to Windsor to Kew until at last arriving at the festival itself, the present.

It's a narrative trick that echoes Woolf's in *Orlando*, which begins in Tudor England and follows Orlando through centuries of history until, at its last page, it reaches midnight on October 11, 1928, the date of the book's publication. What does this form of ending do? It invites the audience to step forth into a continuation, says "you have been carried here, to the present, to this place, in the boat of what has been made for you. It is an imaginary boat, but you might, for a time, feel its support beneath you as you slip back into the daylight, or lift your face up from the page. You might glide, might go on gliding." You might even get to the future.

Today I am meeting Scott for lunch. He works on the other side of the river and will cross over to a restaurant nearby. To get there I have to go farther east than the Spottiswoodes' film traveled, not far, but enough that I feel the difference, see my feet on the pavement, the water to my left, down below. The night I want to understand happened more than a quarter century ago, but yesterday evening in my hotel, as the light outside went from scarrow to full dark, I watched episode after episode of *I May Destroy You*, Michaela Coel's series about a woman whose friends leave her drunk and alone in a club with a man who rapes her, and neither the flatness of the screen nor the intervening years were enough to stop the wave from reaching me, from knocking me down. At the end of the series, the woman's best friend—who has not admitted to her part in the abandonment—is on the verge of confession, when Coel's character stops her. All is understood, even if unspoken. Such love! I sat alone on the hotel bed and wept. If only I could reach that wordless place.

After I dried my tears, I had wanted to talk to Chris, or my sister, but the hours were misaligned; they were in the midst of parenting duties, dinner and bedtime. When I tried calling, Chris couldn't answer. Instead he texted me a photo of Hattie's ankle, which they'd injured at the playground. We conferred, made a plan to see how it was in the morning. Georgia's morning is now and they seem okay. I text back *phew* from the future.

I walk and recite my questions to myself, and then a text arrives from Scott; he's at the restaurant, got a table inside, it's a bit cold. I find him in a corner and he gives me a big hug. I am uneasy eating indoors, all these mouths, these conversations. Everyone is so close together. He has to get back to work soon for a meeting. I have no room in which to place my planned words. It's okay. The moment, I can feel it, is wrong. We have to first fill in the present, an island from which we can sail further back. We begin with his wife, his work, his house, how one finds space amid the hunkering down. I tell him my closet. He tells me the guest room. It is as if we have been diving in nearby waters and now are surfacing, removing our masks and regulators, feeling the air on our faces, sharing what we have seen below.

"I can't believe you came here before you went to see your mum," Scott marvels, and reaches for his drink. I feel defensive, not just because I've chosen to prioritize my imagining of my mother's past over her present, physical self, but because I hadn't really considered doing otherwise until Scott spoke in this moment. I don't feel ready to see her. I'm still too angry. I don't know how to say this.

"We're going for Christmas," I say. "I've been waiting for this trip a long time."

He wants to know my plans, the shape of what's to come. I will go to Kew on Sunday, I tell him, after spending the weekend with his sister. I should come for dinner at his house, he says. I nod a vague agreement. His house is too full for the questions. I do not speak this, but he can sense a needful form between us. Maybe, he adds, he could head over to Kew for lunch someday. I nod again. My own days from now to then are stacked so high and full I can hardly see over them to the week he's planning. Such a crowd. I cannot think. My body has grown accustomed to the sky, and after these days of walking the Downs and the London streets, the seats of today—the library, the restaurant—feel like a return to sheltering in place. I am ready to go back outside.

We part not in opposite directions, but at different speeds, Scott returning to work and I at my leisure, continuing along the Thames. The tide is low and the river bares its edges. Some such rivers, I've read, are subject to periodic reversals; as a strong tide travels in from the sea it forms a wave powerful enough to push against the current. The change does not last. Once the agitating wave has passed the river resumes its customary movement.

At Blackfriars Bridge I cross over en route to the building where the Woolfs bought their first printing press for Hogarth from the Excelsior Printing Company. Now[1] it's a pub, and when I go in I'm tempted to sit by a window and furtively scratch my name

---

[1]   "Now," of course, is a risky word, but I like to bind my own small account of the place into the sequence of pages tracing the building's use. In 2017, for instance, in the introduction to *Two Stories* (which Chris had given me during the early days of the pandemic), Clara Farmer wrote that "a century on, the building that housed Excelsior is a down-at-heel Tandoori restaurant." Some day in the future it should spend time as a bakery, I think, bringing Leonard Woolf's imagination to life: "Nearly all the implements of printing are materially attractive and we stared through the window at them rather like two hungry children gazing at buns and cakes in a baker shop window."

into the glass, but it's too early in the day; nobody else is there and I'd be certain to be caught. On March 23, 1917, the Woolfs came here from Richmond, Virginia breaking off a letter to her sister in order to depart: "I must stop—as we are going to the Farrington Rd. to buy our press." There is no such place (how I love her mistakes) but there is Farringdon Street,[2] and I am on it, and above me are the Victorian red and gold of the Holburn Viaduct passing over the road askew, below me the River Fleet, invisible, underground. A stream of ink.

AT NIGHT I CROSS the Thames again, back to Southbank Centre, where my friend Jack and some others are giving a poetry reading. The sky is dark and the concrete is aglow. Early, I circle the grounds, go back toward the river. It is still moving in the same direction.

Jack comes and finds me, brings me to the green room, where he introduces me to Anthony and Joelle and Rebecca and Safiya and Wayne (whom I already know) and nobody is wearing a mask and they offer me a beer and I give up, give over, think *let me have this one night.* I do not have a precise map to lay over me, but I think the auditorium in which they speak their poems is in roughly the place where a model of the Crystal Palace would have stood during the Festival of Britain in 1951. I am not inside the model. I am inside, says Safiya's poem, Muhammad Ali's fist. Good. There I go.

I turn to Wayne and make my eyes go wide; he nods; I am so happy.

Afterward, in a bar beneath the National Theatre, everyone

---

2   To be fair, Farringdon Road exists too, differing from Woolf's account only in spelling and the fact that it begins a bit farther north from the former site of Excelsior.

foams up with joy and drink. It is the first in-person reading since the pandemic began. Some of us babble, some of us blink, and whatever form our lack of social graces takes is understood and forgiven. Wayne says that behind us is an actor from a show I've never seen, and I tell him a game I like to play, a game I haven't been able to play for ages. Everyone around me, I pretend, is an actor, reciting lines and following stage directions according to a script they've endlessly rehearsed, and it's stunning; they're flawless, the timing so intricate, look! The glass she knocks over has to break just so, her face register—but not too early—her surprise. The props have been perfectly set. Look at Jack in his Jack-ness, about to speak the line from that poem he loves so, *"Wow. The rain. Rose beetles."* How lucky we are to have stumbled into this scene, surrounded by such naturalistic talent.

I cannot play forever. I have plans to attend to, the matter of Knole. (*Happy birthday*, I think, *to me*.) I've stuck to my stubborn idea of getting as close to Woolf's last page as I can, on the grounds of the house where Vita Sackville-West grew up, the house around which the plot of *Orlando* is built. It's not Vita I'm looking for; it's Woolf's imagination. I want it to be a real place, but I am afraid to go there alone, of being caught and thrown out.

"Are we still on for Knole?" I ask Jack.

"Yes," he says, and with the index finger of the hand holding his beer pointed at me like he's hitting a midair pause button, he turns to Anthony. "Are you up for a midnight drive?"

"Yeah, sure, where are we going?" Anthony is putting on a performance of his sense of adventure, but it's based on a true story. His boldness is real. It runs through his writing and his life. "Quickly," one poem demands, snapping me to a doomed attention: "when was the last time / you gargled magnets?" *I don't know! Was I supposed to?* I want him to like me. *Let me start again.*

I explain the plot, how the National Trust said I could not stay at Knole until midnight, how I've scouted the grounds on street-view and found what looks like a scalable fence, but it's more than three miles from the hotel where I'll be staying and I'm nervous to walk that far on my own so late at night.

"So you're asking me to break into a National Trust house," says Anthony.

"No, just the grounds," I say, hoping this sounds reasonable.

"It's just trespassing," says Jack. "If we get caught they'll just ask us to leave."

"I'm in," says Anthony, and for a moment it's as if we actually are—we've made it, it's midnight at Knole and I am with friends.

I have to get back to the hotel. Jack says he'll walk me over the river, then catch a train or a bus home. The concrete is still gold beneath the streetlamps, the Thames black. When a streetlamp illuminates a tree I pretend it is the tree itself that is sending light out from within. Sometimes I am able to untether myself from pretending and coast all the way to belief. Sometimes I don't want to come back.

"So how's it been? How's your trip?"

"Incredible. I can't believe I'm here."

"And part of it's family?"

"Yeah. I saw my cousin today. It's hard though, I have all these questions." I look up at the arch of an underpass and turn back toward him. "I'm trying to put back together this night I don't really remember."

Jack sets his face into a question and waits.

"There was this night, when I was fourteen, my grandfather

died and I came over with my mother for the funeral, but I stayed with my cousin—he was living with someone else then—I stayed with them and they took me out one night and got me really drunk, and then this guy, I never really know how to say this."

Jack is listening with such attention I am afraid to meet his eyes.

"I never feel like *rape* is exactly the right word, but he took me outside, into some alley, and I mean, it's not like I could consent, I was drunk and I was fourteen." I smile, give my hands a little lift, like I am testing the weight of something invisible in the air.

"Then that's all you need to say."

I pull my lips in and nod and we reach the bridge over the river and he does not leave until I'm safe on the other side.

Lock and Key

‡‡

OUTSIDE MY AIRBNB, AN octagonal back garden hut where I will stay for the next ten days, a realistic, framed drawing of a lion's head hangs over a stylized mosaic of a dragon on the nearby table. Green thrums in the cool and humid air. I am delaying my entry into the Gardens, wanting first to orient myself in Kew village and Richmond. It's the latter I begin my walk toward, making my way down Paradise Road. In the two years since I was last here, the occupants of Hogarth House have let wisteria grow thick and wild against the brick, hiding the Woolfs' blue plaque from casual passersby. It reminds me of a photograph I've seen, of Vita Sackville-West in her childhood, in fancy dress, with her mother's caption in cursive at its base: "Vita, as a basket of westiria." Her expression is one of silent, plaintive patience.

On the Woolfs' last day at Hogarth House, before they moved

to Tavistock Square in 1924, Virginia wrote that the weather hid Kew's Pagoda from view. I also cannot see it from here, but this is because I am at street level, whereas she looked out from the top floor. For a moment I think I will try looking out from a window in the Paradise Road Car Park across the street, but then realize its levels exist wholly underground. Still hungry for a view, I walk instead to Richmond Hill, from the top of which a path rolls down to the river. Beyond it, say the signs—on a clear day—one can see Heathrow and Windsor. The day is not clear and so I am not one. I don't mind. I know my way, can imagine myself with ease upon the map. And no one is waiting for me anywhere today.

In the horseshoe of little shops by Kew's railway station, I drop into the Sainsbury's Local to stock up on groceries. When I step back out on the street, the sidewalks are full of children in school uniforms, holding hands with parents and walking home. The girls wear little straw hats, their hair drawn tidily into ponytails or plaits. One catches my glance and smiles, small and bright. The day is darkening, and by the time I walk back to the pedestrian bridge over the rails that will take me over the tracks and back to the hut on North Road, electric lights are lending a pronounced glow to the objects around them. At the crosswalk, a Belisha beacon—a tall blinking light atop a black and white striped pole—matches its golden orange pulse so closely to the berries of the firethorn hedge behind it that it seems as if they must have grown, like a longstanding couple, more and more alike over time. Despite the many years, they remain in deep, contented love. I want to stand near them and bask for ages, but the sidewalk is barely two feet wide and everyone's flowing in one direction from the station to get home. I have to step out of the way.

Next morning, though, I am up early enough that the day is still mostly unpeopled, and I sit on the steps of the pedestrian bridge, watching the scene across the street. The leaves of the firethorn, a deep delicious green, give the berries and light a surface to be orange against. At Monk's House, a tour guide said Vanessa Bell and Duncan Grant mostly disdained green—in gardening and in interior design—sniffing at it as "ubiquitous." They teased Woolf, who adored the color. I'd like to melt into this particular green, to lean against the hedge and give way to its dark. I can imagine mixing the paint, each drop of black a growing sweetness. I could be a place where love, orange, happened.

I walk again to the shops by the station, buy coffee, face the alley my mother pointed out two years ago. This is the path she would have taken from her home to Kew College, where my grandmother taught kindergarten, in order that her children might attend the otherwise unaffordable school for free. Family legend has it that Harold Pinter's son, a student in her class, once lay his head down weary on his desk mid-lesson and sighed, "This bloody writing gets me down."

The alley is beautiful and this hurts me. If it were ugly this would hurt me too. The walls on either side are sometimes wood, sometimes brick, overgrown with squash blossoms and dark vines. It happened, my mother told me, on a bench set into a small recess. The man—she remembers him as "greasy"—approached her on the corner and told her, "Your mother said you were supposed to come help me." She felt uneasy, but wanted to be good. It wasn't until he reached beneath her dress, reached further, that she knew for certain his lie.

When I picture this, the man blurs into Woolf's recollection of her half-brother: "I can remember the feel of his hand going under my clothes; going firmly and steadily lower and lower, I remember how I hoped that he would stop . . . But it did not stop." My mother apologized before running away. I press my hand against the wall. Barbed wire runs in two lines above it. A lost straw hat, ribboned with school colors, lies flattened in the mud. Further on, a single black sneaker. I am leaving footprints. The leaves are lifting; I watch and pretend there's no wind. It's a game I play when I want to imagine the world differently, making myself believe the tree's movement comes from within.

I almost want to see a robin. I'm not ready to talk with my mother, but I could ask it to go find her and make sure that she's okay.

At the other end of my walk, a woman named Jill is waiting for me in the churchyard, whose graves and plants she tends. We've not yet met in person, but we have emailed and talked on the phone, and she has promised to show me round, indoors and out. Jill is wiry and electric, with bright gray hair cut in a plain sharp bob. Her husband's ashes are buried on the far side of the church (so he can watch, she says, the cricket). During lockdown, she noticed plants growing over the graves and began casually to weed. After a conversation with church officials, she took on the task more formally, and now not only scrubs moss away when it grows over the tombstones' engravings, but records the words of each before they further erode.

Marie (not like Antoinette, rhymes with sari), the parish administrator, lent Jill keys to the church. At first, when the door opens, the visual splendor of the space seems to produce the music spilling out into the morning air (as if a film director were pairing scene and soundtrack), until my consciousness adjusts and I realize that what I hear is someone playing the church's organ (and the film reveals the notes to be emerging, diegetic, from a prop).

"Julian," explains Jill. "The organist."

He's still in his running gear from his long morning jog. She consults her binder so she can guide me to the names on marble memorial tablets hung round the walls—Franz Bauer (royal botanical illustrator), and George Englehart (painter of royal miniatures, and ancestor of the Englehart who'd later develop the street where my mother would live). One memorial tablet hangs close to the front of the church, next to the altar, and Jill formally introduces me to Julian. He needs help; he's attempting to record a video, but his tablet—digital, not marble—won't turn on. He bids me to follow him across the nave behind the altar. (I will my parents to catch a glimpse of me as I do so, while they stand in the past, waiting for the vicar to pronounce them wed.) The video, he explains, is for the church's Facebook page, so that parishioners unfamiliar with the hymns he has chosen for Sunday's service can listen and learn beforehand.

Tablet now working, Julian brings it back to the organ and turns to tell invisible viewers that this week's new hymn was chosen in honor of William Tyndale, an early translator of the Bible into English. Tyndale's work was met with royal disapproval and he was forced into exile. In May of 1535 he was arrested and imprisoned, charged with heresy. From prison, Tyndale wrote to his captors asking "to be allowed to have a lamp in the evening; it is indeed wearisome sitting alone in the dark." The following year he was strangled, then burned at the stake. Tyndale's translation of the Book of Matthew contains one of the earliest known occurrences in English of the word "beautiful."

"Ye are like unto painted tombs," he wrote, "which appear beautiful outward: but are within full of dead bones."

Tyndale, says Julian, in his knowledge of language possessed a key. You can use a key to lock people out, or to open a door and let them in.

"Do you want to see the prison?" asks Jill. I almost can't comprehend the question, then rapidly nod my head yes.

We walk down the aisle (my parents are married now and on one side the pews are filled with their smiling friends, while on the other mourners weep for their loved ones as memorials are affixed to the wall) and turn at the back of the church to a staircase on the right. It takes us deep beneath the earth. In front of me, at the center of a brick wall, a short, arched, hopelessly thick wooden door stands open. I peer into the cell and try to imagine its past. There are no windows to which a robin might fly, no ways to offer comfort to whomever the cell once held. It's used as a storeroom now, haphazard stacks of wood and metal grates leaning against the wall. I wonder if they still have a working key to the centuries-old lock, wonder who was the last person to be held here, whether they were permitted a lamp, whether the presence of the church above made them feel the company of some angel, some manifestation of Christ. In the King James version of the Book of Matthew, much of which was posthumously absorbed from Tyndale's translation, Jesus instructs listeners that "inasmuch as ye have done it unto one of the least of these my brethren, ye have done it unto me," offering a list of acts by which their righteousness might be known:

> For I was an hungred, and ye gave me meat: I was thirsty,
> and ye gave me drink: I was a stranger, and ye took me in:
>   Naked, and ye clothed me: I was sick, and ye visited me:
> I was in prison, and ye came unto me.

It is hard to reconcile such instructions with this place. What did people do here to their brethren? Someone used their talent to build this door. Someone worked to forge the metal of the lock. Someone cast another inside. Someone turned the key.

Back upstairs, Marie steps out of the office to say hello. "So you saw the prison then?"

"Yes."

"Do you want to see the mausoleum?"

Again the church expands in space beyond what I knew was there; we walk back to the nave, behind the altar, down a few steps and into a small room lined with shelves of urns, a library of ashes. There's a skull here, and a femur, as sometimes the earth sends long-buried bones up from its depths, and this room is a place of safekeeping. At the center of the space stand funereal candles, waiting for their next use. There is a slight sense of jumble, which feels to me soft and unstaged. I trust it, feel it bring warmth to the lives whose remains are catalogued here. I think they are beautiful.

When we step back out and past the altar, Marie turns to give a brief curtsy, and makes the sign of the cross. I'm suddenly embarrassed, ought not to have seen it; if I am not within the ritual myself then the view feels invasive and voyeuristic. I turn quickly to gaze at the domed blue ceiling overhead, painted with an astronomical figure of the stars and Halley's comet as they appeared in the sky in 1714, the year Saint Anne's was first built. With my head tilted up, I overhear Marie tell Jill that when she was a child, she thought the tabernacle was full of tiny coffins. I give my hosts my fervent thanks. Outside, workers are feeding branches they've trimmed from nearby trees into a loud machine, which grinds them up and sprays them into a pile of mulch.

I cross the Green to Kew's Library and Herbarium, where I sign in and receive a token I can use to open a locker where I can deposit my belongings. From the corner of my eye I spy, on the wall, a flyer whose largest words are WHAT DO ALL THESE SYMBOLS MEAN?

and cringe. They can see me. How awful! I rush myself away, but the words echo after, calling out those much-recited lines of Rilke, whose frequent repetition has done little to diminish their power over me:

> . . . for here there is no place
> that does not see you. You must change your life.

WHEN I LEAVE THE library for an afternoon break, I cross over Kew Bridge and walk a bit further on, to the former site of the public drinking fountain where my grandmother used to bring her father his lunch. I wonder whether he had time to sit with her here, or if he only reached out his hand from the door of the bus before going on with his route. The fountain is gone now, and I cannot stand in its precise former location. The flat black asphalt is marked with yellow lines, for cars, not pedestrians.

Instead, I walk back south, toward the river, where the Kew ecovillagers briefly made their encampment before the St. George development company cast them out and built luxury apartments in their place. I want somehow to honor the people's resistance. An urge, small as a firethorn berry, brightens in me. My hands want to make a sign, as did Marie's back in the church, but they do not know what shape it should take, and I laugh at them, bemused. I crouch down and let them rest on the cold concrete. Behind me, a virtually empty gastropub has plenty of outdoor seating, and though it is chilly, it is where I want to eat my lunch. I order tea for the sake of holding the warm cup.

After, I linger on this side of the Thames, on the footpath that crosses beneath the bridge. Swans tilt their tails into the air, beaks feeding on algae below. A row of workshops is built into the space where the bridge meets the earth, each entrance a uniform arch. Beside the joinery, which makes windows and doors, a separate shop makes grilles and locks. I go back to the water. The small waves of the high tide climb up and retreat from the stairs linking footpath to river, a route to its bank when the water is low. Standing at the top of the stairs, I grow unsteady on my feet. I feel an urge, large now, to climb down the steps and into the river. It is not that I want to drown. I want to transform. I want to be something, anything else.

The Underworld

‡‡

IN NOVEMBER OF 1992, a fire at Windsor Castle destroyed nine rooms, including St. George's Hall, a space that had been home to the Order of the Garter since the time of Edward III. The audio tour to which I'm listening as I walk through the castle begins with a welcome produced from the mouth of Charles, Edward III's nineteenth-great-grandson, who uses the castle's fire and subsequent rebuilding as a metaphor for the present and possible future.

"Perhaps you will be reminded," he tells me, disembodied through sanitized headphones, that "not only have people lived through trying times before—although few like the times the coronavirus has brought—but they have gone on to flourish creatively afterward." The comparisons—castle fire to global pandemic, repair of a royal residence to artistic vitality—feel like something of a stretch.

Meanwhile, a socially distanced queue of visitors proceeds along the corridor, following along with the building's history as portrayed in a very long timeline in which monarchs and their castle-related actions are recorded above, other people and events below. (In 1348, for instance, Edward III founds the Order of the Garter on top while beneath him the Black Death arrives for the first time in England.)

Of all the spaces in the castle, it's the Royal Vestibule, a room of glass cabinets stocked with the spoils of empire, that most makes me blink in disbelief, not at the fact of possession—for which I felt myself prepared—but the brazenness of the display. Here is a carved tiger head from the throne of Tipu, who resisted the East India Company's incursion for years. Here is a gathering of crowns and headdresses from Ethiopia, labeled gifts, but whose presence makes me uneasy knowing that locked away in the castle's library are illuminated manuscripts looted from Maqdala, and that Alemayehu—the prince whose life some link to Woolf's blackface performance—is buried nearby, beneath St. George's Chapel.

Ethiopian requests for the return of looted artifacts began in 1872. More recently, since 2007, the Ethiopian government has been making official requests for the return of Alemayehu's remains, as well as objects taken from Maqdala. While they have met with some recent success—in 2019 the National Army Museum returned a lock of hair a soldier had cut from Alemayehu's father's head—many of those who hold what was stolen say they will continue to do so. The same year the lock of hair was returned, the *Daily Mail* reported that "according to Palace sources," the

Queen's refusal to honor her part of the request was because Alemayehu was buried among many other people, and "it would be impossible to identify and exhume the body without disturbing the 'sacred space.'"[1]

I cannot help but think that the place was desecrated long ago, that it is calling out for disturbance. My final destination here, the plaque in St. George's Chapel noting Alemayehu's burial in the ground below, was installed at the request of Victoria. It's engraved with the pious declaration, "I was a stranger, and ye took me in," as if the boy—could he still speak—would utter Christ's words of gratitude. It does not allow him to continue that he was sick, nor that he was a prisoner. That he loved to play outside, that he laughed at English small talk. It does not say that he wanted to go home.

I had wanted to see Queen Mary's dollhouse while I was here, but the room is closed, I suspect because it is too small for social distancing, though perhaps it is closed for repairs. Maybe the miniature faucets are leaking. It doesn't matter. I want to get away, feel grateful for the slope down to the train station, how gravity pulls me in that direction. I'll get off one stop before Richmond, at Twickenham, where I will meet my cousin Scott and ask him at last my questions. The train is sitting in stillness with its doors open, waiting to depart. Tired, I lower my mask and take little sips of tea, trying to rouse myself from a descending fog.

I turn my mind back to Kew, the story of a tree named Turner's Oak. Planted in the late 1800s, by the 1980s the oak was in poor health, and when the Great Storm of 1987 hit, the wind knocked it askew, lifting its roots up from the ground. The head of Kew's arboretum had it set back upright while he tended to the many

---

1   After her death, the request was repeated to her son, the new king, who repeated his mother's refusal. In September of 2023, a lock of Alemayehu's hair was found and returned by descendants of Captain Speedy. (For a full account of Alemayehu's life, and a directory of objects looted from Maqdala, see Andrew Heaven's *The Prince and the Plunder*, as well as theprinceandtheplunder.com.)

other trees requiring removal. When at last it came time to deal with the oak, the arborist was delighted to find it flourishing. Decade after decade of visitors walking the same circle around the tree, he came to realize, had compacted the soil to such a degree that its roots struggled to grow and gather nutrients. The tree's upheaval had, in fact, saved it, had given it new life.

I force myself to try a moment of hope. Perhaps such a storm or disturbance could—eventually—let relationships I've assumed to be in permanent decline find other ways to grow. The hope is joined by fear. Not every tree survives.

We journey east. The fog remains, as do my hope and fear. I carry them with me off of the train. My cousin told me to wait by the Marks & Spencer, so I sit on a bench just outside the station, watching people step in and out of the shop while traffic flows thick on the road in front. A text arrives from my cousin; am I on the train? *I'm not*, I tap, *I'm here, at Twickenham Station, by the M&S out front.*

Wait there, he says. *We've just parked.* Sirens pass. Another text: do I mean the M&S by the station? He is here; he can't see me. Am I where I think I am? I am. So is he. There are two Marks & Spencers, one large, one small. He calls, tells me which way to turn, that we will walk until we meet. I surrender to the instructions, but have a hard time believing our trajectories will actually cross; something is misaligned, our dimensions askew. In the distance, a patch of color shaped like a man waves at me until he becomes my cousin, and I become the person he's here to meet.

WHEN THE TIDE IS high, the Thames floods over the path that follows the river from Twickenham toward Richmond. Scott seems surprised, stops to take a picture of the bollards sticking up from the water. He wants to show his wife.

"It's mad," he says, "She won't believe how different it looks." I am confused. Doesn't it do this every day? Maybe the river is higher than usual. I don't ask. I am trying to remember my questions, find the place to begin, but the external world is so noisy.

"Eel Pie Island!" I read aloud from a sign.

"There used to be this really famous concert venue there," says Scott, "It's where—"

"—my mom used to go see the Rolling Stones," I finish. "She told me. I watched a documentary." The sign recites the facts, how the floor of the club bounced beneath the dancers. I'm impatient with everything I already know.

"There's this gorgeous park," says Scott. "I want to take you this way."

We turn left and the path grows darker, trees arcing overhead.

"I'm trying to remember what I can about coming here for Grandad's funeral," I say, wanting to set the frame wide.

Scott nods.

"And I can tell you some things I do remember, but I'm hoping you might remember other stuff, so I can kind of fill it in."

"I don't know if we can keep going this way," says Scott. The Thames—is it still the Thames or just nameless water?—is running over the banks to our right, and our path is growing tighter. People walking in the opposite direction tell us the route is blocked. I look around.

"Should we climb up there?" A waist-high retaining wall surrounds a raised lawn. I want him to think me strong and bold. I am not looking for pity, only the story of what happened.

We place our hands atop the wall and heave ourselves up. My ascent is more agile than his and this pleases me. I hope that he noticed, and then feel ashamed.

"Why did I stay with you? Was there just no room at Nannie and Grandad's?"

"Maybe, but I think we sort of wanted to steal you away for ourselves."

Why, I wonder, but do not say, though I notice a small throb of pride at the thought of being wanted.

"I was trying to remember your flat and—"

Scott laughs and shakes his head. "Do you remember the outhouse in the garden?"

"That was real?" Somewhere I'd known this, but hadn't wholly trusted my recollection. In the memory I am crying in the outhouse and will not come out, and Melanie is coaxing me into opening the door. I imagine her sitting with her back against it, her eyes upon the garden's darkness while she tried to soothe me into coming out. Inside, the light was dim, but strong enough to show me the blood.

"Was it your first time?" she asked, her voice gentled into one for addressing a child. How I hated that sound.

"It wasn't so bad in the summer," says Scott, "but in winter we'd absolutely freeze."

"This way?" I ask, pointing forward, unsure of our route.

"I want us to get over there," he says, but we've found ourselves on the wrong side of a wall. Behind it, the heads of statues peak, enormous women and horses.

"The Naked Ladies," says Scott, and this sounds like a personal nickname, but he says it is what everyone calls them. I like seeing them from this angle, incidental, embedded in the green. We walk the other way.

"The night we went out in Camden Town, was that before Grandad's funeral? I can't remember the order of things."

"I'd have to check my diary," he says, and just like that we are in the night now, our true destination, and though we've not said so, the air between us shifts, we set our eyes forward, surrender to what is to come. It feels as if we have climbed onto an amusement park ride of questionable reliability, sitting side by side, and the restraints have just lowered, locking us into place. A man pulls the lever.

Someone cut my hair and dyed it red—Melanie, she was always giving people haircuts—*and I remember my clothes, these white knee socks, and platform shoes, and we went to a pub with*—my friends from Uni, Ian and James, he's dead now, OD'd, we all used to drink, but he never stopped, I thought we'd all be friends for the rest of our lives—*I wanted them to like me, I remember someone told me to pose with a cigarette, but I was so clueless I put the wrong end in my mouth, and I was mortified, like I gave myself away, I just wanted them to think I was cool*—They did, you had that American accent, I mean, that's always a little glamorous, and I remember they were like, "Your cousin, she's really cool, like you were one of us" (and that's all I wanted, I think, and work to not cry), *and then we went to a club?*

Scott breathes, and I can tell he's thought about this, is not taken aback by where we are going, and I begin to consider the effects of the age we are in, when men of his class and politics have been encouraged to understand the ubiquity of such nights, such moments, the vines that snake their way through so many women's lives, but the very ease of that imagined understanding sends me briefly into a feeling of impersonal distance, knowing any such night could be made an example in a corporate training exercise, with words scripted flat and thin, the vines synthetic and arranged for presentation on stage. I bring myself back to the immediate present. My cousin is speaking. The leaves around us are real.

"In hindsight, we should have called it a night then, after the pub, but someone had the idea and we were all a little drunk. So yeah, we went to World's End."

"World's End?" The name is making me blink.

"It's kind of legendary, been there forever, we went down to the club in the basement—the Underworld—and you started dancing with this guy, but I made sure I had my eyes on you, I was watching you the whole time, but eventually I had to go to the toilet—"

And now we are falling—

"So I told someone, I can't remember who, to watch you, and when I came back you were gone, and I just remember thinking *Oh no*, like it just suddenly hit me how old you were, that we were supposed to be looking after you, and we searched all over, I was panicking, but we finally found you—"

His voice fades out and somewhere back in the fog I recollect the illuminated edges of that moment, of feeling surveilled and running away, like a child in a game, and I don't know if the recollection is real, if it happened, but I can imagine, remember, some verb in between, that the self-conception of the group—they were wild, exciting, not subject to the dull limits of proper behavior—made me sense that to belong I would have to go further, go beyond, deeper underground, out of reach—

"You must have been so scared," I say.

"It was awful, and then we found you, and I said *Right, that's it, we're going home*, and I should have insisted—"

I don't remember this part, and I know he is about to speak this regret, this failure, and my heart jumps out to him there in the dark of the club with his soft voice, and to me, drunk, confused, a teeming heap of desire and need refusing to cohere into a person, skinless, pulsing, uncontrollable—

"—but then Melanie said *go say goodbye to your man*—"

Pride glimmers through me, the memory of it, *my man*, I had a man.

"—and you vanished again and this time we found you outside—"

"I remember an alleyway."

"Maybe, I can't remember, but you were upset—"

"I remember the outhouse when we got home. I remember Melanie talking to me through the door."

"—and we were panicking because you couldn't remember if you'd had sex or not—"

I thought he would know, I thought someone would know, and here in the green of the riverside park I realize how much I wanted, *want*, to know and cannot, and though I can see the two of us, the man and me in the alley's dark recess, when Scott says this, a door closes on the scene and there is no way to see what is happening on the other side, no way to reach her, and *I'm sorry* I tell her, I tried—

"—but we had to get you the morning after pill, just to be safe."

"I remember going to a clinic with Melanie, that she told me not to use my real name, something about the NHS."

Scott looks confused. "I don't know why she would do that. It would have been a chemist's, I would have thought. Maybe it would help if you talked to her."

"Are you still in touch?"

They are, things have changed, she's done a lot of work—

"I don't want to upset her," I say.

We've walked away from the river and onto a street leading into a park where, hidden behind discreet bushes, is a beautiful green Victorian pissoir whose signs instruct its users:

PLEASE ADJUST YOUR DRESS
BEFORE LEAVING

When Scott comes out, he speaks in the voice of one who has been thinking.

"You know, I'm really sorry for what happened to you, I'm sure I've already told you that many times, but—"

"You haven't, actually."

I'm so startled that I've said this that I don't go on, I feel us at the top of a final peak, paused in stillness, until Scott leans forward and gravity tilts us downward, the rails holding us to our path, a full and deep apology—he should never have taken me there, he understands how much it affected me, he takes responsibility—

But I can't fully hear him, am descending through another fog, on which projectors are casting the scene from *I May Destroy You* in all its artistry, where confession, apology, forgiveness, reconciliation all occur without being explicitly spoken. I remember how I wept in my hotel room to see the love between the two friends, and now I hunger for such a feeling between me and my cousin, which makes me fear and regret the inferiority of the scene I am in, its requirement that direct words be spoken out loud, but I surrender to it, to the script, hoping that—despite the lack of nuance and subtext—the general shape of the plot will allow something like love to occur.

"I forgive you," I say, "You were so young."

I feel nothing, so try to continue.

"Do you want a hug?"

I don't know if he really does, but he says yes, and I hug him and hope that maybe he is feeling something—catharsis or resolution or some emotional effect of the scene I have caused—because

I still feel nothing, or nothing but fatigue, and from now until I reach home, through the miles of walking a senseless path over Richmond Bridge, past Hogarth House, Lion Gate, my mother's childhood home, the fog will turn to the slow and awful bloom of recognition that the only constancy or connection I can find between that night and this moment with Scott is the awareness that I am performing, that I am reciting the lines and movements I've seen others speak and make, and I cannot bear the flatness of myself, nor the flimsiness of my disguise. I get back home to the octagonal garden hut, untransformed. Twenty-seven years have passed and I am frightened that this flatness is all I have, is all I am: a shabby paper cutout, the person who pretends.

Very Small Flags

++

I AM STANDING ON Birthday Hill, having made another orbit round the sun. I did not mean to make anything more than this happen today, but I told my cousin Alison I would be here, and word rippled out, and now the whole English side of my family is coming. They will arrive soon. I wanted first to be alone. Last night I called my sister and said something to this effect.

"But you did tell Alison," she pointed out, meaning I may want more attention than I would care to admit.

I fear Woolf cursing at me. "The damned egotistical self!"

I missed a call from my mother today, while I was in the shower. A text followed: "Happy Happy Birthday. Hope that someone gets to roly poly down the hill and, of course, a bit of robin's song!" I meant to reply, but was distracted, or it was easier to choose delay.

There's a photograph of my mother and her family here on

Birthday Hill in 1973, on the day she turned twenty-seven. In it, my mother's red hair is long and hangs in a vertical curtain as she leans her questioning face toward Alison, her niece, who's small and blond and clothed in a short white dress, with matching mary-janes and bobby socks. Scott is even blonder than his sister, and the bright fuzz of his head almost obscures his mother's face. His father, my uncle, lounges on the grass, mirroring the posture of my grandfather, who's reading a book. Behind my mother, her friend Maureen is the only person looking at the camera. Who holds it I do not know. Some passing stranger. My grandmother's back, covered in a black and white floral dress, is turned to them, as she speaks to my mother's other friend, Niki, who's leaning back on his hands, in a thin, pale coral T-shirt.

When I was born, Niki flew to the US to visit my mother, in the small New Hampshire town she'd moved to with my father. He was, my mother tells me, the first person to ever give me a bath. Niki was the name he went by with friends, but in his professional life (in fashion, where for a time my mother also worked) he went by Baron Nikolai Soloviev. It was under this name he appeared in *Life* magazine in 1966, in an article about "Swinging London" and the fashions of Carnaby Street. He used to give the most wonderful dinner parties, says my mother, in an elegant dining room whose walls he'd painted black. The curtains were green and long and velvet, and when he and his guests were properly drunk they'd end the night with dancing on the coffee table.

When my mother had her breakdown in 1968, he was one of the only friends who came to see her in the hospital, where she stayed for months. It is this loyalty that hurts me, because my mother's to him eroded during his trip to New Hampshire. She worried he'd gone on with drugs from which she'd turned away, that he would ask her for money or ring up a long-distance phone bill as he'd done at her sister's, that he was making passes at my father, that he was being paid for sex, for kink. She could not see how to square her life—settled, straight, a mother—with his—queer and in upheaval. In some ways, I identify with him, both of us too difficult for my mother to manage. They went adrift. He lived, she thinks, for a time in San Francisco. He lived, she thinks, for a long time with AIDS. That he died she is certain. Where he died she does not know.[1]

ALISON IS THE FIRST to arrive. I remember coming here to Kew with her once when my sister and I were five and six. We all took off our shoes to practice our pliés and jumps in the grass. "Point your toes," she told us, and I felt the line my legs and feet arranged in the summer air grow longer. It was important to me to jump higher than Chelly. Time has settled Alison on the ground. Alongside and behind her are her daughter and son—Sophia and Ethan. They tell me what fun they had coming to visit my parents a few years ago, all the sea stories my father shared from his years in the Merchant Marines.

Conversation shifts to updates from the present. Ethan has grown intrigued by British military history. Sophia is recently back from Calais, where she worked preparing food for the refugees to whom the UK will not permit entry. We walk around the top of the lake. And how is, they ask, your mum?

"Here's the bridge," I say, looking at my watch. "We should cross back."

---

1   The closest I have come to finding Niki is through one of his old friends, Tim, who's been looking for him too. It was Tim who told me of the curtains, and that Niki was Jewish, but decorated lavishly for Christmas. Once he worked as an interior designer for the Shah in Iran. He deserves his own book; these sentences are in this moment the most I can do.

We head toward Victoria Gate, where the rest of our family is waiting for us, carrying blankets and bags of food and gifts. I panic. It is too much; I have caused them to do and to carry too much and now I am responsible for all of it. They do not know how to get to Birthday Hill. My uncle is the only one who would have celebrated there regularly, and it has been years now, and in any case, he is not one to speak up, preferring to let his wife do the talking for him.

"It's this way," I say. I am carrying my pocket map of the Gardens, because it feels friendlier than a phone, because maybe Ethan will find it entertaining.

"Is this it?" asks Kate, when we arrive, surprised. It is such a slight place, little temple atop a small slope.

"I know it doesn't look like much," I say. "It's just, you have to imagine all the birthdays they had here." I am afraid she (and everyone) will have no bigger feelings, or that the feelings will be centered around my birthday, which—beheld alone—is empty, and I do not want this, I want (now that they are here and I cannot stop what is happening) for the ritual to pull us all in together. I should have prepared, I think. I should have gathered the photos on my phone to share, so they could see the ghosts, the layers, the years.

My aunt and uncle settle themselves on the benches behind the temple columns, and concern circulates that they will not find it easy to sit on the ground. It will be okay, I say, panicking. We can set up the blankets and they can sit on the benches and we can all drift back and forth. Unease remains, but I am the only one speaking loudly, and with the particular authority of the day, which I did not want, but now feel grateful for, a bit of sharp light to cut through the fog. Somehow it works. Blankets are spread, food laid out. It helps that they have brought wine.

Ethan has a plastic bag of paper pennant flags on toothpicks.

He distributes them, a different color for each person, along with instructions that we are to use them to mark our territory. We can form alliances, and invade. There will be, he tells us, a war. My flags are yellow. I settle them into the earth.

"I'm invading Mummy's territory," says Ethan. "Whose side do you want to be on?"

"Can't I just grow food and take care of the land?" I ask.

"That's not an option," says Scott, laughing.

"We are not fighting," I say, speaking in the voice of my people. "We are an anarchist collective and we are keeping borders open for the refugees."

I am annoying. Ethan shrugs, but he allows it. A stranger passes and I offer her my phone, ask if she will take our picture. We adjust our gathering into a pose.

"Isn't anyone going to play roly-poly?" asks my uncle, vaguely, not directing his eyes toward anyone. "It's not a proper birthday unless there's roly-poly."

Everyone looks confused.

"Rolling down the hill," I say. There's nodding and a shift back to other conversations, a shared understanding that the question does not contain the expectation of action, only a little wisp of history to add to the fog. A recitation.

"I'll do it!" I say. The ground is wet and I think it is probably a terrible idea, but can't stop myself. "Ethan, do you want to roll down the hill?"

He shakes his head yes, vibrating his whole small frame. I'm afraid I will hurt him.

"You lie down over there," I say. "I'll go over here."

I can hear the family joking and adjusting around us, lifting up their phones, and I try to pretend nothing is being recorded, that the world is just Ethan, me, the grass, and gravity. I'm lying, and my pretending is weak, but I don't know what else to do.

"Ready? Go!"

Ethan disappears. I wrench myself into movement with such force that I can think of nothing but spinning, or rather, thinking stops, and—surprised at the rate of my hurtling—I disappear too, vanishing into my body, whose mouth releases laughter as I roll, leaving a long and helpless peal of it behind me like a strip of ribbon down the hill.

Dizzy, I stand and call out to my family above. "Who wants to go to the pagoda?"

We pack up, we wander southward. We circle the pagoda. We spot the peacock. His name is George. A long queue of people are waiting to enter the Temperate House. We are buffeted away toward the rhododendrons. Everyone needs to pee. I steer us back to the Refreshment Pavilion. We drift northward to the Palm House. I stay outside with Ethan, inspecting the Queen's Beasts, stone replicas of the heraldic figures that were created for the 1953 coronation. He is better at guessing what they represent than I am, though I am at least able to recognize the house of Hanover's white horse.

"Who are your favorite kings?" he asks.

"I don't like any kings very much," I say.

"I like the bad ones," says Ethan. "They're more interesting."

Everyone comes out from the Palm House feeling parched and needing tea. "'Wherever *does* one have one's tea?'" whispers the young woman from Woolf's *Kew Gardens* in my ear, "with the oddest thrill of excitement in her voice."

"Over there," I tell her, gesturing to the Orangery.

Ethan does not want to wait in line. It's okay, I say, we'll go play by Kew Palace.

"Someone can come find us once you're through?" I ask Alison. She nods.

Near the edge of the palace lawn, we settle by a bench and take out our flags. From the bushes behind us, a robin hops out. It pretends not to notice the skeptical look I am giving it, staring back at me innocently. I give up.

"Ethan, look, a robin."

"Hello, robin," he says, and returns to his flags, working out where our conflict will begin. The two nations, we decide, were once joined, though the people were divided in some way, two families perhaps, or two religions. One year, at the Robin Festival, a fight broke out, and such terrible things were said and done that the people parted ways, invented a border through the land. In the intervening time, my people have claimed the robin as a symbol for themselves.

Ethan's people regard the bird with suspicion. For the first time in a century, the Robin Festival is once again being held, and both sides are full of anticipatory tension.

"There you are," says Scott, crossing the lawn. "We've got a surprise waiting for you." We pull up our flags.

Sitting on the table outside the Orangery are three cakes. Kate brought red velvet and Victoria sponge from Waitrose. Alison brought gingerbread from the Women's Institute. Everyone sings and smiles. I am happy, I realize. My bag is full of birthday gifts, their gestures of kindness that threaten to make me feel undeserving. I calm myself by giving them presents in return: honey from Kew's bees for my aunt and uncle, Woolf's *Kew Gardens* for Sophia, cider from Kew's apples for Scott and Kate, a cyanotype kit for Ethan and his parents.

"The paper is sensitive to light," I say. "If you put a flower on top of it and leave it out on a bright day, the sun will make a picture."

"That sounds fun, doesn't it Ethan?" Alison prompts him, and

Ethan nods his head. The paper is blank, waiting to turn blue with decisions and mistakes.

I walk them to their cars, then to the pub by the train station for dinner, its arched glass calling back to the Palm House, which does not look its way. Jimi Hendrix and his band drank here after they had their photo taken for the cover of *Are You Experienced?*, the fish-eye lens curving the blossoms behind them, somewhere in the Gardens. I have given up on trying to find the tree, and the beech under which Woolf imagined her characters in *Night and Day* too. The map inside me has been unfolded and refolded so many times that the whole surface has wrinkled and softened. It's in danger of falling apart.

The waiter takes my order and when he leaves I pick up my phone to look at the stranger's photo of my family. I get an idea. I open the 3D photo app. The left image, I tell it, is this picture. The right one is my mother's twenty-seventh birthday. Am I sure? it asks. Left and right image are not very similar. I tell it they are similar enough. And there we are, the years compressed in a single frame. One temple repeats another, standing beside itself. Alison in her white dress is facing the future she will enter. My grandfather has nearly vanished, his diagonal lean on the ground coinciding with the line of his great-grandchildren today. Branches interrupt themselves, the sky. Niki is there, still sits listening in his pink shirt. My mother's hair hangs down, red and abundant. It brushes across my face.

"October the 10th, 1980, 2:25 AM."

+++

MY MOTHER IS READING to me.

"I wonder if this is it. Pain started at 12:50 and seemed to be coming every five minutes or so and getting stronger. Michael says, 'Go back to sleep and worry about it in the morning. Get some rest now.' Easier said than done. I guess he could be right. It could be false labor. I'll just have to wait and see."

She is reading to me from her diary, because I asked. When I got home to the hut I called her back. She asked if I'd seen robins or rolled down Birthday Hill and I said she'd have to wait and read the book. I'm afraid of giving her the wrong impression, need her to see the whole.

"Hope he manages to work up a bit more interest and enthusiasm, true or false labor. I've been nagging him all day. Don't mean to, but as always, worries will out. And the birth of our child— even if this isn't the start of it—is close. And we have no heating in the house and it's not a clean place to bring a newborn person into. No matter how hard he works, I can't see that he'd be able to get it finished."

"What was Dad working on?"

I'm being a journalist again.

"We were trying to get a furnace to get some heat in the house."

"Were you cold?"

"Yeah, pretty chilly. The whole house leaked all over the place and was such a wreck. We'd been working on it forever. I think your room was done, the bedroom. I remember when we were doing your bedroom, we went out and the light we wanted to get was so expensive. And I'm trying to find another light, and Dad's saying, 'No, I want only the best for my child.' So we bought that light."

"What else do you remember feeling in your body?"

"I felt like a galleon going around, like a ship. All my clothes floated. It was wonderful. I was looking forward to meeting you. I was curious to know who you were."

"Did you talk to me then?"

"Oh yes, you were there inside me, so I would tell you what was going on, what we were going to do. Sometimes you were very, very active, so I played you classical music to help you calm down. Sometimes you moved so much that it seemed . . ." She pauses to seek the right words. "Like something was wrong. Or maybe it's just that I was tired and in need of rest."

"Was the music helpful for you too, to relax?"

"Yes. The house was such a mess and we'd been going and going. You know, when I was first pregnant with you, I was bleeding and they told me to go to bed for three months, have bed rest for three months. And that's when we loaded up all our possessions and drove from Texas to New Hampshire and bought the house. Sorry, I should have stayed in bed."

"Well, I turned out okay. Was it hard for you? Did you have fears about miscarriage?"

"Yes."

"Did you talk to me then?"

"Yes." Her voice wobbles.

"What did you say?"

"That you were going to be okay. When I think about it now—driving all that way, finding somewhere to live, buying the house, then going to England, because we had to wait six weeks for all the paperwork to go through—it was probably not a good idea. But I think I had stopped bleeding by then."

"I didn't know you were in England when you were pregnant with me."

How has this not come up before? Were there no photos?

"I can't remember how long I stayed there, but I know I went back to visit my old neighbor. He was Lebanese, and his mother and I had been friends, even though she didn't speak any English, and I don't speak Arabic. As soon as she opened the door, she looked at me and patted her tummy and said, *Oh,* whatever the Arabic is for *Oh, you're having a baby!* She was happy for me."

I imagine opening the door and seeing my expectant mother. So much still unknown, still undetermined. I am happy for her too.

"But then going back home to New Hampshire, it was very, very hard. I had no one to be close with. I had no idea when we married what Dad would be doing and how much he'd be away. But at the same time I had wanted to change my life, you know, and that's why I decided to get married and leave London and all of that. Sometimes when it was really hard, I said to myself, 'Well, this is what you wanted. This is what you've got, so you have to deal with it.'"

Outside the hut the sun has gone down, and I can barely see the garden through the dark. The windows reflect the room.

"If you could travel back in time to help the younger you," I ask, "What do you think you would do?"

"I think I would've told Dad to go right to deep sea, not to start off on the small ships. It's when he joined the union that things changed for us. We actually had health insurance and things like that."

"I understand that financial security and access to healthcare and all of that is fundamental, but what about at just an emotional level?"

"That's difficult because so much of that time was situational, that we had bought the house in Alton, which was not a place that had a lot going on. It was hard to find friends. So I think I would've told myself to move to a bigger town to start with, but we couldn't do that because we didn't have any money."

I try again.

"If you could travel back in time to any point in your life and just sit, not to say *move to a bigger town* or *choose different work*, but just to talk with the younger you, what do you think you would say?"

"Work harder in school. Don't run away from things that you don't like."

"What age do you imagine speaking to when you say that?"

"My teenage self, because I didn't put any effort into school. I thought it was a waste of time, but now I value education a lot more. So that's why I say go back and work harder. Don't think, 'Oh, I'm only here for another however long, and then I can be out in the world on my own.'"

"So if you could go back and talk to your teenage self, how do you think you would be able to say it in a way that she would listen?"

I realize, as I speak, that I am trying to get her to say now what my own teenage self needed to hear. I wonder if my mother realizes it too.

"I don't know," she says. "I don't know if she would listen. She was pretty headstrong."

"What do you think you would need to say to get her to trust you?"

"That the older me loves the younger me for all her faults."

"What do you think it would've felt like to have somebody say that they loved you for all your faults?"

I ask this out loud to my mother, but I am asking myself too and I don't know the answer. I want her answer to be mine. I want it to feel good. I want us to feel good together. She is quiet for a moment and then she speaks.

"The younger me would probably say, 'Yeah, okay. Fine. Or, 'Thank you. I want to believe you, but I don't know if I can.' It just wouldn't make any difference."

IN MY PARENTS' HOUSE in Maine, on a display shelf and out of reach, my mother has three beautiful blue wineglasses, a gift from a rich friend to my grandmother, who later passed them on with a command: *You must promise never to drink from these. They are too valuable.* A promise my mother has kept.

I should call her back, I think, so I can tell her I want her to drink from them before she dies. That I would join her if she'd let me. We could raise a toast. To ourselves, to our faults.

It would be okay if a glass broke. Even all three! The world would not end. The world would not end and she would still be loved. Silently I practice saying this in the center of the octagonal hut, blue shards scattered around me on the floor.

But that's easy, it's so easy to ask someone else to let go. How much harder to watch your own precious things break. And I know that I must. I can't ask of my mother what I refuse to ask of myself. So:

I never saw any yarrow at Kew, nor on the Downs.

The pub menu I ordered from at the Sunday family lunch called the zucchini *courgettes*, not *vegetable marrow.*

Until I began writing this book I had never heard the word *scarrow* and am not at all sure that I've used it correctly.

I have no idea whether the cows in the fields near Charleston were pregnant or farrow.

Early on, I decided this book must contain precisely two occurrences of every two-syllable word ending in -arrow (*barrow, harrow, narrow, sparrow* . . .) making each one of a pair.

I realize this is unlikely to matter much to anyone beyond myself. I imagine my pairs could seem insignificant next to my mother's blue heirlooms, but I still hope you—and she—might understand what it takes for me to relinquish them now. Through years of composition, across a treacherous sequence of increasingly personal drafts, I maintained my meticulous pattern. It felt like a life vest I could put on when I was afraid that writing the book would kill me.

Now I have broken it.

The Wild Goose

AS MY BIRTHDAY ENDS and the clock tips me forth into October 11, the final pages of *Orlando* begin. I will follow them from Kew to Sevenoaks, the village in Kent that is home to Knole House. On my walk to Richmond Station I pass more named buildings, plucking the words into a bouquet. McDougal Court. Walnut Tree House. One I reach for and then pull back. The house is called CCTV IN OPERATION. I pass shops. A funeral home. Sainsbury's. A gas—a petrol—station. A florist's with yesterday's cut blooms set in a bucket labeled FREE. One shop's awning is so busy with signs that its name is partially obscured, H and O covered up, leaving only ME & GARDEN.

It is late morning, a weekday, and when I change trains at Waterloo the crowd on the platform is sparse. I have the carriage to myself. We pass New Cross, St. John's, Hither Green. "Whither,"

I ask no one "thither"? *Orlando* is on my lap, bookmarked with a scrap of paper to note where this day begins and remind me how swiftly I must go. There's little time left before I fly home.

By *Orlando*'s final chapter Woolf's protagonist is settling into marriage with Marmaduke Bonthrop Shelmerdine,[1] whose gender Orlando is pleased to find is as multifaceted as her own. Sheldmerdine is a ship captain, often away at sea, and in his absence Orlando finishes writing "The Oak Tree" at last, having worked on it for more than three hundred years.

Woolf herself finished writing *Orlando* on March 17, "as the clock struck one," or rather, she finished the first draft, in which the final lines flounder about with Orlando standing on the ground gazing up at her husband, whose career has been shifted by the twentieth century from the sea to the air, and "as Shelmerdine leapt from the aeroplane & ran to meet her a wild goose with its neck outstretched flew above them."

"Shel!" Woolf has Orlando cry, "The secret of life is . . ." but, dissatisfied with the thin joke, she crosses this out and has her start again.

"'Shel!' crie[s] Orlando. 'The wild goose is— is . . .'" but still she cannot finish her sentence, as Woolf pauses, strikes out *wild* and at last writes "The End."

That ending later changed, letting in the sound of the clock that marked its birth. In the copy of *Orlando* that I hold open to finish reading as I stand and gather my things, as the train pulls into Sevenoaks station, and "as Shelmerdine, now grown a fine sea captain, hale, fresh-coloured and alert, leapt to the ground," the book ends on the date of its publication:

---

1   I can present no evidence for the source of Woolf's name for Orlando's husband (Harold Nicolson's avatar) but because it amuses me, I choose to believe he is named for Sir Marmaduke Constable, "who reputedly choked to death on a frog which hopped into his glass whilst he relaxed in the garden of Flamborough Castle" in 1519.

[T]here sprang up over his head a single wild bird. 'It is the goose!" Orlando cried. "The wild goose . . ."

And the twelfth stroke of midnight sounded; the twelfth stroke of midnight, Thursday, the eleventh of October, Nineteen Hundred and Twenty-eight.

IT IS BEFORE NOON when I exit the train station, looking for lunch. I dine alone, in the corner of an otherwise empty Indian restaurant. Jack and Anthony won't get here until this evening. My ticket for the official tour is marked for two o'clock. I set an alarm on my phone. The day has no room for mistakes.

Woolf had mixed feelings about *Orlando* when she finished her first draft, but later came to a deeper sense of satisfaction with the work, spurred in part by a sense of competition with her friend Lytton Strachey. His book, *Elizabeth & Essex*, was published the same year and told too of the elderly queen besotted with a young nobleman, though Strachey's book lingers longer in the story, while Woolf kills the queen swiftly and sends Orlando on his way. She held Strachey in high esteem, but thought *Elizabeth & Essex* deeply flawed.

In her diary, she recollects Strachey saying at some point, "We can only live if we see through illusion," a statement whose phrasing she finds incommensurate with the space it occupies in her mind. It is not only his words she finds there, she explains: "This saying of Lytton's has always come pictorially, with heat, flowers, grass, summer, & myself walking at Kew." Her recollection of this scene leads her to a memory of a more recent visit from Strachey, during which they "talked about Elizabeth & Essex . . . for the first time. And it was painful . . . but it was also a relief, on both sides."

I have to hope that alongside the pain my pages will cause there will also be relief, that I have disturbed but not destroyed. Have I seen my way through illusion? I ask myself this as I exit the restaurant. I look around. I can't find an answer. The sidewalks are empty, and so without fear of an audience thinking me strange I shake my head as if to clear it, as an animal shakes off rain.

The road continues onward up a hill, carrying me toward Sevenoaks' High Street. The village is radiant and clustered, with shop and pub and church all clumped together, peopled at last. Once, in Florence, practicing her craft in her travel diary, Woolf reminded herself of the dangers of description: "What one records is really the state of one's own mind." I do love to be one; it is my favorite pronoun. It conjures me up, over there, where I can see myself, like a word tried out upon the page. One has arrived at the gate to Knole. One will go in.

On October 9, 1927, Woolf wrote to Vita from another such threshold: "Orlando turns out to be Vita; and its all about you and the lusts of your flesh and the lure of your mind." She had already immersed herself in the project: "I am reading Knole and The Sackvilles" she added. "Dear me; you know a lot: you have a rich dusky attic of a mind."

Three years earlier, Vita had written to Woolf to invite her to come away to Spain, distancing herself from her desire for the trip by adding, "Look on it, if you like, as copy, – as I believe you look upon everything, human relationships included. Oh yes, you like people through the brain better than through the heart, forgive me if I am wrong," and I think she is not precisely wrong, but rather that Woolf knew (better than Vita) that the brain and the page are also real places. One moves through life composing, not copy, but the sentences through which the world and one's heart become known. If I am capable of change, I think, walking the long driveway through Knole's grounds, it will begin there, in language. A risk: it may end there too. One cannot trick words with a pratfall; they will only turn away. I have to actually leap off an edge, not knowing whether they will rise up to meet me.

Courage, I tell myself, as I pass by Knole's herds of red deer. It is rutting season and the beasts are on edge. Trees show scrape marks where the deer have rubbed the velvet from their new-grown antlers. Signs everywhere warn me not to proffer food. (I won't.) They tell me to keep my distance. I cannot promise that.

At first approach, the house looks unexpectedly small and low, but circling round its side I watch it grow. The ground slopes up and I spy a vast oak whose invitation I accept, aligning my spine against it. I have just settled into stillness when a ringtone sounds its tiny trumpets, reminding me that my tour will begin in ten minutes, and I leap to my feet.

At the front entrance, I show my ticket and climb the stairs up to the rooms where Vita's cousin Eddy Sackville-West—who as a man would inherit the house and title she could not—began his life at Knole. The furniture and decor is real (the record player, the bedspread, the historically accurate toiletries), while the documents (guestbook, manuscript of *Orlando*) are facsimiles, made to be touched, or to protect the originals from the public. I am tempted to add my own name, but distract myself by pretending— and I actually think this phrase—that I'm *casing the joint*. *Orlando* is under glass on a pedestal, unaware of my gaze or the anniversary it's reached.

I grow dizzy down the staircase (spiraling, stone), cross the courtyard, and enter the main part of the house. Decorative leopards abound, and darkness. There are fewer guides and other guests here than at Monk's House or at Charleston, or the size of the space makes it seem so. The hall of Sackville portraits strain to keep their faces in one's mind. At the end of that dark room, a great staircase stands manned by a friendly white-haired guide who points out the wood, the stained glass.

"Just let me know if you have any questions," he says, while I gaze at the patterns the sun makes on the floor.

A loud moan sounds from somewhere outside and I jerk my head up, alarmed.

"The stags," says the guide, smiling. "They can be rather noisy this time of year." I recollect myself, why I'm here.

"I'm especially interested in *Orlando*," I say, "if there's anything that comes to mind there?"

"Ah," he says, looks up, tilting his head back as if to physically reach the zone where he keeps his helpful facts.

"*Orlando*, as you know, tells the love story of her and Virginia Sackville-West," he says, making the same mistaken blending of the two names that Woolf's nephews wrote into *One Hundred Years After*, as if their Bloomsbury play were not a fantasized future, but a prophetic vision.

Shit. I'm early, I think, one hundred years have not yet passed, or—desperate to not miss my chance—let's say they have; if time would break out of itself anywhere it would be here, and now I must wonder how the world beyond these walls has transformed. We will have sunk more deeply into climate catastrophes. Do we still let billionaires exist? No, those are not real questions, merely recitations, and they read the time-traveling gesture incorrectly; both *Orlando* and *One Hundred Years After* are at heart comedies, intimate teasing born of love. I want that, or to know what it would feel like to live inside such pages, uncircumscribed by fear.

"So love something," I tell myself, retreating down the stairs. I practice. I love the sunlight, the broken quadrangle it draws upon the wall. I love the bannisters, the wood panels, even a pair of mounted antlers, which have—poor things—no head. I pass a sign.

THANK YOU
You have become part
of a 400 year history
of visiting Knole

I will not be made a shilling, I tell Vita. You may not collect me. *Love.*

"Love," says Orlando. And we will not be corrected.

In the courtyard, I seat myself on a bench facing the clock tower, watching its blue face. "Are you all right, love?" asks a guide passing by.

"Yes," I tell her, and point. "I'm just waiting for it to strike." It is very nearly four. The lawn is smooth and unclouded, cut across one side by the house's sharp shadow. The guide walks back to the gift shop. The hour arrives and pulls from me a smile, small and private. I feel like a struck bell, neither seeking nor stopping the vibrations with which I respond. When all is still again I stand up and take my future with me on a slow walk back to the night's hotel.

NERVOUS THAT MY MIDNIGHT plans will break my fastidious sleep routine and send me spinning, I drug myself for a nap. It is a restless one. I do not dream, but rise and fall through consciousness, as if the hotel bed were a wide white pond and I a school of fish. A ship passes over me and in fear I disperse. I wake, I cohere, I eat, I grab my bag.

Jack and Anthony are in the lobby. Anthony is tall and thin and underdressed for the cold, and I am afraid it is my fault. Jack's face is soft beneath his warm hat. We walk to the pub. It is approaching nine o'clock, and when the bartender tells Anthony the kitchen is closed I panic that I have caused him to miss his dinner. He gets a bag of Twiglets.

"Do they have these in America?" he asks.

"No," I say, and he starts to explain them to me.

"I know," I tell him. "I've been trained." I get us beer. Disaster, I think, sinking. Where'd I lose my courage? Did I drop it in my sleep, in the pond? The bartender returns with tidings from the kitchen. Miraculous, they have eked out a burger and chips.

I settle. My Guinness settles. Now we will talk about poems. A mispronunciation of Mary Ruefle's name has been circulating among young British poets: *roo-fleh*, and Jack wants to confirm this is an error. It is. We love her. Anthony is floored by Kaveh's new book. I would like to say something very intelligent and subtle, dressing myself up in a coat I cannot afford, whose meaning reveals itself in the weight of the fabric, the exquisite line of its seam, but it keeps slipping from my hand.

Jack asks me to explain the night, the plan. He's recording our adventure for a podcast he makes for his poetry publishers, thinking it would make for a fun episode. I do not want to disappoint him.

"So you know *Orlando* ends at midnight on October 11," I begin, addressing them both, as well as the podcast's invisible listeners—

"No," says Anthony. "I've never read it."

"Oh! I thought it was like, required," I say, meaning as part of standardized education, vaguely wondering where I picked up this belief. (Dazed, I watch it shrink into a thin ticket I hand to a cloakroom attendant in exchange for my misshapen coat.)

I turn to Jack.

"I read *To the Lighthouse*," he says, "and I got about halfway through *The Waves*."

Anthony explains his literary education, the scholarship to an elite school where he floundered, where a teacher told him he'd no future as a writer. It was Joelle, he says, who saved him, Joelle whom I met the other night at the reading, sharp and butch in her three-piece suit.

"Anyway," I say, "I just want to be at Knole at midnight. I'm hoping we might hear it."

"Hear it?" asks Jack.

"There's a big clock tower at the house. I don't know how close we'll be able to get. It's okay if we don't hear it. I just want to be there."

I'm lying and the words know it. I'm dying to hear it, think if I hear the Knole House clock strike twelve on this day, as Woolf imagined, then I will finally be—what? All the way inside her book? Saved? By who? *WHOM* booms the proofreader's nice pen.

We walk back to the hotel, where Anthony parked his car. It has been repaired, he says, since the night the hood was dented by a friend: a drunk, twerking poet. I feel decidedly sober. I am not going to twerk on anything. I worry I am dull. I show them our destination on my phone.

"It's around the south side of the Deer Park. It's the only place around the whole estate I could find where we might climb over." I switch to streetview. "There's no barbed wire at the top or anything. And there's one of those revolving gates. It's probably locked, but . . ." I shrug my shoulders and try to look hopeful in a small and casual way. Anthony tells the car the coordinates. Jack is narrating our progress into his phone for the podcast. We find an unlit patch of grass alongside the road where we can park. It's eleven.

"We do need to watch out for the deer," I say, unclicking my seatbelt. Anthony turns to me.

"Watch out for what?"

"It's rutting season," I say. "The stags are kind of . . . keyed up."

"So we're breaking into a National Trust property full of horny deer in the dark." Anthony gives Jack a look.

"It's for poetry," he says.

Anthony shakes his head. "I'm from North London. This is some pastoral *nature* poetry." He's not refusing though, only registering his complaint. We get out of the car.

I push against the revolving gate, testing. I will it to resist me, forcing us to climb the fence so that we can give Jack's podcast an adventure, but just like that the bars turn and we are inside. Inwardly reeling—as if from a silent blast—I feel a key disintegrate in my head and its tiny pieces fly outward, to the edges of my skull. In the darkness the stars come clear.

"The stars," I say. "You can see them."

"Astonishing," says Anthony softly.

The air is cold and through it a deer bellows.

"What the fuck?"

I bring my eyes back to earth. I can't tell who the words came from.

"It's okay," I say. "Let's just . . . keep to the path." We've come without flashlights, for fear of drawing human attention, but it's so dark we have to use our phones to cast their weak illumination on the unfamiliar ground. We walk in closer, slowly.

"Is that a car?" whispers Anthony. I squint, peering ahead to where he's pointing.

"It looks like it's parked by a building. Maybe it's a caretaker?"

A deer grunts in the distance, then another from the other side.

"There was a fork in the path back there," I say. "Why don't we try going that way?"

Jack is looking up *rutting deer dangerous* on his phone.

He reads aloud, quietly. *"During the rut, the stags and bucks have sharp and dangerous antlers and are likely to demonstrate aggressive behaviour. Rutting stags, in particular, are often pumped up with testosterone, and you could be putting yourself at risk. There have been a number of cases where visitors to parks have suffered injuries which might have been avoided."*

"Which might have been avoided," Anthony repeats. It's twenty past eleven.

"Why don't we find a tree," I say. "We could stand by it and be pretty inconspicuous. And we could climb it if we needed to. I think that's what you're supposed to do."

"Let's go back to the car," says Jack. "We can come back in the other way when it's time."

An owl hoots.

"Fuck," says Anthony. "Let's go."

We head back to the car, appreciative of its warmth.

"So what else do they have to say about these deer then?" Anthony asks. Jack continues reading from his phone.

"Don't shout or wave . . . Back off slowly if possible . . . Do not run . . . this may trigger the animal into chasing you. Oh, this is helpful—*Do not roll into a ball where you are; this may increase the risk of attack."*

"Who's going to roll into a ball?" says Anthony, perplexed.

"Hedgehogs?" I ask. "You can get them to open up, you know, if you are hunting them. You just beat on the ground rhythmically with a stick. They can't resist." I act it out, curling up and unfurling myself in three-inch thrusts to the beat of an imaginary drum.

"Good to know," says Jack. "Okay, here's another bit. *In the unlikely event that you are threatened or attacked, try to put a barrier such as a vehicle or substantial tree between yourself and the deer. If you can, climb a tree to get out of reach.*"

"I was right!" I say, completely unrolled now, ecstatic.

"I'm not climbing a bloody tree," says Anthony. "I'm from North London."

"Will you read some of the ending for the podcast?" asks Jack. I pull out *Orlando*. She is on the grounds, inside the night, at just such a moment as this.

"*Night had come,*" I read, "*Night that she loved of all times, night in which the reflections in the dark pool of the mind shine more clearly than by day . . .*"

(I glance up at Jack and Anthony while Orlando catches sight of her husband's ship, nearly returned, as her mind cycles through its reflected images of the past.)

"'*Ecstasy!' she cried, 'ecstasy!'*" I read on, "*And then the wind sank, the waters grew calm; and she saw the waves rippling peacefully in the moonlight.*

"'*Marmaduke Bonthrop Shelmerdine!' she cried, standing by the oak tree.*"

(I worry the words I read are not reaching my companions, that some plastic tarp is up between us, that Woolf's campy sentences will sound in earnest against it and fall down flat—)

"*The cold breeze of the present brushed her face with its little breath of fear. She looked anxiously into the sky. It was dark with clouds now. The wind roared in her ears. But in the roar of the wind she heard the roar of an aeroplane coming nearer and nearer.*

"'Here! Shel, here!' she cried, baring her breast to the moon (which now showed bright) so that her pearls glowed—like the eggs of some vast moon-spider.'"

I pause. "Moon-spider!" I repeat, "How good is that?"

"It's good, it's good," says Anthony, eyes closed, nodding.

Marmaduke Bonthrop Shelmerdine leaps to the ground from his plane for the second time today. Again Orlando spies the goose overhead and calls out, and the clock strikes its twelfth note, depositing us in the present.

"I think we should yell that when we get back in the car again, for the podcast," says Jack.

"The wild goose part?" asks Anthony.

"Yes."

"Okay," I say, unsure, poking at the tarp. "Should we go back in?"

We push through the gate. This time we veer leftward. I want to go further in, had imagined we'd go further in, close enough that with luck we might hear the clock.

"It's just so dark," says Jack. It's true. A stag could be ten feet away and we wouldn't know. "Anthony's a bit worried about the deer," he says into his phone. Anthony grabs it from him.

"*Everyone's* worried about the deer."

At the end of January 1928 Vita's father died, Knole was passed on to her uncle, and a few months later she "allowed [her]self a torture-treat," coming here in the dark. "I have a master-key," she wrote to her husband, "so could get in without being seen":

I had the sensation of having the place so completely to myself, that I might have been the only person alive in the world—and not the world of today, mark you, but the world of at least 300 years ago. I might have been the ghost of Lady Anne Clifford.

Jack, Anthony and I have the place to ourselves, but are, I think, very unlike ghosts. I'm glad. I have worked hard to bring myself here, alive and in the flesh. In the present. In the company of misbehaving friends. The grunts of the stags sound at uneven intervals from several directions, as if plotting a constellation whose name I should know but can't quite recognize.

"It's almost time," says Jack. "Let's wait here." He goes to greenwichmeantime.com, so we can properly count down. He narrates this to the podcast. My mind bends into its shape.

"Ten," says Jack, "Nine."

Vita knew that Woolf would die, not "here, over the weekend," she wrote to Harold in 1926, "but just die young." *Stop it*, I tell her, *just stop. You don't have to write it that way. She's alive. Let her have the years still to come.*

"Eight, seven, six," say Jack and Anthony together. I join in, compelled.

"Five," I say, lying. The numbers press themselves over me like a printer's heavy apron, like a full page of lead type. I close my eyes and thrash everything off. For a moment my body stills and I am strange and wild and light.

In the dark a sudden instinct shakes my head. I feel antlers growing from my skull. They are not hard enough, still covered in velvet. *Scrape it off against the oak*, I tell myself. *Yes! Good. Sharper.* They say four. They say three. I ready myself for a bellow. One grows large and then grows larger. There is no need to be scared. Hold on. Just hold on. Here I come. I promise. I'm coming. I am on my way.

EPILOGUE

IT WASN'T UNTIL A year and a half after the night at Knole that I went to see the Parthenon Marbles at the British Museum. I needed time. When enough had accumulated, I finally felt ready to face the Underworld's alleyway wall and call out *Please*. I spoke as if the word were a needle puncturing the thin cloth of the present, and the thread it pulled through would gather the many selves I have been together.

Now even that moment has long since receded.

The problem of writing from life is that it continues.

For years, I have joked with my friends that this book was trying to kill me, highly aware of the melodrama in the sentence.

It wasn't until 2024 that I patched the idea into these pages. Then I sent the full manuscript off to my mother, who had not yet read it, and waited to find out if I had torn our relationship up into irreparable pieces.

When I awoke the next day, I saw that my right arm and hand had swollen up far past their usual size. I went to the emergency room, where I was told I had a pulmonary embolism and a clot in a deep vein near my collarbone. I was admitted to the hospital, put on blood thinners, and taken to the operating room for two surgeries, in between which I stayed in the ICU.

The diagnosis: Paget-Schroetter Syndrome, or "effort-induced thrombosis."

Possible causes: muscle growth from strenuous repetitive exercise crushing vein against bone, potentially exacerbated by years of crouching on the closet floor, my right hand outstretched to put words to paper, to click on one more link.

In my mind I typed out a sentence. It went HAHAHAHHA-HAHHAHAHAHAHAHAHAHHA.

I thought it was funny. I thought it was kind of funny.

Later, post-surgery, in a room crowded with people transferring me from gurney to bed, a nurse pulled my underwear off from beneath my hospital gown and I slipped outside my body to watch it shake while I flashed back to Camden Town.

"Are you cold?" asked the nurse.

I heard my voice try, between gasps, to explain that I had been deep in the work of finishing a memoir about—but honestly I don't remember exactly how the description went, because the book is a challenge to summarize under totally normal circumstances in which my body is hooked up to not even a single IV drip.

But I was writing a book, my voice said, or something like that. "Sort of about Virginia Woolf and my mother and England, but also featuring a recurrent image of the underwear I wore on a night in Camden Town when I was fourteen," and it was *this*, my *art*, that explained my body's reaction, not the placating sentences the room full of medical people offered, like possible captions to set beneath the scene: *Of course I was anxious, I was a "healthy person" who was suddenly in an ICU, I couldn't move my arm or leg*, and so on and so on until the drugs kicked in and the shaking stopped.

In the lull I assembled a sentence of words pinned down to their useful meaning, which I hated even as I spoke. *I was sexually assaulted when I was fourteen and having my underwear pulled down was very triggering.*

They weren't even pinned-down words. They were Styrofoam cut into bite-size pieces. I hated it. I hated it. The nurses fed me Jell-O.

I am afraid of being dismissed as a mediocre practitioner of *the trauma plot.*

In her essay on the overuse of such plots in various forms of fiction, the critic Parul Sehgal praises the way Woolf imagines Mrs. Brown (a character drawn from a woman she saw crying on the train) decorating her house with sea urchins. The sea urchins are allowed to be themselves; they are not made to stand in for a troubling event from the character's past that suddenly explains everything.

Woolf, in a letter: "Whether its right or wrong I don't know, but directly I'm told what a thing means, it becomes hateful to me."

"Unlike the marriage plot," writes Sehgal, "The trauma plot does not direct our curiosity toward the future (*Will they or won't they?*) but back into the past (*What happened to her?*)"

Despite my years of effort, the past remains full of unknowable parts.

My mother texted me the morning of my first surgery: "I am about half way through reading the book, it is all fine, just a few minor detail alterations to be made, but that can all wait until things are a bit more back to normal. I love you!!"

One of the nurses, Mike, was particularly kind. He made me promise that if I put him in a book I had to explain that he is six feet tall.

Mike, the kind nurse, is six feet tall.

I am five foot six, though if you count the antlers you have to add on like thirty more inches. My blood type is AB negative. Pulse: 89. Temperature: 97.7. Blood pressure: 102/70. I am typing with one hand.

The X-rays—the surgeon let me stare at them when they had finished the procedure—made me feel very fond of my skeleton. My spine.

When she finished reading the book, my mother had more corrections, all but one of which were easy to fix: in the chapter I titled "Tides," she said, she *had* warned Scott and Melanie of my vulnerable state. She had no idea, she said, "how badly they would let us down."

I asked Scott about my mother's warning. He does not remember her saying anything about the hospital, the police, my desire to die. It is, he said, the kind of story you'd remember.

I can fashion a past that makes sense: my mother tells Scott he must look after me, and why, but in language vague enough to make both their memories true. Just a few degrees apart. A question of emphasis.

But I am done with such questions. I am tired of upheaval. I don't know which trees will survive. You will please, I hope, forgive me.

In the future. If we get there.

My mother texted me 30 seconds ago.

The kind of sentence that's true until it isn't.

She is still alive. I am still alive.

There is between us a long blue thread.

ACKNOWLEDGMENTS

I BEGAN WRITING THIS book in 2018. To work for so many years inevitably leads to a vast crowd of people to whom I am indebted, as well as the uncomfortable likelihood that I will fail to name some of them here. I hope they will forgive me.

For their faith in my work, their astute commentary, and their willingness to stick with me through the slow and difficult process of discovering precisely what this book required, I am grateful to Michele Christle, Christopher DeWeese, Madeline Jones, and Meredith Kaffel Simonoff. I am also grateful to others who read the manuscript in part or whole at various points along the way, including Kaveh Akbar, Dennie Eagleson, Emily Pettit, Ella Risbridger, and Moriel Rothman-Zecher.

I thank my mother for her courage and our ongoing conversation, my father and sister for their care for my family when I was ill, and my child for their patience, curiosity, support, and wise counsel. I am grateful to my UK family for their acts of hospitality.

I would also like to thank the people whose generosity in conversation and action carried me through years of composition, whether they appear directly in the pages preceding this note, or in the much broader process of how those pages came into being. I cannot list all the particularities (and peculiarities) of everyone's contributions, but please imagine a multitude of shapes gleaming behind each of these names, ranging from single points representing brief but significant exchanges, to tesseracts that stretch far across time:

Samuel Ace, Nuar Alsadir, Anthony Anaxagorou, Deepika Bahri, Dara Barrois/Dixon, Sophia Blackwell, Emily Bludworth de Barrios, Jericho Brown, Blake Butler, Sarah Castleton, Gabrielle Civil, Arda Collins, T Cooper, Barton Creeth, Caroline Crew, Amy Cutler, Caspian Dennis, Claire Donato, Shaunna Donoher, Dennie Eagleson, Charles Fairbanks, Hannah Fallon, Madeline ffitch, Jessica Fjeld, Jason Francisco, Renee Gladman, Betsy Gleick, Nora Gonzalez, Elizabeth Goodstein, Wayne Holloway-Smith, Jeannie Hoag, Eoian Holohan, Tayari Jones, Amy Key, Lauren Klein, Hank Klibanoff, Nora Lewis, Paige Lewis, Ella Longpre, Carrie Lorig, Maya Marshall, Raewyn Martin, Erika Meitner, Linda Merrill, Christopher Moisan, Sirisha Naidu, Laura Otis, Alula Pankhurst, Kate Polak, Rebecca Perry, Emily Pettit, Doug Powell, Sina Queyras, Ben Reiss, Gemma Roundmell, Tharanga Samarakoon, Nicholette Scofield, Dan Sinykin, Robyn Schiff, Daniel Sheerin, Joel Silverman, Timothy Smulian, Nick Sturm, Mandy Suhr-Sytsma, Nathan Suhr-Sytsma, Kim Tallbear, Eleanor Taylor, Jack Underwood, Paula Vitaris, Masha Vlasova, Danielle Vogel, Scott Walker, Elissa Washuta, Jill Wilson, Sam Worley, Michelle Wright, Tiphanie Yanique, Derek Yorks.

My gratitude to the Howard Foundation and Emory University for their institutional support; to the librarians and archivists at Kew, Emory University, the University of Leeds, the Berg Collection at the New York Public Library, the British Library, and the British Film Archive; and to the guides and docents at Knole, Monk's House, Charleston, and the King's Observatory. In particular, I would like to thank Victoria McGrath at the Museum of Richmond, who not only gave a wonderful tour, but also saw I'd left behind a notebook containing the entirety of my notes for my 2021 trip, and scanned each individual page so that I might go on with the work. I still marvel at that kindness.

If you are in emotional crisis, text HOME to 741741 to connect with a trained counselor. The service is free and available 24/7.

SOURCES

PROLOGUE

Balley, Martin. "British Museum's Reading Room Still out of Bounds." *Art Newspaper (International Ed.)*, 32, no. 359 (September 19, 2023). https://www.theartnewspaper.com/2023/09/19/after-ten-years-the-british-museums-reading-room-is-still-out-of-bounds.

Caygill, Marjorie, and Christopher Gate. *Building the British Museum*. London: British Museum Press, 1999.

Ovid. "The Rape of Prosperina." In *Tales from Ovid*, 49–62. Translated by Ted Hughes. New York: Farrar, Straus and Giroux, 1997.

Rose, Greenland, Fiona. "The Parthenon Marbles as Icons of Nationalism in Nineteenth-Century Britain." *Nations & Nationalism* 19, no. 4 (October 2013): 654–73. doi:10.1111/nana.12039.

Stephen, Leslie. *Sir Leslie Stephen's Mausoleum Book*. Oxford: Clarendon Press, 1977.

Woolf, Virginia. "Greece 1906, Acropolis." In *A Passionate Apprentice: The Early Journals, 1897–1909*. Edited by Mitchell A. Leaska. San Diego, New York, London: Harcourt Brace Jovanovich, 1990.

Woolf, Virginia. "April 21, 1932." In *The Diary of Virginia Woolf*. Vol. 4. Edited by Anne Olivier Bell and Andrew McNeillie. London: Granta, 2023. 119–121.

Woolf, Virginia. *A Room of One's Own*. London: Hogarth Press, 1929.

Woolf, Virginia. *Jacob's Room*. London: Hogarth Press, 1922.

PART I

EPIGRAPH

Woolf, Virginia. *Mrs. Dalloway*. London: Hogarth Press, 1925.

GATE

"Kew Gates 1847–1913" (one volume). Kewensia Collection. Royal Botanic Gardens Kew Archives, Kew, Richmond, London, UK.

Allan, Mea. *The Hookers of Kew, 1785–1911*. London: Michael Joseph, 1967.

Blunt, Wilfrid. *In for a Penny: A Prospect of Kew Gardens*. London: Hamish Hamilton in association with the Tyron Gallery, 1978.

Desmond, Ray. *The History of the Royal Botanic Gardens Kew*. London: The Harvill Press, 1995. 39, 234–7, 339.

Dyduch, Amy. "Royalty Opens Kew Gardens' Elizabeth Gate." *Richmond & Twickenham Times*. October 21, 2012. https://www .richmondandtwickenhamtimes.co.uk/news/9993864.royalty-opens -kew-gardens-elizabeth-gate/.

Fish, Margery. *We Made a Garden*. London: Faber and Faber, 1956.

Kawara, On. *I Am Still Alive*. Berlin, Germany: Edition René Block, 1975.

Kincaid, Jamaica. *My Garden (Book)*. New York: Farrar, Straus and Giroux, 1999. 72.

Merriam-Webster.com Dictionary. S.v. "gate." https://www.merriam-webster. com/dictionary/gate.

Rollins, Dorothy S. "Alton News & Notes." Newspaper unknown. 1980.

Vidler, Anthony, Michel Foucault, and Pamela Johnston. "Heterotopias." *AA Files*, no. 69 (2014): 18–22. http://www.jstor.org/stable/43202545.

Woolf, Virginia. *Mrs. Dalloway*.

HALF

"Recent Work on Germination." *Nature* 149 (3789), 1942, 658–59. https://doi .org/10.1038/149658a0.

Bell, Quentin. *Virginia Woolf: A Biography*. New York: Harcourt Brace Jovanovich, 1972.

Crockett, Moya. "A Statue of Virginia Woolf Has Been Given the Go-ahead in London." *Stylist*, 2018. https://www.stylist.co.uk/visible-women /virginia-woolf-statue-richmond-london-2018/207137.

Edwards, Adrian S. "Destroyed, Damaged and Replaced: The Legacy of World War II Bomb Damage in the King's Library." *Electronic British Library Journal*, 2013. https://doi.org/10.23636/1039.

Registration as British Citizen: Chidren of British Parents Version 6.0, (Home Office, UK, August 9, 2019), 4. https://assets.publishing.service .gov.uk/government/uploads/system/uploads/attachment_data/file/824429 /registration-as-british-citizen-children-of-british-parents-v6.0ext.pdf.

Woolf, Virginia. "On Being Ill." *The New Criterion* 4:1, January 1926. 40–41. A revised version of this essay, published in 1930, ends the second sentence at "the depths of the mind," a change brought to my attention by Brian Dillon's essay on Woolf's opening sentence, first published in *Cabinet*, and later at *Lit Hub*: https://lithub.com/on-a-wonderful-beautiful-almost-failed -sentence-by-virginia-woolf/.

Woolf, Virginia. "The Mark on the Wall." In *Two Stories: Virginia Woolf & Mark Haddon*. London: Hogarth Press, 2017.

Woolf, Virginia. *Orlando*. London: Hogarth Press, 1928.

A SKETCH OF THE PAST

"London's Biggest Fire." *LIFE Magazine*, December 21, 1936. 33.

Benjamin, Walter. *The Arcades Project*. Translated by Howard Eiland and Kevin McLaughlin. Cambridge, MA: The Belknap Press of Harvard University, 1999, 184.

Christle, Heather. Unpublished diary, 1997.

Desmond, Ray. *The History of the Royal Botanic Gardens Kew*. 48–57, 159–166.

Foster, Peter. "Kew Cuts Down 60ft Palm That Makes a Break for Freedom." *The Telegraph*, June 12, 2001. https://www.telegraph.co.uk/news/uknews /1308786/Kew-cuts-down-60ft-palm-that-made-a-break-for-freedom.html.

Harris, John. "Sir William Chambers and Kew Gardens." In *Sir William Chambers: Architect to George III*. Edited by John Harris and Michael Snodin. New Haven and London: Yale University Press, 1996, 55–67.

Kohlmaier, Georg, and Barna von Sartory. *Houses of Glass: A Nineteenth-Century Building Type*. Translated by John C. Harvey. Cambridge, MA and London: MIT Press, 1986.

Laing, Olivia. *To the River: A Journey Beneath the Surface*. Edinburgh: Canongate Books, 2011.

Lee, Hermione. "How to End It All." In *Virginia Woolf's Nose: Essays on Biography*, 95–122. Princeton University Press, 2005. https://doi.org /10.2307/j.ctv3f8rcp.8.

Lee, Hermione. *Virginia Woolf*. London: Chatto & Windus, 1996.

Newman, John. "Somerset House and Other Public Buildings." In *Sir William Chambers: Architect to George III*. Edited by John Harris and Michael Snodin. New Haven and London: Yale University Press, 1996. 107–124.

Woolf, Virginia. "22 Hyde Park Gate." In *Moments of Being*. Edited by Jeanne Schulkind. San Diego, New York, London: Harcourt International, 1985. 162–178.

Woolf, Virginia. "A Sketch of the Past." In *Moments of Being*. Edited by Jeanne Schulkind. San Diego, New York, London: Harcourt International, 1985. 61–160.

PARADISE

"Suffragists Burn a Pavilion at Kew." *New York Times*, February 21, 1913. 5.

"Suffragists Work Ruin in Kew Gardens." *New York Times*, February 8, 1913. 1.

Bell, Quentin. "Preface." In *Virginia Woolf and the Hogarth Press in Richmond* by Margaret Evans. Richmond, UK: Richmond Local Historical Society, 1991.

Clarke, Darren. "Duncan Grant and Charleston's Queer Arcadia." In *Queer Bloomsbury*. Edited by Brenda Helt and Madelyn Detloff, 152–71. Edinburgh University Press, 2016. http://www.jstor.org/stable/10.3366 /j.ctt1bh2k6g.14.

Foucault, Michel, and Jay Miskowiec. "Of Other Spaces." *Diacritics* 16, no. 1 (1986). 22–27.

Hull, Stephen. "Going Underground: Mile After Mile of Ornate Brickwork and Labyrinthine Tunnels Which Reveal the Beauty of London's Hidden River Fleet." *Daily Mail Online*, September 19, 2011. https://www.dailymail .co.uk/news/article-2038281/London-underground-photos-Miles-ornate -brickwork-tunnels-hidden-Fleet-River.html.

Jefferies, Richard. *Nature near London*. London: Chatto and Windus, 1883. 185.

Lee, Hermione. *Virginia Woolf*. See esp. "Thoby," "Liaisons," "Bloomsbury," and "Leonard."

Letter from the Home Office to the Justices at Richmond, Surrey. 25 February 1913. HO 144/1255/234788. National Archives, Kew.

Lewis, C. S. *Boxen: The Imaginary World of the Young C. S. Lewis.* London: Collins, 1985.

Merriam-Webster.com Dictionary. S.v. "deflower." https://www.merriam-webster.com/dictionary/deflower.

Moggridge, Donald. *Maynard Keynes: An Economist's Biography.* London: Routledge, 1992.

Moran, James. *Wynkyn De Worde, Father of Fleet Street.* London: British Library, Oak Knoll Press, 2003.

Parker, Lynn, and Kiri Ross-Jones. *The Story of Kew Gardens in Photographs.* London: Arcturus Publishing Limited, 2013. 110.

Rhein, Donna E. *The Handprinted Books of Leonard and Virginia Woolf at the Hogarth Press, 1917–1932.* Ann Arbor, MI: UMI Research Press, 1985.

Ryan, Derek. "Bloomsbury Group." In *Oxford Bibliography Online* in British and Irish Literature, https://www-oxfordbibliographies-com.proxy.library.emory.edu/view/document/obo-9780199846719/obo-9780199846719-0185.xml.

S. P. Rosenbaum, and J. Haule. *The Bloomsbury Group Memoir Club.* Basingstoke: Palgrave Macmillan, 2014.

The Cambridge Companion to the Bloomsbury Group. Cambridge: Cambridge University Press, 2014.

Woolf, Leonard. *Growing: An Autobiography of the Years 1904 to 1911.* New York: Harcourt Brace Jovanovich, 1975.

Woolf, Virginia. "April, 18, 1918." In *The Diary of Virginia Woolf.* Vol. 1, 178–182. Edited by Anne Olivier Bell. London: Granta, 2023.

Woolf, Virginia. *Mrs. Dalloway.*

BIRTHDAY HILL

"The Weather." *Times,* March 17, 1883, 12.

"How 'Space Weather' Affects Planes and Power Grids." Transcript of *Science Friday: Talk of the Nation,* January 27, 2012. https://www.npr.org/2012/01/27/145990089/how-space-weather-affects-planes-and-power-grids.

Al-Khalili, Jim. "Quantum Life: How Physics Can Revolutionise Biology." Royal Institution Friday Evening Discourse. January 30, 2013. https://youtu.be/wwgQVZju1ZM.

Christle, Valerie. Account of childhood home. 1992. Unpublished. By permission of Valerie Christle.

Desmond, Ray. *The History of the Royal Botanic Gardens Kew.* 139.

Griffin, Donald R. "The Sensory Basis of Bird Navigation." *The Quarterly Review of Biology* 19, no. 1 (1944): 15–31. http://www.jstor.org/stable/2808564.

Günther, Anja, Angelika Einwich, Emil Sjulstok, Regina Feederle, Petra Bolte, Karl-Wilhelm Koch, yov, Ilia A. Solov, and Henrik Mouritsen. "Double-Cone Localization and Seasonal Expression Pattern Suggest a Role in Magnetoreception for European Robin Cryptochrome 4." *Current Biology* 28, no. 2 (2018): 211–223.

Harris, John. "Sir William Chambers and Kew Gardens."

Kennedy, Maev. "Kew Gardens to Breathe New Life into Great Pagoda Dragons." *Guardian*. June 2, 2015. https://www.theguardian.com/science/2015/jun/02/kew-gardens-great-pagoda-dragons-london-restoration.

Kincaid, Jamaica. *My Garden (Book)*. 112.

Lack, Andrew. *Redbreast: The Robin in Life and Literature*, based on the book *Robin Redbreast* by David Lack. Pulborough, UK: SMH Books, 2008.

Lee, Hermione. *Virginia Woolf*. 191, 473–6.

Paris, John Ayrton. *The Life of Sir Humphry Davy*. London: Henry Colburn and Richard Bentley, 1831. 138.

Stevens, Wallace. "Thirteen Ways of Looking at a Blackbird." In *The Collected Poems: Corrected Edition*. Edited by John Serio and Chris Beyers. New York: Vintage Books, 2015.

Wiltschko, Wolfgang, and Roswitha Wiltschko. "Magnetic Compass of European Robins." *Science* 176, no. 4030 (1972): 62–64.

Woolf, Virginia. "November 28, 1928." In *The Diary of Virginia Woolf*. Vol. 3. Edited by Anne Olivier Bell and Andrew McNeillie. London: Granta, 2023. 264–266.

Woolf, Virginia. "Old Bloomsbury." In *Moments of Being*. Edited by Jeanne Schulkind. San Diego, New York, London: Harcourt International, 1985. 179–202.

Woolf, Virginia. *The Voyage Out*. London: Duckworth, 1915.

Woolf, Virginia. *To the Lighthouse*. London: Hogarth, 1927.

WALL

Lewis, C. S. *Surprised by Joy*. New York & London: Harcourt Brace Jovanovich, 1955.

Spicer, Jack. "Any Fool Can Get into an Ocean." In *My Vocabulary Did This to Me: The Collected Poetry of Jack Spicer*. Edited by Peter Gizzi and Kevin Killian. Middletown, CT: Wesleyan University Press, 2008. 23. By permission of Peter Gizzi on behalf of Jack Spicer's estate.

Merriam-Webster.com Dictionary. S.v. "marrow." https://www.merriam -webster.com/dictionary/marrow.

Woolf, Virginia. Virginia Woolf to Janet Case. March 20, 1922. In *The Letters of Virginia Woolf*. Vol 2. Edited by Nigel Nicolson and Joanne Trautmann. New York and London: Harcourt Brace Jovanovich, 1976. 515.

MODEL

"Observations on the Transit of Venus." Manuscript notebook. 1768–1769, King's College London Archives: The George III Museum Collection, Ref: GB0100 KCLCA K/MUS 1/1. https://kingscollections.org/media /arc_cat/pdf/000643/KCL.KingsCollections.GPP.K-MUS-1-1.pdf.

"Vanessa Bell / The Making of a Pioneer." *TOAST* podcast. November 28, 2019. https://podcasts.apple.com/us/podcast/ vanessa-bell-the-making-of-a-pioneer/id1440135011?i=1000458098905.

Allan, D. G. C. "Royal Science." *RSA Journal* 142, no. 5447 (1994): 70–71. http://www.jstor.org/stable/41376395.

Bennett, Alan. *The Madness of King George: The Complete and Unabridged Screenplay*. New York: Random House, 1995.

Brooke, Rupert. "The Soldier." *Poetry* 6, no. 1 (April 1915): 19. https://www .poetryfoundation.org/poetrymagazine/browse?contentId=13076.

Chen, Chen, Matthew H. Schneps, and Gerhard Sonnert. "Order Matters: Sequencing Scale-Realistic versus Simplified Models to Improve Science Learning." *Journal of Science Education and Technology* 25, no. 5 (2016): 806–23. http://www.jstor.org/stable/45151175.

Colley, Andrew. "Bekonscot Have Always Had the Royal Seal of Approval." *Bucks Free Press*, June 8, 2014. https://www.bucksfreepress.co.uk/news /11262127.bekonscot-have-always-had-the-royal-seal-of-approval/.

From Our Correspondent. "Royal Visit to Bekonscot." *Times*. April 16, 1936. 10. *The Times Digital Archive*.

Herdendorf, Charles E. "Captain James Cook and the Transits of Mercury and Venus." *The Journal of Pacific History* 21, no. 1 (1986): 39–55. https://doi.org/10.1080/00223348608572527.

Hodgson Burnett, Frances. *A Little Princess*. 1905; reis., New York: J.B. Lippincott, 1963.

Moore, John E. 1998. "The Monument, or Christopher Wren's Roman Accent." *Art Bulletin* 80, no. 3: 498. doi:10.2307/3051302.

Musgrave, Tony. *The Multifarious Mr Banks: From Botany Bay to Kew, the Natural Historian Who Shaped the World.* New Haven and London: Yale University Press, 2020.

Padan, Yael. *Modelscapes of Nationalism.* Amsterdam University Press, 2017.

Roberts, Jane. "Sir William Chambers and George III." In *Sir William Chambers: Architect to George III,* 41–54. Edited by John Harris and Michael Snodin. New Haven and London: Yale University Press, 1996.

BIBLIOMANCY

Fordy, Tom. "Inside the Box of Delights: 'You'd Never Have JK Rowling without John Masefield.'" *Telegraph*, December 21, 2020. https://www.telegraph.co.uk/tv/2020/12/21/inside-box-delights-never-have-jk-rowling-without-john-masefield/.

From our own Correspondent. "The Spanish Epidemic." *Times*, June 3, 1918, 5. *Times of London Digital Archive.*

Grim, Ryan. "Rikers Island Prisoners Are Being Offered PPE and $6 an Hour to Dig Mass Graves." *Intercept*, March 31, 2020, 11:54 AM, https://theintercept.com/2020/03/31/rikers-island-coronavirus-mass-graves/.

Kincaid, Jamaica. *A Small Place.* New York: Farrar, Strauss and Giroux, 1988. 32.

Slotnick, Daniel E. "Molly Brodak, Poet and Memoirist of Her Father's Crimes, Dies at 39." *The New York Times*, March 19, 2020. https://www.nytimes.com/2020/03/19/books/molly-brodak-dies.html?unlocked_article_code=1.zko.brLi.vLhqybvfaN8m&smid=url-share.

Sooke, Alistair. "The Elgin Marbles Don't 'Belong' to Greece—They Belong to Us All." *Telegraph.* February 19, 2020. https://www.telegraph.co.uk/art/what-to-see/elgin-marbles-dont-belong-greece-belong-us1/.

Woolf. "July 2, 1918." *Diary* 1. 210.

Woolf. "July 4, 1918." *Diary* 1. 210–211.

Woolf, Virginia. *The Years.* London: Hogarth Press, 1937.

PART II

EPIGRAPH

Woolf, Virginia. *Night and Day.* London: Duckworth, 1920.

BRIDGE

"A Note on the Text." In *Two Stories: Virginia Woolf & Mark Haddon.* London: Hogarth Press, 2017. xxiii.

Carmel, David, Michael Arcaro, Sabine Kastner, and Uri Hasson. "How to Create and Use Binocular Rivalry." *Journal of Visualized Experiments* 10, no. 45 (January 1, 2010): e2030.

Good, Jonathan. "Royal St. George, 1272–1509." In *The Cult of St George in Medieval England.* Woodbridge, Suffolk, UK; Rochester, NY, USA: Boydell & Brewer, 2009. 53.

Grasp the Nettle. Dir. Dean Puckett (2013). Available on Vimeo: https://vimeo .com/64705880.

Klein, Holgera A. "Refashioning Byzantium in Venice, ca. 1200–1400." In *San Marco, Byzantium, and the Myths of Venice.* Edited by Henry Maguire and Robert S. Nelson. Washington, DC: Dumbarton Oaks Research Library and Collection, 2010. 193–150.

Riches, Samantha. *St. George: Hero, Martyr and Myth.* Stroud: Sutton, 2000.

Ryan, William Granger, and Eamon Duffy. "Saint George." In *The Golden Legend: Readings on the Saints.* Princeton, NJ: Princeton University Press, 2012. 238–242.

Sebald, W. G. *After Nature.* Translated by Michael Hamburger. New York: Random House, 2002.

Setton, Kenneth M. "Saint George's Head." *Speculum* 48, no. 1 (1973): 1–12.

Walsham, Alexandra. "Introduction: Relics and Remains." *Past & Present* 206, issue supplement no. 5, 2010. 9–36.

Woolf, Virginia. "The Mark on the Wall."

Woolf, Virginia. *Mrs. Dalloway.*

ON FIRE

"Hallmark Recalls Jumbo Snow Globes Due to Fire Hazard." *United States Product Safety Commission.* December 23, 2008. https://www.cpsc.gov /Recalls/2008/hallmark-recalls-jumbo-snow-globes-due-to-fire-hazard.

"Snow Globe Causes Charity Shop Fire." *Guardian.* December 25, 2014. https://www.theguardian.com/uk-news/2014/dec/25/snow-globe-causes -charity-shop-fire.

Adorno, Theodor W. "A Portrait of Walter Benjamin." In *Prisms*, 233. Translated by Samuel and Shierry Weber. Cambridge, MA: MIT Press, 1981.

Bal, Mieke. "The Discourse of the Museum." In *Thinking About Exhibitions*. Edited by Reesa Greenberg, Bruce W. Ferguson, and Sandy Nairne. London and New York: Routledge, 1996. 145–158.

Benjamin, Walter. *The Correspondence of Walter Benjamin, 1910–1940*. Edited by Gershom Scholem and Theodor W. Adorno. Translated by Manfred R. Jacobson and Evelyn M. Jacobson. Chicago: University of Chicago Press, 1994.

Brodak, Molly. "Inlet." In *The Cipher*. Warrensburg, MO: Pleiades Press, 2020.

Cashmore, Amanda. "Home Set on Fire by SNOW GLOBE in the Window That Acted as a Magnifying Glass in the Bright Winter Sunshine." *Daily Mail online*. December 14, 2017. https://www.dailymail.co.uk/news/article-5180671/Home-set-fire-SNOW-GLOBE-window.html.

Chodziesner, Georg. "How I Came to Australia." Manuscript shared on *Stories from the* Dunera *and the* Queen Mary. https://www.dunerastories.monash.edu/dunera-stories/153-the-voyage-the-testimony-of-georg-chodziesner.html.

Christle, Valerie. "Memorial Day Weekend" in diary. 1995. Unpublished. By permission of Valerie Christle.

Cummings, E. E. "Sonnets–Unrealities: IX." In *Complete Poems 1904–1962*. Edited by George J. Firmage. New York: Liveright, 1991. 144.

Jasanoff, Maya. "Misremembering the British Empire." *New Yorker*. October 26, 2020. https://www.newyorker.com/magazine/2020/11/02/misremembering-the-british-empire.

Jay, Martin, and Gary Smith. "A Talk with Mona Jean Benjamin, Kim Yvon Benjamin and Michael Benjamin." *Benjamin Studien/Studies* 1, Perception and Experience in Modernity (2002): 111–125.

Jennings, Ashley. "Snow Globe Starts Fire in Oregon Man's Home." *ABC News*. March 21, 2012. https://abcnews.go.com/blogs/headlines/2012/03/snow-globe-starts-fire-in-wisconsin-mans-home.

Jones, Tamsin Treverton. "Harwich, Essex." In *Windblown: Landscape, Legacy and Loss: The Great Storm of 1987*. London: Hodder & Stoughton, 2017. 69–76.

Satia, Priya. "The Past and Future of History." In *Time's Monster: How History Makes History*. Cambridge, MA: Belknap Press of Harvard University Press, 2020. 271, 285, 297.

Sharpe, Christina. *Monstrous Intimacies: Making Post-Slavery Subjects*. Durham, NC: Duke University Press, 2010. 115.

Stein, Gertrude. "Portraits and Repetition." In *Lectures in America*. New York: Random House, 1935. 165–206.

Taussig, Michael. "Walter Benjamin's Grave." In *Walter Benjamin's Grave*. Chicago: University of Chicago Press, 2006. 16–45.

Walter Benjamin's Archive: Images, Texts, Signs. Edited by Ursula Max, Gudrun Schwarz, Michael Schwarz, and Erdmut Wizisla. Translated by Esther Leslie. London: Verso Press, 2007.

Woolf, Virginia. "A Sketch of the Past."

NIGHT AND DAY

Ash, Susan. *Funding Philanthropy: Dr Barnardo's Metaphors, Narratives and Spectacles*. Liverpool: Liverpool University Press, 2016.

Benjamin, Walter. "Theses on the Philosophy of History." In *Illuminations: Essays and Reflections*. Edited by Hannah Arendt. Translated by Harry Zohn. Boston/New York: Mariner Books, 2019. 196–209.

Cadava, Eduardo. "'Lapsus Imaginis': The Image in Ruins." *October 96* (2001): 35–60.

Christle, Valerie. Barnardo's information request form. 2020. Unpublished. By permission of Valerie Christle.

Fitzgerald, Penelope. *Edward Burne-Jones: A Biography*. London: Joseph, 1975.

Fyfe, Paul. "Accidental Death: Lizzie Siddal and the Poetics of the Coroner's Inquest." *Victorian Review* 40, no. 2 (2014): 17–22. http://www.jstor.org /stable/24877707.

Gernsheim, Helmut. *Julia Margaret Cameron: Her Life and Photographic Work*. New York: Aperture, 1975.

Kingsley, Joey. "Bodily Filth and Disorientation: Navigating Orphan Transformations in the Works of Dr Thomas Barnardo and Charles Dickens." In *Rereading Orphanhood: Texts, Inheritance, Kin*, 123–4. Edited by Diane Warren and Laura Peters. Edinburgh: Edinburgh University Press, 2020.

Lee, Hermione. "Maternal." In *Virginia Woolf*, 79–94.

Matthews, Samantha. *Poetical Remains: Poets' Graves, Bodies, and Books in the Nineteenth Century*. Oxford: Oxford University Press, 2004. ProQuest Ebook Central.

McNees, Eleanor. "The 1914 'Expurgated Chunk': The Great War in and out of The Years." In *Virginia Woolf: Writing the World*. Edited by Pamela L. Caughie and Diana L. Swanson, 55–62. Liverpool University Press, 2015.

Murdoch, Lydia. *Imagined Orphans: Poor Families, Child Welfare, and Contested Citizenship in London.* New Brunswick, New Jersey, and London: Rutgers University Press, 2006.

Olsen, Victoria. *From Life: Julia Margaret Cameron & Victorian Photography.* London: Aurum Press, 2003.

Priestley, J. B. "Men, Women and Books: Tell Us More About These Authors!" *Evening Standard*, October 13, 1932.

Trachtenberg, Alan. "The Camera and Dr. Barnardo." *Aperture* 19, no 4 (1975): 68–77.

Watts, M. S. *George Frederic Watts: The Annals of an Artist's Life Vol. 1.* London: Macmillan & Co., 1912.

Wolf, Sylvia. *Julia Margaret Cameron's Women.* New Haven and London: Yale University Press/Art Institute of Chicago, 1998.

Woolf, Virginia. "A Sketch of the Past."

Woolf, Virginia. "Craftsmanship." In *The Death of the Moth, and Other Essays.* 1942; New York: Harcourt Brace Jovanovich, 1974. 198–207.

Woolf, Virginia. "Middlebrow." In *The Death of the Moth, and Other Essays.* 1942; New York: Harcourt Brace Jovanovich, 1974. 176–186.

Woolf, Virginia. *The Pargiters.* 1932–1934. Notebook 5. MS Berg 42. York Public Library.

TIDES

Ardam, Jacquelyn. "How the Alphabet Helped Virginia Woolf Understand Her Father." *LitHub* June 26, 2019. https://lithub.com/how-the-alphabet -helped-virginia-woolf-understand-her-father/.

Bell, Quentin, and Julian Bell. "A Hundred Years After or Ladies and Gentlemen." MS. British Library. London.

Bell, Vanessa. Vanessa Bell to Virginia Woolf. May 11, 1927. In appendix to *The Letters of Virginia Woolf.* Vol. 3. Edited by Nigel Nicholson and Joanne Trautman. New York and London: Harvest/HBJ, 1977. 572–573.

Christle, Valerie. Valerie Christle to Heather Christle. Letter. December 2020. Unpublished. By permission of Valerie Christle.

Christle, Valerie. "Memorial Day Weekend."

Christle, Valerie. Account of funeral. July 1995. Unpublished. By permission of Valerie Christle.

Christle, Valerie. Barnardo's information request form. By permission of Valerie Christle.

Hoblyn, Harry. "Restoring Charleston's Studio Border." Charleston. org. February 21, 2020. https://www.charleston.org.uk/stories/ restoring-charlestons-studio-border/.

Lee, Hermione. "A Haunted House." In *Virginia Woolf*. 469–477.

Woolf, Virginia. "A Sketch of the Past."

Woolf, Virginia. Virginia Woolf to Vanessa Bell. May 22, 1927. *Letters* 3. 379–382.

Woolf, Virginia. *Orlando*.

Woolf, Virginia. *To the Lighthouse*.

PORTRAITS

"Action Looks at Life." *Action* 1, no 6 (November 12), 193. *British Online Archive*, https://microform-digital.proxy.library.emory.edu/boa /documents/19982/action-october-to-december-1931.

"Jews Desecrate Nelson's Column." *The Blackshirt*. September 14, 1934, 3. *British Online Archives*. https://microform-digital.proxy.library.emory.edu /boa/documents/729/the-blackshirt-july-to-december-1934.

"Max Levitas." *Times*. November 16, 2018, 57. *The Times Digital Archive*.

"Nelson Monument Defaced." *Times*. September 7, 1934, 9. *The Times Digital Archive*.

Brown, Jane. *Vita's Other World: A Gardening Biography of V. Sackville-West*. London: Penguin Books, 1987.

Cannadine, David. "Portrait of More Than a Marriage: Harold Nicolson and Vita Sackville-West Revisited." In *Aspects of Aristocracy: Grandeur and Decline in Modern Britain*, 210–41. Yale University Press, 1994.

De Courcy, Anne. *Diana Mosley*. London, Vintage Books, 2003.

Dennison, Matthew. *Behind the Mask: The Life of Vita Sackville-West*. London: William Collins, 2014.

Diestelkamp, Edward. "The Curvilinear Range National Botanic Gardens, Dublin." *Curtis's Botanical Magazine* 12, no. 4 (1995): 209–20. http://www.jstor.org/stable/45065130.

Flood, Alison. "Miniature Book Said to Have Inspired Virginia Woolf's *Orlando* to be Published." *Guardian*. October 11, 2017. https://www .theguardian.com/books/2017/oct/11/quick-read-tiny-book-that-inspired -virginia-woolf-to-be-published-vita-sackville-west.

Kincaid, Jamaica. *My Garden (Book)*. 82.

Lammers, Benjamin J. "The Birth of the East Ender: Neighborhood and Local Identity in Interwar East London." *Journal of Social* History 39, no. 2 (2005): 331–44. https://doi.org/10.1353/jsh.2005.0143.

Lee, Hermione. "How to End It All."

Lee, Hermione. "Vita." In *Virginia Woolf*. 478–504.

Nicolson, Harold. "Election Will Annoy You." *Action* 1, no. 1 (October 8, 1931), 10–11. *British Online Archives*. https://microform-digital.proxy .library.emory.edu/boa/documents/19982/action-october-to-december-1931.

Nicolson, Nigel. *Portrait of a Marriage*. New York: Atheneum, 1973.

Private communication from Eoin Holohan (location manager for *Vita & Virginia*). January 31, 2021.

Rose, Norman. *Harold Nicolson*. London: Jonathan Cape, 2005.

Sackville-West, Vita, and Harold Nicolson. *Vita and Harold: The Letters of Vita Sackville-West and Harold Nicolson*. Edited by Nigel Nicolson. New York: Putnam's, 1992.

Sackville-West, Vita. "Endless Pleasure in Miniature Gardens." *Action* 1, no. 7 (November 19). *British Online Archive*. https://microform-digital .proxy.library.emory.edu/boa/documents/19982/action-october-to-december -1931.

Sackville-West, Vita. *The Garden*. London: Michael Joseph Limited, 1946.

Sackville-West, Vita. *The Land*. London: Heinemann, 1926.

Schuyler, James. "February 13, 1975." From "The Payne Whitney Poems" in *The Morning of the Poem*. New York: Farrar, Strauss and Giroux, 1980. 50.

Stein, Gertrude. *The World Is Round*. New York: William R. Scott, 1939.

Strachey, Lytton. *Eminent Victorians*. London: Chatto and Windus, 1918.

Woolf. "July 23, 1927." *Diary* 3. 186–189.

Woolf, Virginia. Virginia Woolf to Clive Bell. January 23, 1924. *Letters* 3. 84–86.

Woolf, Virginia. Virginia Woolf to Vita Sackville-West. May 3, 1938. *Letters* 3. 225–226.

Woolf, Virginia. *Orlando*.

Woolf, Virginia. *Roger Fry*. London: Hogarth, 1940.

CORRECTION

"Geoffrey de Havilland, Obituary." *Journal of the Royal Society of Arts* 113, no. 5108 (1965): 617–19. http://www.jstor.org/stable/41367885.

Alt, Christina. "'To Pin through the Body with a Name': Virginia Woolf and the Taxonomic Tradition." In *Virginia Woolf and the Study of Nature*, 72–105. Cambridge: Cambridge University Press, 2010.

Pascal, Roy. "The Elusiveness of Truth." In *Design and Truth in Autobiography*, 68. London: Routledge & Kegan Paul Ltd, 1960.

Silver, Brenda R. "'Anon' and 'The Reader': Virginia Woolf's Last Essays." *Twentieth Century Literature* 25, no. 3/4 (1979): 356–441. https://doi.org/10.2307/441326.

Woolf, Virginia. "A Sketch of the Past."

Woolf, Virginia. "Craftsmanship."

Woolf, Virginia. "Flying Over London." In *The Captain's Death Bed and Other Essays*, 186–192. Edited by Leonard Woolf. London: Hogarth Press, 1950.

Woolf, Virginia. "Sunday 9 June, 1940." In *The Diary of Virginia Woolf*. Vol. 5, 390. Edited by Anne Olivier Bell and Andrew McNeillie. London: Granta, 2023.

Woolf, Virginia. *Orlando*.

PART III

EPIGRAPH

Woolf. "October 15, 1930." *Diary* 3. 412–413.

HITHER

Gladman, Renee. "Untitled (Environments)." *e-flux journal* 92 ("Feminisms Issue One"): June 2018. https://www.e-flux.com/journal/92/203283/untitled-environments/.

Hill-Miller, Katherine. *From the Lighthouse to Monk's House: A Guide to Virginia Woolf's Literary Landscapes*. London: Duckworth, 2001.

Lee, Hermione. "Monk's House." In *Virginia Woolf*, 415–428.

Olterman, Philip, Kate Connolly, and Andrew Roth. "Briton Suspected of Spying for Russia 'Kept Himself to Himself.'" *Guardian*. August 12, 2021. https://www.theguardian.com/world/2021/aug/12/briton-accused-spying-russia-kept-himself-to-himself-david-smith.

Richter, Max. 2017. "Memory Is the Seamstress." *Three Worlds: Music from Woolf Works*. Deutsche Grammophon.

Woolf, Virginia, and A. V. Stephen. "Literary Geography." *Times Literary Supplement*, March 10, 1905, 81. *Times Literary Supplement Historical Archive*.

Woolf, Virginia. "Haworth, November 1904." *Guardian*, December 21, 1904. (Unsigned).

Woolf, Virginia. "March 24, 1941." *Diary* 5. 477–478.

Woolf, Virginia. *A Room of One's Own*.

Woolf, Virginia. *Between the Acts*. London: Hogarth Press, 1941.

Woolf, Virginia. Virginia Woolf to Leonard Woolf. 28 March 1941. In *The Letters of Virginia Woolf*. Vol. 6. Edited by Nigel Nicolson and Joanne Trautmann. New York and London: Harcourt Brace Jovanovich, 1980. 486–487.

Woolf, Virginia. Virginia Woolf to Vanessa Bell. Sunday [23? March 1941]. *Letters* Vol. 6. 485.

Woolf, Virginia. *Orlando*.

THITHER

"Don't Overmilk the Cow!" Tripadvisor post by username ashdown2011. July 29, 2019. https://www.tripadvisor.com/Attraction_Review-g186275 -d613868-Reviews-or40-Charleston-Lewes_East_Sussex_England.html. Accessed October 30, 2021.

Bell, Quentin, and Julian Bell. "A Hundred Years After or Ladies and Gentlemen."

Clarke, Darren. "Duncan Grant and Charleston's Queer Arcadia."

Woolf, Virginia. "Haworth 1904."

TOURIST

"Maqdala Collection." *The British Museum*. Undated. Accessed November 5, 2021. https://www.britishmuseum.org/about-us /british-museum-story/contested-objects-collection/maqdala-collection.

"Percussion Revolver, 1860–62." *Royal Collection Trust website*. Undated. Accessed November 2021. https://www.rct.uk/collection/61616 /percussion-revolver.

Allingham, William. *A Diary*. London: Macmillan & Co., 1907.

Amulree, Lord. "Prince Alamayou of Ethiopia." *Ethiopia Observer* (1970): 8–15.

Jones, Danell. *The Girl Prince: Virginia Woolf, Race and the Dreadnought Hoax*. London: Hurst & Company, Oxford University Press, 2023.

Garnett, Angelica. *Deceived with Kindness: A Bloomsbury Childhood.* London: Chatto & Windus, 1984.

Gullick, John M. "Captain Speedy of Larut." *Journal of the Malayan Branch of the Royal Asiatic Society* 26, no. 3 (163) (1953): 3–103. http://www.jstor.org/stable/41503024.

Heaven, Andrew. *The Prince and the Plunder: How Britain Took One Small Boy and Hundreds of Treasures from Ethiopia.* Cheltenham (UK): History Press, 2022.

Hunt, Tristram. "Should Museums Return Their Colonial Artefacts?" *Guardian.* June 29, 2019. https://www.theguardian.com/culture/2019/jun/29/should-museums-return-their-colonial-artefacts.

Johnston, Georgia. "Virginia Woolf's Talk on the Dreadnought Hoax." *Woolf Studies Annual* 15 (2009): 1–45. http://www.jstor.org/stable/24907113.

Lee, Hermione. *Virginia Woolf.* 278–83.

Nurhussein, Nadia. "Fashioning the Imperial Self." In *Black Land: Imperial Ethiopianism and African America*, 72–89. Princeton University Press, 2019. https://doi.org/10.2307/j.ctvdmwzxj.8.

Olsen, Victoria. *From Life: Julia Margaret Cameron & Victorian Photography.*

Pankhurst, Richard. "The Napier Expedition and the Loot from Maqdala." *Présence Africaine*, no. 133/134 (1985): 233–40. http://www.jstor.org/stable/24351450.

Pulp. "Common People." By Steve Mackey, Russell Senior, Nick Banks, Jarvis Cocker, and Candida Doyle. Recorded 1995. Track 3 on *Different Class.* Island Records, CD.

Ransome, Cyril. *An Advanced History of England from the Earliest Times to the Present Day.* New York: Macmillan and Co., 1895.

Ransome, Cyril. Manuscript of autobiography, 1888–1896. Arthur Ransome Collection. Library Special Collections, Leeds University, Leeds, UK. https://explore.library.leeds.ac.uk/special-collections-explore/40083.

Young, Kevin. "The Time Virginia Woolf Wore Blackface." In *New Yorker*, October 27, 2017. https://www.newyorker.com/books/page-turner/the-time-virginia-woolf-wore-blackface.

THE DISTANT THAMES

"The Hogarth Press." British Library, May 25, 2016. https://www.bl.uk/20th-century-literature/articles/the-hogarth-press.

"The Jubilee." *Times*, August 2, 1814, 2+. *Times Digital Archive.*

Anaxagorou, Anthony. "Meeting the End of the World as Yourself." In *After the Formalities*. London: Penned in the Margins, 2019.

Appleyard, David, and Richard Pankhurst. "The Last Two Letters of Emperor Tewodros II of Ethiopia (April 11 and 12 1868)." *Journal of the Royal Asiatic Society of Great Britain and Ireland*, no. 1 (1987): 23–42. http://www.jstor.org/stable/25212066.

Coel, Michaela, creator. *I May Destroy You*. Season 1. Released June 7, 2020. https://www.hbo.com/i-may-destroy-you.

Darrah, William C. *The World of Stereographs*. Gettysburg, PA: W. C. Darrah, 1977.

Johnston, Keith M. "'An Unlimited Field for Experiment': Britain's Stereoscopic Landscapes." In *British Rural Landscapes on Film*, 71–85. Edited by Paul Newland. Manchester University Press, 2016. http://www.jstor.org/stable/j.ctv18b5gnk.10.

Johnston, Keith M. "Now Is the Time (to Put on Your Glasses): 3-D Film Exhibition in Britain, 1951–55." *Film History* 23, no. 1 (2011): 93–103. https://doi.org/10.2979/filmhistory.23.1.93.

Kilalea, Katharine. "Hennecker's Ditch." *PN Review* 195, Vol. 37:1, September-October 2010. https://www.pnreview.co.uk/cgi-bin/scribe?item_id=8078.

Kinshasa, Safiya Kamaria. "Cinderella." In *Cane, Corn & Gully*. London: Out-Spoken Press, 2022.

Legg, Stuart. "Mr R. Spottiswoode." *Times*, 21 Aug. 1970. 10. *Times Digital Archive*.

Maitland, Frederic William. *The Life and Letters of Leslie Stephen*. London: Duckworth, 1906.

Robinson, David. "Films in 1951." *Twentieth Century Architecture*, no. 5 (2001): 88–94. http://www.jstor.org/stable/41861912.

Silverman, Robert J. "The Stereoscope and Photographic Depiction in the 19th Century." *Technology and Culture* 34, no. 4 (1993): 729–56. https://doi.org/10.2307/3106413.

Smith, Brian, dir. *The Distant Thames*. 1951. UK: International Realist. London: British Film Institute Archives.

Spottiswoode, Raymond, and Nigel Spottiswoode. *The Theory of Stereoscopic Transmission & Its Application to the Motion Picture*. Berkeley & Los Angeles: University of California Press, 1953.

Spottiswoode, Raymond. "Things to Come." In *Film and Its Techniques*, 364–387. London: University of California Press, 1951.

Woolf, Virginia, Vanessa Bell, and Thoby Stephen. *Hyde Park Gate News: The Stephen Family Newspaper*. Edited by Gill Lowe. London: Hesperus Press, 2005.

Woolf, Virginia. "The Cinema." *The Nation & Athenaeum*. 3 July 1926: 381–3.

Woolf, Virginia. *Orlando: The Holograph Draft*. Edited by Stuart Nelson Clarke. London: Stuart Nelson Clarke, 1993.

LOCK AND KEY

Brown, Jane. *Vita's Other World*. 37.

Daniell, David. "William Tyndale, ?1494–1536." In *The Bible in English: Its History and Influence*, 133–59. Yale University Press, 2003. http://www.jstor.org/stable/j.ctt1dszxtb.13.

Oxford English Dictionary, s.v. "beautiful (adj., n., & adv.)," September 2023, https://doi.org/10.1093/OED/6632057087.

Tyndale, William. *Tyndale's New Testament*. Edited by David Daniell. New Haven [Conn.]: Yale University Press, 1989.

Carroll, Robert, and Stephen Prickett. *The Bible: Authorized King James Version*. The World's Classics. Oxford: OUP Oxford, 2008.

Rilke, Rainer Maria. "Archaic Torso of Apollo." In *The Selected Poetry of Rainer Maria Rilke*. Edited and translated by Stephen Mitchell. New York: Vintage Books, 1982.

Woolf, Virginia. "A Sketch of the Past."

Woolf, Virginia. "March 12, 1924." In *The Diary of Virginia Woolf*. Vol. 2. Edited by Anne Olivier Bell and Andrew McNeillie. London: Granta, 2023. 369–371.

THE UNDERWORLD

"India—Tiger's Head." *Royal Collections Trust*. Catalogue entry from "Gold." London, 2014. https://www.rct.uk/collection/67212/tigers-head.

"The Ancient Oak Tree That Taught the World a Lesson." *BBC Witness History*, January 28, 2020. https://www.bbc.co.uk/programmes/p081llyy.

Heavens, Andrew. *The Prince and the Plunder: How Britain Took One Small Boy and Hundreds of Treasures from Ethiopia*. Cheltenham, Gloucestershire: The History Press, 2023.

Hookham, Mark. "Give Back Our Stolen Prince, Your Majesty." *Daily Mail.com*, May 12, 2019. https://www.dailymail.co.uk/news/article-7018909/Queen-sparks-diplomatic-row-rejecting-Ethiopias-plea-return-stolen-king.html.

Jasanoff, Maya. "Collectors of Empire: Objects, Conquests and Imperial Self-Fashioning." *Past & Present*, no. 184 (2004): 109–35. http://www.jstor.org/stable/3600699.

Kinver, Mark. "Lessons Learned from Great Storm." *BBC News*, October 14, 2007. http://news.bbc.co.uk/2/hi/science/nature/7044050.stm.

Pankhurst, Richard. "The Napier Expedition and The Loot from Maqdala."

Tamirat, Jibat, and Cecilia Macauley. "Ethiopia's Prince Alemayehu: Buckingham Palace Rejects Calls to Return Royal's Body." *BBC News*. 22 May 2023. https://www.bbc.com/news/world-africa-65588663.

VERY SMALL FLAGS

"Spread of the Swinging Revolution." *LIFE International*. July 1966.

Akram, Razwana. "The Queen's Beasts." *Kew.org*, 2 December 2016. https://www.kew.org/read-and-watch/the-queens-beasts.

Christle, Valerie. "October the 10th, 1980, 2:25 AM." Diary. Unpublished. By permission of Valerie Christle.

Sablich, Justin. "A Jimi Hendrix Experience in London." *New York Times*, January 14, 2020. https://www.nytimes.com/2020/01/14/travel/jimi-hendrix-london.html.

Woolf, Virginia. "Kew Gardens."

Woolf, Virginia. *Night and Day*.

THE WILD GOOSE

"The Deer Rut." *British Deer Society*. Undated. https://www.bds.org.uk/information-advice/about-deer/the-deer-rut/.

Bell, Quentin, and Julian Bell. "A Hundred Years After or Ladies and Gentlemen."

Clarke, Matthew. "Queer Elizabeth: Early/Modern Feeling in Orlando and Elizabeth and Essex." In *Virginia Woolf and Heritage*. Edited by Jane de Gay, Tom Breckin, and Anne Reus, 134–40. Liverpool University Press, 2017. https://doi.org/10.2307/j.ctt1ps32z5.23.

Forster, E. M. *Virginia Woolf: The Rede Lecture*. Cambridge, UK: Cambridge University Press, 1942.

Sackville-West, Vita. Vita Sackville-West to Harold Nicolson. November 30, 1926. *Vita and Harold*. 175.

Sackville-West, Vita. Vita Sackville-West to Harold Nicolson. May 16, 1928. *Vita and Harold*. 195–196.

Sackville-West, Vita. Vita Sackville-West to Virginia Woolf. July 16, 1924. In *The Letters of Vita Sackville-West to Virginia Woolf*, 50–51. Edited by Louise DeSalvo and Mitchell A. Leaska. New York: William Morrow and Company, 1985.

Woolf, Virginia. "February 24, 1905." In *A Passionate Apprentice: The Early Journals, 1897–1909.*

Woolf. "June 15, 1929." *Diary* 3. 298–299.

Woolf. "March 18, 1928." *Diary* 3. 222.

Woolf. "November 28, 1928." *Diary* 3. 264–266.

Woolf, Virginia. *Orlando.*

EPILOGUE

Sehgal, Parul. "The Case Against the Trauma Plot." *New Yorker*, January 3, 2022. https://www.newyorker.com/magazine/2022/01/03/the-case-against-the-trauma-plot.

Woolf, Virginia. "Mr. Bennett and Mrs. Brown." In *The Captain's Death Bed*, 90–111.

Woolf, Virginia. Virginia Woolf to Roger Fry. May 27, 1927. *Letters* 3. 385–387.

IMAGE SOURCES AND CREDITS

14 Christle, Heather. "Light Indicates Approval." Photograph. August 20, 2015.

14 Christle, Heather. "Wild Deer Roam Freely in the Park." Photograph. September 16, 2018.

25 Christle, Michael. "Temple of Aeolus." Photograph. May 1979. By permission of Michael Christle.

25 Christle, Heather. "Temple of Aeolus." Photograph. October 11, 2019.

28 Hortop, Scott. "Richmond Riverside." Photograph. March 2009. Licensed via Alamy.

28 Dizengremel, Laury. "Virginia Woolf Sculpture Planned Installation." Photograph. [2018?] By permission of Laury Dizengremel.

37 "Exterior of the South Front of the Great Exhibition Building." Illustration. From "A Guide to the Great Exhibition of Industry." *Illustrated London News*, May 3, 1851, [359]+. The Illustrated London News Historical Archive, 1842–2003.

37 "Famed Landmark's Fiery Shell." Photograph. In Daily Sketch, December 1, 1936, 1. Licensed via Alamy.

55   Christle, Valerie. "Heather on Nannie's Lap at Birthday Hill."
Photograph. [Summer 1981?]. By permission of Valerie Christle.

55   Christle, Heather. "Birthday Hill." Photograph. October 10, 2019.

71   "Julia Stephen with Virginia." Photograph. 1884. Leslie Stephen
Photograph Album, Mortimer Rare Book Collection, MRBC-MS-00005,
Smith College Special Collections, Northampton, Massachusetts.

71   Christle, Michael. "Heather on Valerie's Lap." Photograph. [1985?].
By permission of Michael Christle.

79   Popper, Paul. "Princess Elizabeth Visits Model Village." Photograph.
1936. Licensed via Getty Images.

79   Christle, Valerie. "Heather and Michele at Bekenscot." Photograph.
[1986?] By permission of Valerie Christle.

97   Christle, Heather. "For there she was." Partially erased photograph.
2024.

97   Christle, Heather. "For it was a snail." Partially erased photograph. 2024.

97   Goldberg, Julia Ty. "Illustration of Piecemeal Rivalry." 2024.
Commissioned for this text, based on "Figure 7" from "How to Create
and Use Binocular Rivalry," cited fully in sources for "Bridge."

112   "The Refreshment Pavilion, Kew Gardens." Picture postcard. Gale &
Polden Ltd., London, [c1910?].

112   "Tea House, Kew Gardens, destroyed by suffragettes." Photograph. Bain
News Service, March 1913. From Library of Congress: Bain Collection.
https://www.loc.gov/item/2014691574. Library of Congress, Prints &
Photographs Division, LC-B2- 2535-3 [P&P] LOT 10825.

117   "Home for Working and Destitute Lads." Photographic cards. Undated.
From Barnardo's Archive.

121   Stone, Benjamin. "The Library Gallery in Holland House, Kensington,
London." Photograph. 1907. © Victoria and Albert Museum, London.

121   Harrison. "Readers Browsing Shelves of the Post-Bombing Remains of
the Library at Holland House." Fox Photos, October 23, 1940. Licensed
via Alamy.

227   "Valerie in Front of Rhododendrons at Kew." Photograph. Undated.
[c1956?]. By permission of Valerie Christle.